D1490969

THE
RUNAWAY
GENERATION

by

BIBI WEIN

DAVID McKAY COMPANY, INC.

New York

THE RUNAWAY GENERATION

Library of Congress Catalog Card Number: 77–120173

MANUFACTURED IN THE UNITED STATES OF AMERICA

VAN REES PRESS • NEW YORK

For my brother, Gerald Wein

ACKNOWLEDGMENTS

THE research for this book could not have been done without the cooperation and generosity of many people. I owe special thanks to Jean Rouverol Butler and Irving and Betty Shapira for opening their Los Angeles homes to me, to Susan Lee for arranging for my stay in San Francisco, and to my parents, Jack and Claire Wein, whose apartment I had overflowing with kids for many days. Of the many professionals who were so generous with their time and the knowledge gleaned from years of experience with teenagers, I have space to name only a few: Joe Tortelli, Executive Director of the Human Rights Commission in New Rochelle, New York; John E. Hoy, former Sheriff of Westchester County; John Lambrosa, Westchester's Special Assistant for Youth Services; Lieutenant James Burns of the New York Police Department; Father Robert Benedetto; Tom Cox and Paul Johnson of the L.A. Diggers; Charles Sansone; Marjorie Rynerson; Don Robinson; and Irving Shulman.

The help and encouragement of the following friends contributed much to the writing of the book: Judy Lent, Debby Lent, Debby Butler, and Dennis Gura, the very special kids whose enthusiasm for the project doubled mine;

Elaine Ewing and Vikki Power, who typed much of the manuscript; Jonathan Rosenbaum, who provided me with many ideas when the book was just a vague notion, and who came up with the title; John Bragin, who looked over my shoulder as I wrote Parts I through III; Tom Ewing who, at a crucial moment, helped me renew my enthusiasm for writing; my brother, Gerald, who was a tireless source of information; Gene and Arlyn Hobel, from whom I learned much about conducting interviews.

I am especially grateful to my husband, Allan Zola Kronzek, who cheerfully put up with my lapses in housekeeping, and whose editorial suggestions were, as always, precise and invaluable; and to my daughter, Edith, who waited until the book was almost finished to be born.

Finally, I would like to express my deep appreciation for the honesty, warmth, and candor of all the young people who granted me interviews.

CONTENTS

ix

PART I

Introducing the Kids

1

THE CHILDREN ON BLEECKER STREET

A YEAR AGO, I was living in the West Village, which is not for the most part, a very wild or "bohemian" place. I had moved there when it was still just the Village, the "West" being unnecessary because there was no East Village yet. Earlier, when I had lived in what is now the East Village, it was just the Lower East Side; and on the Lower East Side, some time between the death of the word "beatnik" and the birth of the word "hippie," I partook of a life style similar in many ways to the life now enjoyed by many people in the East Village.

When I moved to the West Village, I had been through pot, hash, and what is now known as speed, bypassed acid, graduated from college. Later, I held a few uptown jobs, published a novel, got married. The Village was no longer THE VILLAGE in the bold-face caps of my high school and early college days. It represented no bohemian mecca to me. Just little streets, low buildings, and an occasional tree.

When I moved into the West Village at the end of 1964, the tourist-trap streets, Macdougal, West Third, Bleecker, were still populated during the non-tourist hours by people of about my own age, which was then 21. When I moved out, in the middle of 1968, those streets were populated by people much younger than I, which seems natural enough. But they seemed younger than I had ever been. They were younger than I or any of my friends had been when the name *Greenwich Village* took on meaning for us.

They were 12, 13, 14 years of age. They had not yet achieved their full growth. Most of them were not more than five feet tall. They looked to us like Lilliputians—tiny in size, monstrous in sophistication. They filled the sidewalks and the streets and the shops and the pizza parlors. The policemen who dotted the crowds on weekends and summer evenings stood out like giants among them.

When my husband and I went walking on summer nights, even at 2 A.M. or later, the kids were there, in droves. We marveled at them as if they were creatures of extra-planetary form. They were so young, so separated by their very size from any adult world, yet *in* an adult world, dressed for adulthood, eager for it, and apparently free for it—as we had been free for it at 18, 19, 20. We found ourselves wondering why they weren't home in bed at 2 A.M., and were embarrassed at the thought, feeling that we must be ready to take to rocking chairs in our mid-twenties for having the philistinism to question the doings of a "younger generation" when we were only old enough to be their siblings, and were hardly members of anything that remotely resembled an establishment.

We first became aware of the phenomenon in the summer of 1966. We watched the kids, were shoved around by them, put uptight by them, and puzzled by them for two years. Then one day I decided to find out who they were, where they came from, what they did, what they wanted to do, and what they thought about whatever they thought about.

That is what I did, and that is the subject of this book.

If you are anticipating a sociological study substantiated by charts and tables and statistics, you will not find it in these pages. I am not a sociologist, and I do not pretend to be. In this book, you will find only people, young people of today and of yesterday—or what seems like yesterday to the parents of the children out on the Bleecker Streets of America tonight, but what seems almost like another lifetime to us, we who were the children on Bleecker Street ten years ago.

2

KIDS IN CATEGORIES

AS my interviews for this book progressed, and I walked through Macdougal Street in the West Village, Tompkins Square in the East Village, Sunset Strip, or Fairfax Avenue, or the Topanga Canyon Shopping Center in Los Angeles, looking for and at subjects; as I wandered into Huckleberry House in San Francisco, or on Telegraph Avenue in Berkeley, as I rode the New York Central to one of the half-dozen or so Westchester suburbs I visited, or sat in the living room of my parents' Pennsylvania apartment and watched my younger brother's friends wander in and out, I became more and more aware that there was little I could predict about an individual's answers to my questions.

There are only a few things that I can, even now, say in general about the long-haired, open-faced, brightly dressed kids I met on the street, or the conservative-looking kids whom I picked out in the same wild places, or the kids who were summoned to the offices of school or youth board officials to meet me. And these few things became so predictable, even in radically different individuals, that I would expect to receive the same impressions from at least

90 percent of the kids I talked to anywhere in the continental United States.

But before I discuss these few generalities, I would like to emphasize the differences between the particular kinds of middle-class adolescents whose appearance or behavior has earned them the often inaccurate label of "rebellious," "alienated," "troubled," or generally tuned in, turned on, and/or dropped out. The answer to the question "Who are they?" is that they could be anybody. They can look and generally behave as straight and proper as the preacher's kids, but have all hell going on in their hearts. They can seem as far out as the Yippies in dress and manner, but not actually be doing very much, or feeling a sense of rebellion very deeply. The kids with the psychedelic posters all over their bedroom walls may only like the way psychedelic art looks and the atmosphere it creates and the sense of belonging to the "NOW" generation that it gives them— and that may be where their "rebellion" begins and ends. It is both foolish and dangerous for us to assume that all the young people whom we know or think are engaging in some activities that challenge the American Dream are motivated by the same reasons, have the same problems, are on the same quests. For example, S.D.S. members and other radicals generally don't have drug problems, while, conversely, drug abusers do not engage in much political activity or thought.

I have found the real rebels divisible into three broad, non-overlapping categories, in no particular order of importance or estimable number, as follows:

1. The Dopers
2. The Street Dwellers
3. The Radicals

Readers may be puzzled by the absence of a category such as "love" or "peace" children. Although many of the young people who fall into the rough classifications listed above sport peace symbols on buttons or pins, or hanging from chains or strips of cowhide around their necks, there are really no "peaceniks" or "love people" in this younger-than-hippie generation. Those that are really into politics are activists of one persuasion or another. The ideal of, and the need for, world peace is of great importance to many of them, but even those most dedicated to it are neither "peaceniks" nor pacifists. They are both more cynical and more pragmatic than that. Many have marched and participated in other kinds of non-violent demonstrations, and many still do, but with less enthusiasm than young marchers had two or three years ago, and with less of a sense of potency in this particular act.

On the other hand, many have been completely discouraged, as have many of their elders, and their elders' elders, about the efficacy of peaceful political action. But those who have stopped marching and vowed never to canvass or waste their breath singing "We Shall Overcome" again have not necessarily turned revolutionary. Some have. But others have turned apathetic. They are waiting and watching to see whether there will be something else, something active but not drastic that they can do—but they do not always expect that something to come along.

There are also those who have found themselves able to do nothing but talk and think, because although they acknowledge the Vietnam War and the rights of minorities as burning issues, they do not feel strongly enough, or want to *do* badly enough, to oppose parents who have forbidden them to get involved. And there are the wearers of the peace symbol who have never found a particular course of action that felt right for them—and who may not have looked for it very hard.

It is interesting to me that the political thinking of the teenagers I have spoken to breaks down in very much the same pattern as adult political attitudes do, and I find that I could apply the above statements just as easily to adults I know, without stretching a single point. But there is one important difference.

One of the most interesting characteristics of the adolescent, and one that is both exciting and frustrating—to himself as well as to those (including his peers) who are lucky or unlucky enough to have to relate to him—is his capacity for rapid and often radical change. A politically minded 15-year-old (and saying this amazes me, because there was no such animal when I was 15 in 1958!) may easily switch from pacifist to revolutionary in the course of a month or less. He may consider marijuana to be as dangerous as arsenic one day, and as harmless as Coca-Cola the next. He may have respected and admired his parents' world view for the fifteen years he has been a thinking entity, and suddenly, in the course of one dinner-table conversation, conclude that his parents are fools. He may have passionately believed every word he has ever read or heard about America the Beautiful, and in one evening of watching T.V. live from Chicago in August 1968, know beyond a doubt that he's been duped.

Many of the kids told me themselves:

"If you'd interviewed me last month, you would have been talking to a different kid."

"This is what I feel right now, but if you talked to me tomorrow, I'd probably give completely different answers."

The frustration of being unable to trust their own feelings, however passionate, will keep some kids in a state of insecurity well into their college years. Yet, the majority,

aware as they are of their chameleon nature, do not basically mistrust themselves. They are aware that they are
learning and growing. They know and admit they have
been wrong. They are able to say, "Man, was I ever stupid
to believe that crap!" and they are ready to operate under
brand-new principles, with the same fervor and certainty—
and with more self-awareness. Bear this in mind as you listen
to what they have to say, but do not discredit them for it.

3

SEX, DRUGS, AND THE INFORMATION GAP

WHILE a 15-year-old can shake a lifetime of conservatism, obedience to authority, and general belief in the American Dream of the Good Life in an amazingly short time, he cannot so easily shake off the sexual inhibitions that have been imposed on him since birth, and that have been imposed on his parents and their ancestors since the beginnings of Western civilization.

It is almost certainly true that there is more sexual activity among 17- and 18-year-olds today than there was in that age group ten years ago. It is probably true that younger kids have more opportunities for, and fewer taboos against, experimentation with sex than they have had in the past. But it is my impression that it is only the rare young teenager who might be called sexually liberated— that is, free of guilt, doubts, fears, and unaskable questions about the sex act itself, or, at the very least, about reproduction and birth control.

Most kids seem to find the *idea* of premarital intercourse quite acceptable. In fact, they take it for granted—at least for other people. Yet, I saw evidence of very little promiscuity or belief in "free love," but rather a strong tendency

11

toward monogamous or secure relationships. A "sexual revolution" among young adolescents has yet to arrive. A substantial change in sexual mores is slowly occurring, but revolutionaries generally have a certain amount of information at their command, and a degree of confidence. In regard to sex, these kids have neither. They are confused and cautious.

A girl of 15 can turn on to everything that can give her a high from cleaning fluid to heroin and be almost totally ignorant about birth control, embarrassed to discuss sex in the most general way, and scared to death to try it.

A boy of 15 may be familiar with the theories of Marx, Lenin, and Trotsky, may have picked and chosen among them, and may have his own plans for the radicalization of the working class, and may be utterly unable to decide on the morality of sexual intercourse before marriage, though he finds himself able to make confident choices in every other area of his life.

Parents may find this heartening news. But the point is not how concerned should a 15-year-old be with sex, but how concerned is he? Not, should be have to make such choices, but does he? The answer is, he does.

Through education, books, television, music, and movies, we offer him the world. Through the mass media we offer him every high-producing drug known to nature or science. We offer him all the material goods of life, and somehow, almost against our adult will, we offer him the possibilities of concepts that can supersede materiality. We also at least pretend to offer him the right, and encourage his desire, to decide what is for him. As part of this bountiful bequest, we open the door to sex as well. But in this area most of all, we deny him the background he needs to deal with it.

Early in his college years, he is likely to come to terms with sex. Many parents and educators think this is soon enough, if not too soon. It may or may not be for any individual. But the fact that our sophisticated adolescents are for the most part so insecure about their sexuality is not simply a "natural" phenomenon due to the bodily changes of puberty. It is not inevitable, and it is especially unfortunate in an age when sex, sex, sex is flashed before our—and their—eyes at every turn. We are all familiar with the omnipresence of sex in mass-media material that is directed primarily toward adults. But let's look for a moment at some of the advertising in a 1968 issue of *Seventeen* magazine.

Most of the models look much older than the readers of the magazine, and present an extremely sophisticated image. They do not suggest innocence. They do not suggest virginity. The young couples in the perfume ads look as if they are going to do far more than kiss goodnight at the end of their date.

In an ad for a hair coloring product, sex is frankly exploited: "Like all good lures . . . beautifully simple . . . No retouching for six seductive months! Why hide the secret siren inside of you? . . . You're not the type to be timid. And this is no time to be tame!"

References to "looking younger" in an ad for facial make-up seem very much out of place in a magazine intended for high school girls, and another cosmetic company, using the phrase, "Remember the Way Girls Used to Be?" in advertising the "innocent" look in make-up, implies that the audience for this ad has lost its innocence and needs to gain it back in order to be "in."

A bathing suit ad: "Curvy, Clingy. Cleverly designed to make you that special sun body with the high eye cue."

An ad for a dress: "To get in the mood: Think fuschia. Think slink. Wow."

And this is to say nothing of the adult movies, periodicals, and advertising of all kinds that kids come in contact with every day and cannot easily (if indeed they should) be protected from.

Why rate movies General, Restricted, and Mature, to say nothing to suppressing sex education in the public schools, when we are presenting our kids with the idea and image of sex and seduction in material that is intended exclusively for them? We are teasing them unmercifully, giving them all the superficialities and romanticizations of sex, and none of the facts to deal with the realities of it. If we can extend our imaginations for a moment and regard all American culture as one big, glossy magazine, it is obvious that our house policy is to make a point of shrouding the specifics of the act itself in mystery, then capitalizing on this mystery by playing on real desires, heightening them with false glamour. Obviously we have learned from experience that this kind of treatment of sex will sell a product.

It will probably sell a product better than it would if we were all sane and certain on the subject.

It is not that adolescents today do not need information about sex. They needed it ten years ago, and they need it just as much today. And all they are getting besides the ads is a newspaper or magazine story now and then about trial marriages and coed dorms. It has been my impression that parents are being led to expect their kids to experiment with sex once they go away to college. But when a kid needs to have a heart-to-heart talk about sex is not while he's packing his tennis rackets and bright new sweaters to go away to school, but any time he feels the need for communication about it, even if he's only 8 or 10 years old. Most of the kids I spoke to had never had such a talk with their parents. They had been led, by inferences, to an idea, perhaps mistaken, of what their parents' attitudes were, and how they would react to their child's experimentation. The kids said that the greatest influence on their own attitudes toward sex were the attitudes of their peers—the only case in which they freely admitted following the group. Most said they did not learn the facts of life from their parents. Many got the facts from friends, or from books their parents had hidden not quite well enough to keep desperately interested children from finding out what they wanted and needed to know.

What our advertisements have done for the glamorized superficialities of sex is nothing compared to what the editorial content of the media has done for drugs. It is my opinion that 90 percent of American high school and junior high school students, no matter how sophisticated in other areas, are insecure and ill-informed about sex, and that the same number have a vast amount of information— though in many cases, it is misinformation—about drugs. There is enough of that in the press to choke an entire cavalry of horses. And whether the press says it's good or bad, every kid who reads the newspaper knows what pot looks like and how it is smoked; has ideas, right or wrong, about the kind of effect it will produce in him if he tries it. And drugs are now easy to get in almost every part of the country.

Every teenager I spoke to, in the course of my research, regardless of how isolated his community, regardless of how sure he might be that drugs did not and would never appeal to him, said he knew where he could easily obtain marijuana should he want some.

Usually his source would be a friend, or a friend of a friend. This friend's source? Ultimately, it is difficult to say. But while most of the hard stuff—heroin, morphine, cocaine—is imported from the Near East via France in quantities of huge size and black-market value, marijuana does not always have to travel so far or go through such a maze of underworld machinations to end up in the school-yard. It could even be growing there.

While the best of it is supposed to come from Mexico or Vietnam or North Africa, depending on whom you're smoking with, there is probably enough growing on U.S. soil, either wild or cultivated, to turn on the entire nation. Several years ago, I saw 500 pounds of it that had been planted and cultivated on a rented farm in Kansas by a university undergraduate, who carefully tended his illicit crop undetected, and, upon completing his education, harvested it and brought it to New York for sale. Yet until recently, legitimate researchers couldn't get or cultivate pot for study, and had to be supplied by the cops, who have bought it on the street or obtained the contraband from apprehended smokers or dealers.

But, while there should really be no mystery about the availability of the stuff in our traditionally wholesome Mid-west, the fact that it is so popular among even the most conservatively bred of our young teenagers can be blamed more on mass media than anything else. It's the news-papers, magazines, and T.V. that have really sold pot to our kids, and not the amateur pusher who gets hold of a pound somewhere and distributes it among his friends.

Which is not to say that data about drugs should be withheld by the press. On the contrary, I feel that the media are now obliged to attempt to undo some of the damage they have done in their misrepresentation of drugs by replacing the myths with the facts. But myths notwith-standing, the phenomenon of drug use among hippies and college students need not have been presented with enough fanfare to encourage every parent to be suspicious of his child, and every normally alert adolescent to be at least curious about turning on.

Ten years ago, the average high school student did not need very much data about drugs in order to cope with his daily life. Now, so much has been gratuitously supplied to him that he needs more.

Most of the kids I interviewed want and need to know a lot about a lot of things. The number of things they are interested in and the degree to which they have become independently informed about them is admirable. Almost every kid I talked to answered at least one of my questions in a way that impressed me with his intelligence or with the subtlety or depth of his perception. In few people did I discover general irresponsibility, frivolousness, or a defensive or unbecomingly aggressive "know-it-all" attitude.

I didn't always agree with what they had to say, and I was sometimes a little disturbed at their knowledge—knowledge that I felt could not be sanely used without greater understanding, or knowledge that meant an unequivocal loss of innocence. Most horrifying to me was the apparent innocence with which so many middle-class teenagers are toying with the hard drugs, such as speed (the amphetamine compounds) and heroin.

But on the whole, I liked the kids. I liked them a lot, and I think most of their parents have reason to be proud of them. Yet I am afraid that most of their parents are deeply disappointed in them. I hope that once you get to know them a little better, you will like them, too. If you wants to change them, perhaps you'll have a better idea of what you are up against. If you want to know your own teenage son or daughter a little better, perhaps you'll have a better idea of where to begin.

Kids have always been wild. The "younger generation" has always been fearful of, and a mystery to, its elders.

But as long as individual kids are approached with these conditions taken for granted, communication will remain poor and adults will continue to throw up their hands in despair and wish that their 14-year-olds were 4 or 24.

What they need, more than anything, is a willinginess to communicate, and your willingness to receive their communication and give yours in return. Things have broken down between the generations. Neither is unworthy of trust, but they have come to mistrust each other. Being in between in age and life style, I feel I have come into the role of a kind of mediator. I believe I have received honest answers to my questions—not only from the teenagers, but from many adults concerned for their well-being. And the willingness of both generations to communicate to me is largely a gesture of their willingness and need to communicate to each other. Therefore, this book is not meant to be an analysis of the generation gap, but rather a step toward closing it.

I propose that today's teenagers are quite unlike those of previous generations. Even in *my* day, a mere ten years ago, things were different. Times have changed so rapidly that it no longer seems accurate to think of a "younger generation" in terms of a difference of twenty or thirty years. In my day, too, there were kids who were interested in drugs, kids who espoused an anti-middle-class morality, kids who looked out longingly from the comfortable confines of suburbia to the "free" life of a slightly older, widely publicized bohemian subculture. These kids lived in the same places, even grew up in some of the same houses and families as the kids of the Runaway Generation. And they had an intimation of some of the same needs and desires.

But they expressed themselves through different media, they behaved differently, they had different kinds of experiences. The suburban world they lived in was a newer, slightly happier, slightly less jaded world. A familiarity with the kind of lives teenagers led in the Fifties places the Runaway Generation in the perspective of some of the changes all of America has seen in the past ten years. And so it is with the story of an older generation that this book begins.

PART II

The Shadow of Things to Come
Kentwood, Pennsylvania, 1956–1960

"But of course!—the *feeling*—out here at night, free, with the motor running and the adrenaline flowing, cruising in the neon glories of the new American night—it was very Heaven to be the first wave of the most extraordinary kids in the history of the world—only 15, 16, 17 years old, dressed in the *haute couture* of pink Oxford shirts, sharp pants, snaky half-inch belts, fast shoes—with all this Straight 6 and V-8 power underneath and all this neon glamour overhead, which somehow tied in with the technological superheroics of the jet, TV, atomic subs, ultrasonics—Postwar American suburbs—glorious world! and the hell with the intellectual badmouthers of America's tail-fin civilization . . . They couldn't know what it was like or else they had it cultivated out of them—the feeling—to be very Superkids! the world's first generation of the little devils—feeling immune, beyond calamity. One's parents remembered the sloughing common order, War & Depression—but Superkids knew only the emotional surge of the great payoff, when nothing was common any longer—The Life! A glorious place, a glorious age, I tell you! A very Neon Renaissance—And the myths that actually touched you at that time—not Hercules, Orpheus, Ulysses, and Aeneas—but Superman, Captain Marvel, Batman, The Human Torch, The Sub-Mariner, Captain America, Plastic Man, The Flash—but of course! It was a fantasy world *already,* this electro-pastel world of Mom&Dad&Buddy&Sis in the suburbs. There they go, in the family car, a white Pontiac Bonneville sedan—*the family car!*—a huge crazy god-awful-powerful fantasy creature to begin with, 327-horsepower, shaped like twenty-seven nights of lubricious luxury brougham seduction— *you're already there, in Fantasyland,* so why not move off your snug-harbor quilty-bed dead center and cut loose—go ahead and say it—Shazam!—juice it up to what it's already aching to be: 327,000 horsepower, a whole superhighway long and *soaring, screaming* on toward . . . Edge City, and ultimate fantasies, current and future. . . .

Tom Wolfe
The Electric Kool-Aid Acid Test *

* Tom Wolfe, *The Electric Kool-Aid Acid Test* (New York: Farrar, Straus & Giroux, 1968). Used with permission.

4

SAFE FROM THE CITY

SUSAN GOLDBERG was 13 years old when her family moved to Kentwood, Pennsylvania. Bobby Goldberg was 6. The year was 1956, and Kentwood was just beginning to grow from a semi-rural town into a fashionable suburb. The Goldbergs purchased a seven-room split-level house in a new development called Kentwood Hills. The house cost $16,000, payable via 25-year mortgage. French doors in the dining room and tile in all the three baths were extra. When the Goldbergs had started looking for a new home, they had considered $12,000 their limit.

The urban neighborhood they were leaving was considerably better than many in the "changing" city. (Definition: "Changing": Negroes moving in, white people moving out.) Mrs. Goldberg insisted that it was not the Negroes who were moving into the neighborhood that had "driven her out." (Definition: "Driven her out": Forced her by their very proximity to sell her house as quickly as possible, making no minor repairs or improvements, taking the first offer received.) The row house in which they had lived for thirteen years was simply too small for the family now.

Actually, Sarah Goldberg was afraid of the possibility of

23

little Bobby being beaten up by neighborhood toughs; she was worried about her "well-developed" Susan in a junior high school that was 70 percent black *already*.

Her husband, Sam, was not afraid of anything but a 25-year mortgage. The idea of caring for a large lawn, after a fifty-hour, six-day week (not counting commuting time), did not appeal to him. But it seemed they would be able to manage somehow, if that was what the rest of the family wanted. It was obvious that Sarah wanted it. And so did Susan.

Susan's awareness of the hostilities of the city was limited to the few minor fears her mother had succeeded in worrying into her. But her life was narrow. The boys and girls with whom she had grown up in the two- or three-block area that was hers to roam freely had all moved far away. She had friends at school, but she was permitted to visit them only rarely because of the five or six blocks she'd have to walk alone. And most of them weren't allowed to visit much either.

Susan was a little shy, but she looked forward to meeting new people in Kentwood, especially boys. She looked forward to more freedom. Hopefully, her mother would worry less. She was also pleased with the status that the move to the suburbs gave her with her friends—both those whose families were planning to remain in the city and those who would also soon move.

But Bobby was scared. He wasn't scared of being beaten up on the city street. He had friends on that block whom he liked. He was scared of going into the second grade at a brand-new school, scared of a new place where he knew no one. He was afraid of doing poorly at school, of not fitting in. He found it impossible to imagine what his new life would be like. He felt safe where he was.

Bobby ran away on the mild September day the Goldbergs were to move. He was found by his father near the forbidden territory of the park, three blocks from home, about twenty minutes after he disappeared. He was a mischievous little boy, and it seemed that, with everyone's attention on things other than himself, he had just mischievously wandered off. His arrival home with his father was coincident with the very late arrival of the movers, and his mischief was soon forgotten.

It was still light when the Goldbergs arrived in Kentwood to stay. Except for the movers and their van, there was no sign of life on the unfinished street. Four hours later, when the movers were gone, the Goldbergs, sitting uncomfortably in their new living room on their very old furniture, suddenly remembered that none of them had eaten anything since lunch. They closed the house up quickly and went out to look for a restaurant. With all the long day's dirt and grime still upon them, they settled for a small, dingy roadside luncheonette. From the outside, it looked like a truckstop. But it turned out to be nothing of the kind.

When Susan pushed open the screen door, she was immediately confronted by a group of teenage boys and girls, not much older than herself. And she was desperately embarrassed to be seen by them, even though they were complete strangers, in the company of her parents. They were out on their own, clustered around pin-ball machines, stuffing dimes, their own dimes, into the jukebox. The boys had thick, slicked-down hair cut in ducktails. The girls wore tight jeans or short shorts, with wide plastic belts and sleeveless blouses. She did not look like them. The room was ablast with the voice of Elvis Presley, which mingled strangely in the air with the fresh, cool smells of the country and the hot, pungent odors of cheap franks and burgers, and the low rumblings of cars and trucks on the highway. It made her dizzy.

Her parents were speaking to her, but she couldn't answer. They were uncomfortable. These loud teenagers, who bore no relation to their own daughter, annoyed them. The music jangled their nerves. Susan, however, felt suddenly quite detached from her parents. She did not look like any of the other girls, and she did not think she could act like them, she did not think she thought as they did, though she had no idea how or what they thought. She was not particularly attracted to any of the boys. She did not even like Elvis much. But she knew the moment she walked into the room that she was linked to them, she was one of them, and she wanted them somehow to know it, and she knew that they could not guess how willing she was to be whatever they were and do whatever they did.

And what, exactly, did they do?

Did they drink? Some of them had begun to.

Did they smoke? A few of them did.

Did they have sex? None of them had, as yet, gone all the way, but most of them probably would have by the time they turned 18.

Did they take drugs? Only whatever vitamins their mothers were able to force down their throats.

Had they ever heard of marijuana? Some had. It was rumored that marijuana was a narcotic jazz musicians used to make them play better.

What did they do for kicks? Joy riding, drag racing, necking and sometimes petting, in their cars or in older friends' cars.

What were their interests? Rock and roll, dances, cars, the opposite sex, in reverse order.

Did they have opinions about current events? If put on the spot, they would think of something to say. Otherwise, they thought little about anything outside of their own families and friends and favorite rock stars and the day-to-day events of their own lives.

Were they happy? To the extent that the average adolescent is happy, given what we in America consider his normal and forseeable difficulties in coping with his newly sexual body and the often incomprehensible demands of his environment, they were happy, yes.

The town of Kentwood developed around two main roads, which ran parallel to each other in the area where the Goldberg house was situated. The house was on top of a hill, and with their picture window, the Goldbergs had purchased an excellent view.

Perpendicular to their street, four others rolled downward, and the neat little homes built on the slopes were cheerful and gumdrop bright. Their roofs were shingled in light blue and rose and tan. Their wooden siding was painted white or pastel pink or blue or yellow. They were built on treeless new roads that twisted their way down into a thin strip of woods, scarcely as wide as a city block. The developers had given each homeowner a skinny sapling to plant on his lawn. But their children would be grown and gone before the saplings grew into trees. The sapling Sam Goldberg received was to die in its third year.

On the other side of the wooded strip was another new development, called Kentwood Heights. The houses in the Heights were built on lower ground than those in the Hill, but they were larger and more expensive and designed with many more internal possibilities for variety than the Hills homes were. On the outside they were identical gray stone trapezoids, trimmed with a little clapboard. The clapboard on all the houses in the Heights was painted white.

The people who lived in the Heights had more money than any of the other new people in Kentwood, and the fact that this was considerably less than what many of the older residents had mattered little. The people from the Heights separated themselves from the rest of the town, old and new, with an invisible shield that seemed to be provided them by some intangible not altogether unlike the use of a superior toothpaste. They had to patronize the same shopping centers and schools as the other towns-people, but they quickly gained exclusive control of the Jewish religious organizations, and from this stemmed both their social influence and their social isolation.

On the other side of the Heights was a four-lane high-way, known as the Pike. It was the main thoroughfare of fifteen or twenty towns of varying size, and its character changed from town to town. On the Pike in Kentwood, there were a few stores and office buildings that had served the town before its growth, a diner, one excellent restaurant, a couple of luncheonettes, a greasy spoon, and a post office.

From Sam Goldberg's picture window, the moving cars as far away as the Pike could be seen clearly during the day (which Sam never saw except on Sundays). As dusk came (which Sam never saw either) and darkness crept slowly over the sky, hundreds upon hundreds of lights appeared one by one—white street lamps and headlights, red tail-lights, yellow lanterns and porch lights, all blinking and twinkling like a huge machine from some unprecedented time.

In the city there had been nothing for the Goldberg children to see except their neighbors' carefully blinded windows. They were not allowed on the streets after dusk, whether playing in front of the house or returning from a visit to a friend. Once inside, they did not look out.

From the back windows of the Goldberg house, Spring Road, the other main thoroughfare in Kentwood, was visible. Between the house and Spring Road stood a new elementary school in spacious, well-kept grounds. A wild field bordered their back lawn, while the long, low building spread into two modern floors several blocks' distance away. Three playgrounds, carefully equipped for different age levels, huddled close to the school building.

When Sarah Goldberg saw this elementary school, and new houses going up so near it, she felt she had to live in one of those houses—where she could watch her little boy from the time he walked out of the back door of the house to the moment the school bell rang and he disappeared into the safety of the second grade.

Several miles south on Spring Road, a new high school was being built. To the north, ground had been cleared for Kentwood's first modern shopping center, including the town's first movie theater, first big supermarket, first chain variety store. But because of zoning laws, the shopping center and the adjacent development of 2,000 small split-level homes on tiny lots would remain unsightly and unfinished for several years.

To the west of Spring Road the old Kentwood stretched from tidy little bungalows and two-story homes into miles of private farms and forests. There were many charming winding roads, lined with low white fences. Behind the fences splendid trees and carefully tended shrubbery concealed great houses. In spring, the roadsides were green and smelled of roses. In summer, they were shady and cool, and a big blue reservoir and a few private lakes sparkled invitingly. In autumn, the countryside glowed with volatile color, and in winter there was color nowhere. The trees were black, and the white fences were swallowed up by snow.

In the winter Sarah Goldberg and her daughter Susan often watched the sunset from their kitchen window while they prepared dinner. Sometimes the sun would descend in lavender and pink and blue. Sometimes there would be a long streak of slowly fading orange and crimson against the sky. The countryside could not be seen from their house at all. But they were reminded of the greeting-card idea of American country life (though of course they didn't see it that way) by the old red brick church, trimmed in whitest white, that stood across Spring Road from the elementary school. At night, the light below the belfry illuminated its white spire against the black sky. And every Sunday morning, its bells played melodies and woke up Sam.

5

KENTWOOD HIGH: KIDS AND SUPERKIDS

WHEN Susan Goldberg entered the ninth grade at Kentwood High School, a week after her family had moved into town, she thought that the boys and girls she had encountered in the luncheonette that first night were the people with whom she must make friends. In the city, Susan had been aware of only two kinds of kids: white and black. She was relatively unaware of subdivisions within these two groups.

In Kentwood, also, she quickly noticed a dichotomy: the kids divided up into Jews and gentiles. She could easily join the gentile group even though she was Jewish, but her doing so would exclude her from the Jewish group. So, parental pressure aside, she was free to choose between the two groups, although they were mutually exclusive.

But "in" groups in a high school are not limited in number to one or two. The members of any group are "in" in that group, and the non-members are "out" to varying degrees. The social strata of Kentwood High School apparently divided itself into five groups. These are probably typical of the non-integrated, middle-income suburban schools of the late Fifties, and, as we will see later, some, but not all, of the classifications exist in today's schools as well.

1. *The Greasers* (in some places, simply *the grease*). The people Susan met in the luncheonette were greasers. Their name probably came from the boys' predilection for longish, sleekly oiled hair, or from their concern with motorcycles or hot-rod type cars, which they spent a good deal of time lubricating. Greaser boys were usually recognizable by their hair, their walk, and a general appearance that was reminiscent of James Dean, or Elvis, or both. There were also, however, greaser girls, who were a little harder to spot. Most, but not all, of the girls who wore extremely tight sweaters and skirts and make-up that seemed heavy even for an adult were greasers.

But most of the female business students (and about 90 percent of the business students were female) were greasers, and they did not all look like that. Some of them dressed "sharply," though in a different and less costly way than other "sharp" dressers in the school. More awareness of their own sexuality was evident in their appearance than in the appearance of the other girls. (These were the girls who dated young servicemen or boys from a nearby military college, as well as some of the high school greaser boys.)

Among the greasers, both boys and girls did some drinking and probably by the time they were seniors, or 17 years old, their sexual activities had progressed beyond petting. Many of them came from the lower-income families in the community ($5,000 to $6,000). The others had well-to-do but uneducated parents.

One or two were out-and-out rebels like Carla Bross. Both of Carla's parents were college educated, and they had a charming old house in the rural part of the township.

Carla seldom studied, but was in the top 5 percent of her class. She was a peroxide blond, wore cheap, tight skirts and sweaters, and carried cans of beer in her enormous black plastic handbag. She talked a lot about her promiscuity, especially about sneaking out of her window several nights a week to rendezvous with a 22-year-old garbage collector. She stayed out of trouble at school, but got into plenty at home. Despite her appearance and her occasionally disruptive conduct in class, the school took no notice of her at all.

In general, though, the greasers were the least financially privileged, the most potentially delinquent, and the most often in trouble. Trouble meant:

Suspended for smoking (or expelled if suspended three times)

Failing more than one course in a semester

Losing a driver's license for speeding

Being kept in detention hall regularly after school for one or more minor infractions, usually involving repeated disorder in the classroom (such as spitball or airplane throwing, and/or failure to obey orders docilely)

Among the greasers were 99 percent of the small number of students who dropped out or failed to graduate, the one or two girls who left because of pregnancy, and a slightly lower percentage of those guilty of the offenses listed above.

2. *The Sports Crowd.* This group included athletes and their girl friends, who were usually girl athletes, cheerleaders, or majorettes. The activities of this group brought them automatic, undisputed status (especially with those two or three teachers of academic subjects who doubled as

sports coaches, or more often, vice versa). Their status
among the other students was based on the cultural ideal
of the All-American Kid. This was what we were all supposed to be like. A combination of athletic ability and good
grades was unbeatable, but the good grades were altogether
dispensable. This was the clean-cut, crew-cut, brown, mus-
cular guy, more often blond and blue-eyed than not, polite,
relaxed, confident, secure. It was the girl with the bobby
sox and loafers and pleated skirt and soft crew-neck
sweater, the shiny hair with a natural curl, the rosy cheeks,
the loving parents. The girl who was not expected to get
terrific grades, the girl whose parents would be proud to
send her to college, but the girl who was the breeder, more
than anything else, of happy homes and apple pie and rosy
children, who would marry at 20 or 21, and who, meanwhile, while she was in high school, would have a wonderful time, would hang her boy friend's class ring from a
chain around her neck, might have trouble with math, but
would be queen of the prom and queen of her universe.

Members of this group did not have to try to be anything. They just were. Some were wealthy, some were not,
but all had a sense of order in their environments and lives.
Often, it was the order of conservatism (the town, the whole
county actually, was largely Republican), of a solid world
view that neither invited nor required examination. They
were not given to questioning their elders about anything
much besides curfew and car privileges. They found desirable much of what their parents had and held, and could
ask for little more for themselves.

3. *The Brains*. The brains were, more often than any
other group, the ones elected to student council and other
offices. They, along with Group 4, which we shall discuss
later, were the most academically competitive students, the
most concerned not only about college, but about which

college. A brain was so-named by his peers on the basis of little else besides teacher approval. The brains associated more with each other than anyone else, partly out of real snobbery, and partly out of assumed snobbery on the part of the less successful students. Most were extremely cliqueish and dependent on each other. There were one or two super well-rounded athlete-brains, but they definitely fell into the brain classification rather than the athlete group. Carla Bross, for example, who was definitely a brain, fell into the greaser classification because of her concerted efforts to be a greaser.

4. *The Jews.* The Jews were ghettoed off into a category by no one but themselves. Although they were the newest minority to move to Kentwood (which had a few Italians, fewer Greeks and Armenians, and one Negro family), they met with no anti-Semitism, and among the high school students, no special notice. On the whole, they tended to self-segregate. At least the wealthiest of them did. The less affluent, like the Goldberg family, were not wholeheartedly accepted into any social cliques. But among the Jewish students, there were no intellectual barriers, and fewer age barriers than one usually finds among adolescents. Junior high and high school students would often be involved in the same social activities. There was a strong urge to "stick together" as if against the threat of an imagined enemy, and there was also a strong sense of superiority, often with an economic basis. These were the war babies.

Many of the Jews belonged to the brain class, and 50 percent or more of the brains were Jews. One Jewish boy became a greaser. A few others chose not to participate in the various Jewish social groups (B'nai Brith Girls, A.Z.A., United Synagogue Youth), and much to the consternation of their parents, dropped into the *average* group.

5. *The Average.* Into this group fell everyone who did

not fall into any of the others. The "average" kid was not necessarily average. He simply had or did nothing to give him the kind of status that was recognized as status in Kentwood High School. The average were an anonymous, heterogeneous group, consisting of C and D students and A students, students who were talented in non-academic areas, as well as the truly average students who displayed no special abilities in, or enthusiasm for, anything at all. Thus most of the students who were active in the music and drama programs fell into the average class because little value was placed on these activities. Other average kids were extremely bright, but too shy to make a point of it, even in the classroom, and straight A students did not make it into the brain class if they were not overt enough about it to keep their peers aware of them.

More average students were from the middle- to lower-income group than the upper-income group, from which came many of the brains, the sports kids, and the Jews. But money was by no means a major factor in defining a student's social class. Each group perpetuated itself on the basis of certain values, and in some cases, traditions. Any individual who shared these could join. Any individual who did not, was left out—in some cases shunned, and in others treated with friendship and respect, but nonetheless, left out.

6

THE FIRST OF THE ANOMALIES

SOME time in 1959, however, a sixth group began to form. It emerged slowly from beneath the surface of a set of social strata that had qualitatively changed little in half a century, and by the time the existence of a new group was clearly recognizable, its original members were long graduated and gone.

It apparently started with a boy named Barney Katz. His father was a painter, his mother a dancer, his older brother a Yale drama student. In 1959, Barney was a 14-year-old tenth grader, and had lived in Kentwood Heights for two years. He played the saxophone and wrote poetry. He had gone to school in Paris and in Mexico. He was an anomaly.

Barney's parents were anomalies in Kentwood, too, but for adults who had cars, Kentwood was within easy reach of other communities, several of them busy with sophisticated people doing sophisticated things. But a teenager had no such social choices. Even with a car (and of course you had to be at least 16 for that), it was hard to meet kids outside the high school environment and its many programmed activities. There were *some* alternatives open to *some* people—for example, the greasers from all over the county attended dances regularly at a large, rather greaser-oriented school, and the activities of the Jewish groups always included the small, new Jewish populations of other nearby schools—but most of the students at any given high school are more or less stuck with each other, and Kentwood was no exception.

Barney Katz was not as disoriented by his social life at Kentwood, however, as he was by the school itself. He was accustomed to teachers who did not rely on textbooks, and who had both the time and ability to deal with each student individually. Barney was intimidated by the classroom situation at Kentwood. He had a genius I.Q., but did not participate. He was one of the average.

Then there was Ansel Bloom, in Barney's class, a doctor's son, also from Kentwood Heights. Ansel was short and thin, with kinky brown hair, an ivy-dresser. He came on smart-assed and snotty, like a brain. But he shunned the brains and he shunned the Jews and went home after school and read Gide. He was one of the average.

There was Tony Morrell, born in the older section of Kentwood. He was a senior. He played the trumpet in the school band. He was a quiet, seemingly dull boy. He dressed more like his father than like his contemporaries. He was not very attractive. He looked old. He was one of the average.

There was a girl in Tony's class named Betsy Jones, a tall, handsome girl who had waist-length hair and drove a red MG. No one knew anything about her, except that she was rich and had no mother and spent a lot of time in New York. She lived in one of the mansions. Rumor had it that Betsy was a beatnik. Rumor also had it that she had anonymously given the high school library its subscription to the *Village Voice*. She was one of the average.

In the junior class, there was Louise Schenk, another Kentwood native, from a large family with an alcoholic father and lots of sibling rivalry. Louise, whose friends were mostly greasers, was naturally gifted with a high fashion model's face and figure. She appeared in one school play and had vague ideas about being an actress and "making it" in New York. She did poorly in school in everything but Home Ec. She was one of the average.

Older than Louise, but in the sophomore class, was Steve, just moved into Kentwood Heights from the city, a clergyman's son who had, somehow, at 16 already completely failed to live up to his influential father's expectations for his intellectual skills and social finesse. At the end of his young rope, he suddenly discovered that he had some talent as a pianist. He was one of the average.

And then there was Susan Goldberg, now in her senior year, who had lived a pretty normal life. Susan, who was pretty enough and smart enough and *average* enough, and had enough dates and had gone steady enough times and was invited to all the dances and football games and fell in love and out of love, and got along tolerably well with her parents, was utterly dissatisfied with the whole thing, suddenly, after three fun-filled years.

Somehow, they all found each other. Ansel and Barney were in the same class. They met Tony and Steve in the band. Susan and Louise took the same school bus, and a long series of coincidental proximities brought the whole bunch of them together. What, precisely, did they have in common? A dissatisfaction with Kentwood. Some were happy at home, some not. Some did well in school, some did poorly. Some had all the material things they desired, others considered themselves lacking. But all wanted more

excitement
mobility
self-expression

and perhaps most important, more contact with *the outside world*. The outside world was often more cultural than social. Real participation in it was something no one had any clear idea of. It did not mean having a job or an apartment or taking on social responsibilities or necessarily meeting certain kinds of people, or even in the most general way, doing something about something. It vaguely meant being a little more free.

Even the personal associations within this group were limited by lack of independence, lack of transportation. This was not a telephone-talking bunch of teenagers. They had to get together. Usually, logistics were so difficult that they seldom gathered in a group of four. They remained so "underground" that they were not known in the school as a group. Susan's association with Louise, for example, was noticed, as was Barney's with Ansel, but no one connected these 14-year-old boys with those 16-year-old girls.

Let us ask the same questions of this group as we did of the greasers earlier:

Did they drink? Most of them took advantage of opportunities to raid the liquor cabinets of absent parents. Almost all looked too young to be served in bars or liquor stores. A few had tried and failed.

Did they smoke? Almost all did.

Did they have sex? Their experience was more limited than that of the greaser group, and probably would remain limited for longer. Sexual interest within the group was only peripheral, but a blasé attitude toward sex was affected by both boys and girls. Dirty jokes could be handled with some sophistication in a mixed gathering, but the individuals were certainly as preoccupied with sex as those in other groups, and neither better informed nor less hung up about it. However, they differed from others in that, whether they knew it or not, they were adapting themselves to a culture in which "free love" was not only condoned but encouraged, a culture that would make it seem possible for them to openly and happily, rather than surreptitiously and guiltily, shake off the standards by which they had been raised.

Had they ever heard of marijuana? A number of them were interested enough in the drug to make a point of reading about it. Several thought they knew a good deal about all the drugs available at that time.

Did they take drugs? None had, but each knew someone who had, and a few had had the opportunity but chickened out. All would try at least marijuana before the age of 20.

What did they do for kicks? Drank, if they could.

What were their interests? Beat poetry, jazz (the music of Miles, Coltrane, Bird, Mingus, Monk in particular), writers such as Ginsberg, Ferlinghetti, Becket, Ionesco, Burroughs, Sartre, Kerouac, and Gide. Most had had a memorable experience with *Catcher in the Rye*. They had little interest in dancing, actively abhorred rock and roll (and the greasers as a group, though not usually as individuals).

Did they have opinions about current events? Mostly generalities, and the opinions of their idols, the writers and the musicians. Let us say that they did have a world view; whether it was an independent one or not is another matter.

Were they happy? No.

Hanging on at the edge of the group were two older boys, Teddy and Herman, from the city, occasionally joined by a third. The presence of these hangers-on was much appreciated, because no one else, except Betsy, who tended to observe the others rather than join them, was old enough to drive or had access to a car. These boys, who were freshmen in three different local colleges, were introduced to the Kentwood scene by Steve, whom one of them had known in the city, and Teddy and Herman, a bass player and a drummer respectively, had started taking the long drive to Kentwood for jam sessions at Steve's house. The third boy was looking for girls and, in fact, they all found girls.

Herman, who was 18 and told fantastic stories about his adventures, and Barney, who was 14 and cooler than Camus, were the focal people in the scene, but everyone had something to contribute. Teddy, the bass player (also an R.O.T.C. student, which no one noticed particularly), most often had a car. Ansel, the runty little smart-aleck, most often had access to his parents' booze. Tony, according to Barney, was a pothead, and though he had never offered to turn anyone on, he was considered a source of grass should anyone want it. Tony also looked the oldest, and under pressure, might be convinced to purchase liquor.

In general, status within the group was marked by the right combination of coolness and weirdness. Coolness was comprised of equal parts of cultural sophistication, personal detachment with a dash of good old beat *angst* thrown in, and distaste for the greaser vision of the rockin' rollin' hot-rodding gum-chewing teen. Weirdness meant simply having idiosyncrasies—the more the better. To some extent, possessions, such as books and records, were also status. Visits to New York were tops. Even visits to Philadelphia on a frequent basis were not bad. *Downbeat*, the *Village Voice*, and the wonderful old *Evergreen Review* were the periodicals on the required reading list, which was quite a long and impressive list indeed. Familiarity with certain music was also essential, of course, and one could actually get into the group by doing the required reading and listening. Susan, Louise, and Steve, in fact, got in that way. Teddy did the listening, but not the reading. But Teddy was an exception, because he had a car.

The following scenes, based on interviews I did in 1959 for an article that appeared in the *Philadelphia Bulletin,* are typical of some of the experiences the group shared. All sections appearing in quotes represent exact transcriptions of these interviews. I quote them at length because of the connections and contrasts they offer to the life styles of comparable groups of teenagers today.

7

CHRISTMAS VACATION, 1959–1960

SUSAN and Teddy go out on a week-night date. First, they go to a pizza parlor near the university at which Teddy is a freshman history major. It is a clean, well-lit restaurant, with white tablecloths and comfortable chairs. They spend over an hour there. Teddy is very involved in Thomas Jefferson, and Susan has just given him a book of Jefferson's writings as a Christmas present. Teddy has given her his fraternity pin. They talk about the possibility of going to hear some live jazz on New Year's Eve. Lionel Hampton will be in town. Will they pass for 21? They quickly exhaust their few ideas for obtaining false identification, and decide that they will just have to try to look old.

Can they pass? Susan more easily than Teddy. Teddy has a short crew cut, required by his R.O.T.C. program. He is wearing desert boots, a charcoal gray crew-neck sweater over a pin-striped shirt, and continental pants. He has a slim, hard body, a mealy complexion, slightly puffy looking nose, and watery brown eyes. He looks very young.

Susan has fluffy medium length hair. She is wearing a black wool sheath dress, black tights, grayed sneakers, and Teddy's fraternity pin. With her hair in a French twist, and with nylons and high heels, she'll look old enough. Usually, she wears stockings and heels for any date, but tonight is different. Susan and Teddy are going on a special adventure. They are going to visit a coffee house.

The coffee house scene is new to the city, and there has been a great deal of controversy about it even though there are only three coffee houses and two of them are old. One has been an off-beat after-theater spot for some thirty years, with —until recently—a very respectable clientele. The other is more than a hundred years old, and has recently become a folk-singers' hangout, with hoots every Sunday afternoon, and two or three good banjo pickers in almost constant attendance.

But Susan and Teddy are not going to either the folky place or the arty place. They are going to the new place, and they have no idea what it will be like. The newspapers have recently called the coffee houses the breeding grounds of vice, and amid threats to close them all, espresso coffee is receiving as much bad press as pot is to come by later.

Teddy stops his car on a small dark street that is only a few blocks away from the main streets of the city. He and Susan get out and walk down eight uneven, half-broken steps from the sidewalk, and go through a heavy, chintz-curtained door that won't close all the way.

They are in a basement room with dim lights over the counter at the far end, and a single curtained window. They stand awkwardly just inside the door and look around. The floors, walls, and ceilings are of rough white plaster. The bare radiators exude a thick, oppressive warmth. There are shelves along one wall, and on the shelves are copies of *Life, Harper's,* the *New Yorker*. Near the window, there are two shelves stacked with old books, mostly paperbacks, for sale at a dime apiece. Two titles that catch Susan's eye are Scott's *Waverly Novels* and *Lavender and Old Lace*. The

wall opposite the magazines is covered with white cork-
board, on which an exhibit of line drawings has been
mounted. It seems an acceptable action to go over and
study the drawings, so Susan and Teddy do that, although
Teddy is not very interested. The subjects of the drawings
are mainly musicians and painters and death. The first
depicts a one-eyed man, bared to the waist, hanging from a
noose with a spread-winged vulture clawing at his throat
and remaining eye. In the background is a dark red sun.

Susan and Teddy sit down at a table. The room is nearly
empty. There are four people who seem to work there: two
heavy-set young men, one Negro, one white, wearing jeans
and bulky sweaters; a slim, bearded young man in dirty
work clothes, and a boy of perhaps 17, wearing a heavy
plaid wool lumber shirt, tails out. At two tables by the
counter sit two college girls in slacks and sweaters, and
three young men in military academy uniforms. Show music
is playing loudly from a phonograph on the counter, and
the girls are singing along with the records.

The boy in the lumber shirt comes over to Susan and
Teddy, and they order two cups of espresso, their first act
of testing what they have read about as the beat life. The
coffee is hot and thick and bitter. It smells very good with
the tiny piece of lemon peel in it. Susan likes the coffee.
Teddy says he will finish his to please Susan.

Susan notices that each of the waiters is wearing a large
charm of metal or carved wood around his neck. The bearded
waiter is sitting at a corner table with a knife and a long
wooden stick, from which he is carving angular, little
heads. Susan wants to talk to him. She wants to know if he
is a beatnik, and what a beatnik is. And, to Teddy's dismay,
she goes over to this man and awkwardly engages him in
conversation.

Close up, he looks younger. His brown beard is scraggly

and thin. His hair is just a little too long to be a crew-cut, but it is uncombed, and looks as if he has cut it himself. His hands and his dark gray workshirt look very dirty. The amulet hanging from a piece of twine around his neck is a carved rectangular head, with expressionless features and two horns rising from the top corners.

The man's blue eyes are young, and his slight smile is boyish. His name is Clem, he is 23, and he thinks Susan is a curiosity-seeking square, and he is annoyed, but she's just a kid. What he says to her is mostly what he thinks she wants to hear—by now almost a prepared speech, so often is he approached by "interested" strangers.

"I'm not a beatnik," is the first thing Clem says. "Beatniks are *beaten* by someone or something. They have given up on life completely. All we want is to be left alone, to follow life our own way. Most of us are artists—painters, poets, who find average living too high. We can't stand hypocrites. The man who goes to church on Sunday and says he's sorry for something he's going to do all over again on Monday. It's unfair to down the men who want to see for themselves. This carving around my neck is a bare-faced devil," he volunteers. "It stands for me, because that's what I am."

Susan interprets his defensiveness as an "inferiority complex." At the same time, she realizes that her attempt to look *beat* has completely failed, and that she should have taken off her fraternity pin before coming into a place like this, and she wishes that Teddy didn't look so square.

"Beats are looking for God in their own way," Clem goes on. "I believe He accepts what I do. He understands me. Beats are some of the most truly religious people. There's no beat generation. A great many non-conformists are beats. Some aren't. We're not afraid of what people think. We're not making ourselves neurotic with suppressed desires. Beats are pacifists, against war and gruesome things like that. It's a gentler way of life. And we're not all bums. We work for a living."

"Are you rebelling against society?" Susan innocently asks, with very little idea of what she means, and Clem says, "Yes. I want interracial equality."

She asks him what is the "gentler way of life." He says it is "the wayless way of Zen Buddhism." She doesn't dare ask him questions about that. Barney has already told her it is ineffable.

Having made his speech, Clem goes on to talk about himself, and his history, in an impassioned narrative about the ultimate drop-out and his adventures, which bears much resemblance to Kerouac's *On the Road*. He looks at the girls and the military academy boys, and including Teddy in his glance, says "Now I look at these smart kids who stayed home and went to college, and I laugh when I think of how much more I know than they do."

Teddy catches the intention, if not the words, and he rises and interrupts the conversation with a sharp, "Let's go."

Christmas Eve. Susan and Teddy and Barney and Steve and Nina, a girl from New York whom Susan met at camp last summer, and who is staying with Susan for a few vacation days, are gathered in the "recreation room" of Susan's house.

The room is paneled in cheap mahogany and furnished with two attractively covered old couches, a couple of basket chairs, Sam Goldberg's desk and bookcases, and a cheap monaural phonograph. In the living room upstairs, there is a piano, and Teddy has brought his bass, and Barney an alto saxophone. Barney has also brought some records—three by Miles Davis, one by Thelonius Monk, and one by Charlie Mingus—*Bags' Groove, Birth of the Cool,* and *Kind of Blue; Thelonius Alone,* and *Mingus Ah Um.* The five of them sit around for a while listening to the tracks that Barney has selected. And when the music is on, no one speaks. To Barney, foot-tapping is sacrilege, too. And among the members of the group present in this room, at least, no one disregards Barney's wishes. He speaks with authority. He commands respect. He and Nina, who is two years older, are immediately attracted to each other. Steve is attracted to Nina, too, but he, in his hysterical need to belong, can hardly compete against Barney, who is serene in his opinions, his knowledge, his sophistication, serene in everything apparently except for the fact that he lives in Kentwood and is forced to attend Kentwood High.

Nina has straight black hair, down to her waist, and she is dressed entirely in black, except for her sneakers and silver and turquoise jewelry. She is small, fresh-faced, and freckled, and despite the get-up, looks younger than her 16 years. In a letter to a friend, Susan described Nina as follows:

> She doesn't believe in God, or in the morals of our society, but she's scared of the consequences, so she's gone along with the morals so far. She says her motto is "no experience is a bad experience," but I think she thinks the proms we go to, and the prom gowns, and rock and roll and American movies are bad experiences. I think she's missing something. But maybe not.
>
> I call Nina a beatnik, but she insists she's not. She says she loves life and isn't a sadist or a defeatist, and therefore couldn't possibly be a beatnik. But I'll bet she'll think we're all a bunch of hicks.

After listening to the records for a while, the boys wanted to play. They jammed a little in the living room, but Susan's parents said *they* wanted to use the living room, so everyone went downstairs again. There was a piano at Barney's house, too, but Barney said they couldn't go there. Teddy suggested they go visit another bass player he knew who might even have some drums.

The bass player was a Negro boy with whom Teddy had gone to high school. He lived in the city. Teddy didn't have his phone number. It was about 10 o'clock. Susan decided she had better not tell her parents where they were going. She had never visited the home of a Negro before. She knew that they would be upset, and might forbid her to go. In fact, she was a little scared herself. She did not know what she feared might happen to her, but she was game to find out. She told her parents they were going into the city to visit a friend of Teddy's. Reluctantly, they let her go.

Susan, Teddy, Barney, Steve, and Nina piled into Teddy's car, along with the bass and Barney's horn, and drove into the city. When they got to Teddy's friend's house, Teddy got out and went to the door himself. He came back and said that it was okay to go in for a while, but it was too late to jam.

In the small, darkened living room, toward the back of the house, they sat for a while, talking about music. They played some of Barney's Mingus records on a phonograph that was not very much better than Susan's and then they left.

In the morning, Barney, Steve, Susan, and Nina went to the city by bus, and met at the flower shop where Teddy worked. Teddy had to spend the morning making sprays for a funeral. So the others went on, without the aid of Teddy's car, in search of a copy of *No Exit* in French. Teddy met them in the afternoon. They were still making the rounds of basement bookstores, and by dusk Barney decided to settle for the translation, which both he and Nina had already read. Nina, Susan, Barney, and Steve would read through the play that night, while Teddy played the bass in a combo at a Bar Mitzvah.

But somewhere along the way, Steve disappeared, and Barney, Susan, and Nina ended up at Ansel's house in Kentwood Heights. Ansel's parents were away; their bar was well-stocked. They all descended into the basement playroom—a long, lavishly paneled room, with white floors, black leather furniture, a custom-built bar, fine stereo equipment, soft lighting, dark corners. Barney and Nina and Ansel drank a lot of vodka and orange juice. Susan didn't drink. She also didn't know Ansel very well and couldn't think of anything to say to him. She stood by the bar in the dimly lit room, played with the French poodle, and was impressed with Barney, as he stood in the middle of the room and read aloud from *Howl*, which Susan only pretended to understand.

Nina went home the next day, and a few days later, Susan and Teddy took the train to New York. Teddy checked in at a hotel, and Susan settled in at Nina's. Barney was already in New York somewhere, with his parents, and was expected to show up at Nina's party that night.

They spent an hour or so putting up decorations for the party, and then took the subway down to the Village. It was the first time Teddy and Susan had seen the Village. They were a little disappointed. It was a rainy, cold afternoon, and the streets were almost empty. They wandered around for a while, and Nina didn't see anyone she knew, and Susan and Teddy didn't see anything much that interested them. The people they did see were in their twenties and were dressed just like anyone else, bundled up against the weather. They were not strolling around casually, but seemed to have specific reasons to be out in the rain—they were on their way somewhere. And Susan and Teddy had no idea where people out walking in the Village went.

They arrived at the corner of Macdougal and Bleecker

and looked around. Susan was drawn toward a place across the street called Café Bizarre, which had a canopy and streamers flapping outside in the rain, but Nina said that was a tourist trap. They went into the Café Borgia, and took a round table near the window, where Nina could see her friends if they should happen to pass by.

The first to arrive was Danny, 17, a junior at Bronx High School of Science, very thin. Under a parka, he wore tight jeans, a big dark green sweater, and sneakers. His mousy brown hair was spread in a thick, uncombed wave across his forehead, resting on the top edge of the frame of his glasses. Danny, Nina said later, was asthmatic, and hooked on Benzedrine.

It wasn't long before Danny and Teddy were arguing violently. Teddy made the mistake of mentioning that he was in R.O.T.C., and Danny got very upset.

"What's the matter?" Teddy said. "I love my country and I'm willing to die for it. Someone has to defend the ideals of democracy, can't you see that?"

"Nothing, no ideal, is worth the sacrifice of human life. People who are willing to kill are brainwashed for an ideal. And if you are willing to kill for democracy it's no longer an ideal, it's madness. In World War II, we weren't killing Hitler, we were killing Germany's 18-year-old boys. And when the atomic bomb falls, you and all your ideals will be nothing but cruddiness on the ground. What good are you when you're dead?"

"The bomb's going to fall on you, too," Teddy cried. His voice was getting high and squeaky. "At least I'm trying to do something about it. What are you doing?"

"Nothing. This is only talk. There is nothing to do. All I can do is sit and fold my hands and hope I've got the guts to wait there and take it and not give in. And that's a lot harder than going out and being a hero."

"That's cowardice!"

"That is not cowardice! The only cowardice is fear of what other people think."

"Don't you believe in anything?" Teddy challenged.

"I believe in Pooh-Bear. It's a lot better than believing in God. I can imagine such a being as Pooh-Bear, but I can't imagine such a being as God. It's no use trying to explain anything. If you don't understand it, it's ridiculous, and if you do, it's even more ridiculous. Communication is a difficult thing. Ideas are not made up of words. They are made up of feelings, and words are inadequate."

Danny then sank sulkily into the depths of his big coat, and sipped a grenadine and soda through a straw. Teddy's face was flushed and hot. He wanted to leave, but he knew Susan would be disappointed. He knew he had made a fool of himself. He also felt betrayed. Barney knew he was in R.O.T.C., and Barney had never said anything about it.

Nina introduced another boy, Neil, who had silently joined them at the table. Neil, 16, was a Brooklyn College freshman, pre-med. He was well-built and healthy-looking, with curly blond hair not much longer than Teddy's crew cut. Neil and Teddy shook hands, but Neil did not smile.

Somehow the conversation continued between the boys while Nina and Susan listened restlessly. Neil, it turned out, was a very vocal atheist, and when he got finished making that clear, he wanted Teddy to know what he thought about beatniks. First he denied their existence, then he described them.

"If there are such things as beatniks, I look upon them as animals. Some of their ideas are good, but I'd like to see them a little more civilized. Being beat is a state of mind. There is a little bit of the beatnik in everyone. Everyone has a secret desire to rebel against something. But some of the

things they do are so purposeless, like walking across Macdougal Street with no shoes on.

"But if someone wants to take dope or indulge in sex, let
him. Let him think for himself. And people say beats make
a lot of noise. What's wrong with noise? Ike makes a lot of
noise, and nobody ever says anything about him. Basically,
I'll always be concerned with thinking for myself and getting
others to think for themselves, and not caring about the
consequences. These squares who live by the idiot box are
the most pitiful things in the world."

Susan became annoyed at Neil's arrogance. "If you want
people to think for themselves and do what they want, what
do you have against people walking across Macdougal Street
with no shoes on?"

"I think it's stupid because I don't think it's what they
really want to do. They're just trying to make an impression.
They just want the tourists to think they're getting their
money's worth. They want their friends to think they're
cool."

Neil went on to put down the idiot box some more, and
the bomb, and religion again, and the suburbs, and the bomb
again.

Then Danny said, "There's absolutely no privacy in the
suburbs. It ruins the children's minds, stifles the intellect.
Two cars in one-car garages, books they don't even dust,
much less read, cheap prints of paintings by artists whose
names they don't even know how to pronounce . . ."

Then Neil and Danny left, and Nina, Teddy, and Susan
went back uptown. Teddy went straight to his hotel.

Nina said that Danny had an inferiority complex and was
trying to escape the awful world by withdrawing himself
into his own little shell. She said Neil wasn't as well-liked
as Danny because he really was conceited. She said she liked

them both. Susan apologized for Teddy. Nina said he was all right—just a little scared.

Nina's mother had prepared the party food, which the girls put out in the living room. Nina's mother knew that some of the kids would bring liquor (just wine or beer, she hoped), and that she really couldn't do anything about it, since some of them were over 18 anyway. She warned the girls to go easy on drinking, and she and her husband warned everyone who came in to be careful about cigarette butts and ashes, and anyone who was visibly carrying liquor was urged to hold the drinking down. But soon the party got so large that they were unable to greet each person at the door. They moved among the groups of kids, directing them toward the ashtrays and telling them again and again to be careful about the carpet.

They failed to notice that the bathroom was quickly becoming a very popular place, and after a while, people stopped closing the door all the way when they went in to turn on, and the groups sharing the joints spread out into the hall. Susan was offered a drag. She turned it down. She saw Teddy turn away from a joint with disgust. She saw Barney turn one down, too, laughing and shaking his head, because he was so high on gin that he had no use for anything else.

When Nina's parents finally did catch on to the fact that the bathroom was overly much in use, her father burst in to discover not pot-smokers, but Barney, lying in the bathtub fully dressed, clutching a nearly empty gin bottle to his chest, with the shower streaming down on top of his head. Nina's father rescued him gently, and Barney damply stumbled into Nina's room, where he sat on the floor for the rest of the evening, hovering over the stereo, with earphones on his head, listening to records he had brought.

The rest of the party didn't miss the music of the stereo.

There were guitars, and bongo drums, and corners filled with couples necking or small groups arguing.

Nina had turned on, but said she hadn't really gotten very high. She drank a lot of wine, and so did Susan and Teddy. The party broke up around 3 a.m. Teddy went back to his hotel. Susan and Barney and Nina helped Nina's mother clean up. Nina went to sleep in her bed, and Susan and Barney slept near each other on Nina's floor.

Barney left for home the next day with his parents. Nina went to hear Nina Simone at Town Hall that night, and Susan and Teddy went to Birdland, where they heard a not very famous and not very good group for an enormous sum of money, and were sorry that they hadn't been in town early enough to go with Barney to the Village Vanguard to hear Coltrane. But at least they had seen Birdland.

They went home the following afternoon, picked up Teddy's car, and drove over to see Barney. The beard Barney had allowed to grow over the holidays was beginning to come in like the real thing, and he was using a long cigarette holder he'd bought in New York. He said he was going to keep the beard as long as he could get away with it at school, and that he'd had his last haircut until they threatened to suspend him; he figured it would take until around the middle of May before they got around to that.

He told them about his adventure in getting admitted to the Village Vanguard without so much as a phony I.D. They told him about their meeting at the Borgia with Danny and Neil. Danny was okay, Barney said. He was apparently stoned on bennies all the time, but he liked him. Neil, however, was an arrogant son-of-a-bitch. Barney said he was going to write an essay about beatniks for a composition assignment at school.

Later he changed his mind. He decided he didn't feel like

going to so much trouble for something that would not be appreciated. But he had already made some notes.

BARNEY'S NOTES ON BEATNIKS

The people's idea of a beatnik is a guy in a sweatshirt and sandals, a beard, long hair, who goes around the streets spouting incoherent poetry, or who sits in a coffee house drinking espresso.

With real beatniks, it's more of an internal thing, an internal rather than external non-conformity. They aren't external non-conformists just to put on a show, at least. That doesn't make them phoney necessarily, but it doesn't assure their authenticity.

Real beatniks are very good. There has always been a rebellious movement of some kind going on, like the lost generation of the Twenties. But in America today, with our mass communication and mass commercialization, it's become a real big fad, and kids walk around saying "like man," wearing boatneck sweaters and continental pants and saying they're beats.

A real beatnik could look like anybody, maybe even like the man in the gray flannel suit. But the beat abhors all the phoniness and ideas of our present society, particularly security as the ultimate goal. Some beatniks are out going after their goals, while others are just sitting around being bums and looking for kicks and the truth. The trouble is they're looking for kicks first and the truth last.

A real beat has an authentic desire to search for what really is true, and to get away from this degrading society. He should know something about all forms of art. Not just jazz, jazz, jazz. Serious music, modern art, poetry, literature, not just modern stuff, but what was going on before, too. They should be intelligent, and if they're not, they should try to be. They should dig everything.

I hate the word beatnik. It was coined by some commercialist to sell books by Jack Kerouac and jazz records by Bill Potts. And everyone wants to be one. Weekend beatniks are only teenagers in slightly different clothes.

Nine-tenths of present beats will grow up and become solid, respectable citizens. Most of their poets and artists are lousy anyway. And if they sell their works it becomes strictly a business venture, to become a beatnik, and they run around in twenty-dollar sweatshirts. The real beats will always be around, like Henry Miller, who is 60 years old and ran around with Hemingway in the lost generation of the 20s. The beat generation of today is just an outgrowth of that.

Beatniks as a whole will never find the truth, but each one who devotes his existence to it can. The ones who think it's too much trouble will end up running butcher shops.

I've been to coffee houses, but they're usually more like holes than houses. I approve of them. There's usually some music and a poet around. Maybe a lousy poet, but still a poet. It's full of real beats, and people who come to watch. Nobody can really tell who is a real beat, and who isn't. Only the real beats know who they are.

I guess I'm sort of an oddball. I consider myself beat in the pure sense of the word.

8

TUNING IN

CULTURALLY, we of the would-be-beat generation ten years ago were quite different from today's kids. The dichotomy between beat and square was not one of the Revolutionary versus the Pig, the Peace Marcher versus the Hawk, or even the turned on awareness versus the closed off. Our battle was very much a battle of and against the middle class: the unique, the individualist, the non-conformist versus the mediocre, the ordinary.

The fact that our heros, the older beat poets and artists, were more or less at war with an academic establishment had little to do with us. Our battle was against the "silent majority": our parents, our neighbors, the grease, the rahs. There were no extremes to fight. There were no Hawks, no Pigs, no threats but the mere existence of the bomb, about which our young pacifists ranted for hours in the gloom of ill-lit coffee houses. Our dread enemy was simply mediocrity and the stasis of the land.

Art was our answer to the stasis. It was an art characterized by a sense of suffering and pain, an art that virtually stuck pins into our psyches, as if nothing less brutal would serve to remind us that we were alive. The communication was basic, often crude. The message was: feel the pain, end your numbness, know that you live. It was an art that claimed that breaking the shackles of middle-class comforts (buffer to all feeling) was the first step toward freeing the soul.

The art we worshipped was almost exclusively poetry and jazz. The poetry was mostly Allen Ginsberg's, bursting with agonized joy out of the white middle class. The music, jazz or folk, was generally from the black culture or from the oppressed whites of America's past. The music was not always an anguished wail, but even at its most uplifting, it was bittersweet in quality. It was the music of Miles Davis, Thelonius Monk, and Charlie Parker—the great Bird, whose happy music kids didn't listen to as much as they talked about his tragic life and tragic death. Martyred by this unfeeling, mediocre world, he was made a saint by kids who climbed railroad bridges to write in great streaks of white paint, *Bird Lives,* who scrawled it on subway posters in the very same spaces where *Flower Power* was lately scrawled, where *Make Love, Not War* is still seen now.

We were not as much captivated by the message or example of our heros as we were drawn by the timeless romantic appeal of art itself, and the stereotype of the Artist and his sacrifice and suffering and unconventional life style. It was only later that we began to sense, often in only the vaguest way, what it all meant.

It was *Life* magazine that really made clear the connections of the new art with the beat way of life, and that really described for us—with the aid of a number-keyed photograph, no less—what this life was like. We had notions about it, but not the faintest idea of how to live it. There was not enough data around to piece "A Day in the Life" together. We knew that not all beats were on the road, like Kerouac. We knew the pain of *Howl,* and the beatitude of the music. And we grooved on that in our paneled basements and bought black turtlenecks on our parents' charge accounts.

We lived as comfortably as we always had, and it never occurred to us to run away from these comforts as the grown-up beats had. It never occurred to us to leave school, or even to forgo our homework. We may have been apathetic about homework; we may have been underachievers. We may have been apathetic about almost everything in our daily lives. And we may have let these daily lives martyr us, especially after we had all seen ourselves in the image of Holden Caulfield. But we did not really want to run away, even to the extent that Holden Caulfield ran away. We were too comfortable. And we did have each other. We spent much of our time together commiserating about how few of us there were, putting down the grease and the other people who didn't dig what we dug, and alternating between feeling sorry for them and feeling sorry for ourselves.

I don't think kids today feel nearly as sorry for themselves as we did. And how unlike our morose little world is their world today—a world in which awareness is both the beginning and the end and the means to the end. They don't need to stick pins in themselves to know they are alive. They have the Vietnam War to do that for them. They've had Nixon, Agnew, Johnson, Wallace, Goldwater, and three assassinations. They do not need an art form to illuminate America's fall from a state of grace. They need only the news on T.V.

The art of the young today, despite its theme of protest, attempts to remind its audience that everything is not, or does not have to be, so horrible. It proclaims the joys of life and attempts to make converts to the pursuit of joy. This art is rock music in all its varieties—folk rock, soft rock, acid rock, hard rock. It is virtually the only art kids know or care about. Often at its best it is artless, simple, humorous, or naïve. And whether the message is protest or serenity, it is presented matter-of-factly, as *what is,* without great emphasis on significance, because the reality of life is there for the taking. Kids can find it on the streets without giving up the comforts of home. Or they can give them up, do the runaway thing, seek reality elsewhere. If they feel isolated in their community, they know where to go to seek the kindred spirits. They are tuned in to each other as easily as they tune in their radios. They, too, can buy their uniforms on Daddy's charge account. But the bill runs to a little more than $2.98 for a black turtleneck and 39 cents for enough bleach to age a new pair of jeans.

As all was black and faded then, all is color now. The cultivated sobriety of the coffee house has been replaced by the psychedelic brilliance of the discothèque. The intense, quiet talking, and the ritualistic silent listening to music has been replaced by the hysterical rap of the speed freak, the intensity of sound in the music that makes talk impossible, the dancing, the tripping in the park, the wearing of flowers and bells, in proclamation of joy, of love, of freedom achieved rather than freedom sought. The feeling is not sublimated through art. It is real. It is tangible. It can be smoked, swallowed, shot up, seen, heard, worn, danced, screwed. And it can't be read, not really, anywhere at all. It does not exist in words, not even in talking. Between people, it exists in vibrations—spirits touching. There are good vibes and bad vibes, but vibes they are, and they have nothing to do with words. Words are too abstract, too indirect, too much of a medium. Vibes are the medium and the message at once. They are not analyzed, they are not considered, they are more than felt. They are known.

PART III

The Dopers: Suburban Aliens and Anomalies

Kentwood, Pennsylvania, 1966–1970

9

KENTWOOD HIGH TODAY

IN 1960, Kentwood was a small school. It had less than 1,000 students, 25 or 30 to each class, and its disciplinary problems were minor. It had enough money to build its own swimming pool and continually expand its quarters, which were brand-new in 1958. Its library was more attractive and more comfortable than any public library in the county. Its auditorium was posh, and it had a gymnasium and outdoor athletic facilities that any small college would have been proud of.

But 80 percent of the books in the library were geared to the lowest common denominator of teenage reading ability, and only seniors were permitted access to the "adult" books. Use of the library was limited to short periods that allowed students enough time to check out and return books, but no opportunity to do reference work. Use of the auditorium was confined to dull, bi-monthly assemblies, three evening plays a year, and study halls that could not be accommodated in classrooms—the only thing the school didn't have enough of. On the other hand, anyone who neglected to make enthusiastic use of the school's excellent athletic facilities was considered ungrateful and a little strange.

Despite its size and its financial and physical resources, Kentwood's approach to education was nearly as impersonal as that of the computerized multiversity.

Nonetheless, one could say that, in the late 1950s, Kentwood was providing a relatively healthy atmosphere for most of its teenage population. In 1957, for example, while there were a number of teenagers arrested locally, all of them were from other towns. Not a single Kentwood youngster that year was involved with the law for anything more serious than minor traffic violations. Very few high school or junior high students failed to be promoted to the next grade, and even fewer dropped out. The education Kentwood offered was neither the most creative nor the most comprehensive that a small school system with a fair amount of money could have provided, but it was adequate.

Those students who wanted to go to college got into colleges. They didn't break their necks getting in, they didn't all "make" the schools they wanted, they didn't all aim very high, and few, if any of them, were as well prepared as they might have been.

But they weren't tested to death, they weren't nervous wrecks, they didn't take or need tranquilizers, and they learned something about something, if not a lot about very much. And a handful of the teachers were pretty good: i.e., they thoroughly understood what they were teaching, and had a strong intention to communicate their knowledge. And the fact that there were no serious disciplinary problems is a fair indication that either a) the school was relatively well-suited to the students and their goals and general orientation toward life, or b) the students were so apathetic that they would have responded like sheep to almost any situation.

In the past ten years, Kentwood High has grown. It has expanded its curriculum to include more languages, a wider variety of social science courses, a few college-level science courses, and a selection of "accelerated" or honors courses in all major subjects. Standardized testing has become an increasingly prominent part of the educational process at Kentwood, as elsewhere, and it is now much easier for faculty and advisers to select those students who may accelerate. It is easier for them to advise students on how they must prepare for the college of their choice, and what college they should choose. Of course the physical plant has had to be expanded in order to accommodate a student body that has nearly doubled over a ten-year period. And there are more books in the library.

The town of Kentwood has more than doubled its population and nearly quadrupled its commerce. At first, every little gas station proposed was fought by zoning committees; but the committees have not won a single battle, and by now they have just about abandoned their opposition. There are fewer trees, more elementary schools, more churches and synagogues, and, of course, more houses. There are even several complexes of apartment buildings. Kentwood is still rural enough to be a highly desirable suburban area, close enough to the city to be convenient for commuters, and exclusive enough in cost and quality of housing (as well as in the fact that no non-Caucasians have attempted to move there) to retain some snob appeal. Kentwood has everything—from virgin woods to country clubs to department stores to a fleet of brand-new elementary schools. Not only that, but its school system is reputed to be one of the finest in the tri-county suburban area.

In the past ten years, Kentwood has grown, but it hasn't changed much. Kentwood High has grown, but it hasn't changed much. But the kids who were in elementary school or kindergarten in 1960 have grown, and they are not at all like the kids who graduated from Kentwood High in 1960.

The five groups that stratified high school social life in the 1950s still exist in Kentwood, as they do elsewhere. But some of their characteristics and values have changed, and new groups have emerged.

1. *The Greasers*. While retaining most of the same characteristics they had ten years ago, the greasers are tougher, more inclined toward crimes such as vandalism, breaking and entering, and general fight-picking, and are considered not so much cultural philistines as racial and political bigots by the *brains* and other "higher" social classes. They still play pin-ball machines in the steak and hoagie shops along the Pike, and they still drink lots of beer. They also smoke pot and take pills of various kinds, though, I am told, they are "very uncool" about drugs, which they use in about the same way they use beer. They have more money, better clothes, more motorcycles, make more noise, have more power. There is really no such thing as a greaser girl any more. She is a *teenybopper* (which see) and she has no more to do with the greaser male than with the men and boys of any other group.

2. *The Sports Kids*. Now generally known as the *rahs* in most places, the athletic and school-spirited All-American types are also turning on. After all, it's part of the good life, isn't it, to have a good time, and pot is supposed to be fun, no? These are four-years-younger counterparts of some of the Goldwater kids Norman Mailer described so well in his coverage of the Republican Convention of 1964—except I really don't think that the kids who worked for Goldwater in 1964 could have smoked pot—but I've run into several very young pot-smokers who worked for Nixon in 1968. Another drug some rahs, like greasers, have come into contact with is speed, usually in pill form. Acid, the other hallucinogens, and the downers aren't really suited to the per-

sonalities of rahs and greasers, because it's too hard to do things while under the influence, and these are two basically physically active groups.

3. *The Brains.* The few real brains that remain are more pressured, more aware of their braininess, and perhaps more obnoxious than the top 10 percent of the class of 1960. The certainty that comes from taking so many tests and seeing so many figures in black and white on charts and graphs certifying one's brilliance becomes almost an end in itself. Brainy high school kids have a peculiar bland kind of self-confidence that one doesn't find in such quantity in comparable groups of college students. Perhaps it is because, despite the tremendous pressures inherent in constant standardized testing, minds and beings are left, at their most basic level, unchallenged by the system. It isn't really a very alive and active thing to be a *brain* any more. It doesn't really offer enough to survive on as a person. Perhaps this is why the brains are falling more and more into additional roles and social structures, such as politics and dope. There is also such a thing as an *intellectual* (not enough of them to rate a category of their own), which existed only as part of the beat group ten years ago, and bore no relation to the *brains*. But the intellectual can just as easily now be an *under-achiever* (which see) as a brain.

4. *The Jews.* Over the past fifteen or twenty years, the suburbs have been attracting great numbers of people from various ethnic groups who had been previously confined to an urban existence, and were experiencing a rising standard of living that seemed to go beyond the potential they could see in city life. Often a particular suburb will almost exclusively attract members of one particular ethnic group, and so it happened that Kentwood attracted Jews. Though there are many many more Jews in Kentwood than there were ten years ago (as evidenced by three synagogues where there

were none), the Jews as a group in the high school are much fewer. The kids, if not their parents, have assimilated much more and are generally more inclined to make their own rather than their parents' choices. Also, many more of them are kids who have been raised in the amalgam of the suburban town, rather than in the city ghetto, where there was a sharp dichotomy of white and black or Jew and black.

5. *The Average.* The average are no longer an interesting group because all those weirdos and misfits who found themselves so classified in the fifties have found out who they really are. So there scarcely is an *average* class anymore. It has defined itself out of existence into three new groups:

a). *The Teenyboppers.* The teenyboppers are a splinter group drawn from the greasers, the rahs, and the average. One usually thinks of teenyboppers as girls, but very rock-oriented boys under 15 are sometimes considered teenyboppers, too. We'll limit our discussion to the girls. Teenybopperism starts at about age 11 on the East Coast, about 9 on the West Coast, and is usually "just a stage I went through" by time the girl reaches 15. Thus it is more of a junior high than a high school phenomenon, but some girls still haven't grown out of it by the time they graduate.

The word was coined by a California disc jockey, and the teenyboppers themselves appeared around 1965, about the same time as miniskirts and little white boots. They are small girls who try very hard to be sexy and are a source of endless temptation, irritation, and delight to many older young men. They smoke lots of cigarettes, chew lots of gum, read rock and fashion magazines, buy lots of clothes, spend lots of time and money on their hair and make-up, and in general appear to devote most of their efforts to trying to appear to be something, rather than actually doing anything. What else they really do is open to speculation. A number of girls I spoke to admitted with some shame that they *had been* teenyboppers. An ex-teenybopper can become just about anyone or anything from a groupie (camp follower of a rock and roll group) to a classics major at Harvard.

b). *The Underachievers.* These are people who have been told at a very early age that they are not living up to their potential. They may be C students, or they may be doing worse (possibly even better), but whatever it is, it's not good enough. As a group, the underachievers could almost be said to be the product of standardized testing. Of course, they existed before standardized testing came into such widespread use, but they were invisible then. Most often, they become visible in, and are sorted out of, what used to be the average group, but they emerge from all other groups as well, with the exception, of course, of the brains. Some of the underachievers now in the high school were so labeled as early as the first or second grade, or wherever they happened to be when the standardized testing program got down to them.

Once discovered, a Kentwood underachiever is watched closely, tested regularly, informed upon to his parents, and generally bugged by the administration. Sometimes more testing, for which special personnel must be called, and high fees paid, is recommended. Sometimes family counseling, or other therapy for the underachieving child, is urged. I suppose sometimes underachievers grow out of it, or get counseled out of it, whatever "it" is that has put the stigma on them, but more often, they do not.

Some underachievers (expecially those who are also intellectuals) have made the decision not to bother with *achieving* in the required sense. These are the people who refuse to go to classes they find dull or stupid, despite the damage to their grades. They are people who do not believe in adjusting and compromising in order to gain the rewards that others think they should want, but that they consider worthless. In other words, these underachievers do not want to achieve just for the sake of achieving, nor can they find other reasons for doing so.

Other underachievers would actually like to achieve, but if they have any more of an idea of what is holding them back than their counselors do, they can't bring themselves to confront it.

Since either kind of underachiever is a person who has been repeatedly told that he is less than he is, or less than he should be, it is not surprising that he goes around dramatizing this in one way or another. His general tone is apathetic, or sad, or maybe fearful. He is the kid no one can do anything with.

Socially, the underachievers quietly recognize each other as fellow-misfits, and make a kind of half-hearted attempt (the same level of attempt many of them make at everything else) to laugh the whole thing off, and do what they want to do with their time. Some of them feel around for *something* they can do well, or want to do well, and sometimes they find it. Some of the ones who don't find it become dopers, and so do some of those who do.

c). *The Dopers.* It was very difficult for me to get used to using the word "dope" as it is used today, for anything from a light tranquilizer or "downer" like Librium, on up to heroin and the other opium derivative narcotics. To me, heroin, cocaine, opium, and the like were dope; anything else was just drugs. In the old days, anyone referring to pot as dope (such as somebody's mother calling a pot-smoker a "dope fiend") was really to be put down. Today, pot-smokers call themselves, among other things, "dopers," as do the speed freaks, the acid-heads, and the users of heroin. So I use the word here to include all of those.

The dopers are often underachievers. Either the same thing that has led them to underachieve has led them to dope, or dope has led them to underachieve. Dopers can start out as brains, rahs, greasers, teenyboppers, or anything else, but when dope becomes more important to them than being any of these other things, they become dopers. However, in Kentwood and elsewhere, especially in the East, the hard-core dopers of the middle class, whether just potheads, speed freaks, or in a mixed dope bag, are more or less intellectual or spiritual types who reluctantly admit resenting the fact that greasers and rahs are using dope (which is in some circles almost a sacrament), as they would booze, which is in most doper circles the poison of another generation.

10

CHILDREN OF PARADISE

A REPORT made public in the spring of 1969 indicates that, in the opinion of the administration, one-sixth of Kentwood's then 1,800 high school and junior high school students have tried marijuana. People who graduated from Kentwood before 1960 say that if as many as one-sixth of the student body in their time had ever gotten drunk, they would be most surprised. I would be most surprised if *as few* as one-sixth of Kentwood's students in 1969 have tried pot.

A statistic like this, however, is significant and disturbing enough to most parents. What too many fail to realize, I think, is that it is merely a sympton of other problems. Drugs have received a fair amount of attention in this book, and will receive more. But the use of drugs is not really where it's at with these kids. Drug use is merely the most easily measurable index of this generation's differentness. Unfortunately, in most communities, it has not been regarded as such. There has been a tendency to attack the dope problem as if it were measles. The tremendous emphasis on the drug problem by the press in its running coverage of the ever-widening generation gap has tended to lead too many adults, many if not most of them in a position to take positive action

74

against drug abuse, to the conclusion that if there were no drugs there would be no problem. This is somewhat understandable in view of the fact that, until the recent increase of student militancy and radicalism at the high school level provided a new focal point for our attention, drug abuse was the one characteristic problem of the runaway generation that could be pinpointed sufficiently to be attacked at all.

But I cannot stress strongly enough how dangerous I feel it is, and how destructive it has been, to allot all the attention units we as an adult society can invest in the problems of youth on stopping drug users from using drugs and preventing potential drug users from using drugs, as if drugs were themselves a virus that has appeared in the air of a previously whole and healthy community, whose members of all ages were previously sound of mind and spirit, and whose young just happen to be, by virtue of their youth alone, extremely susceptible to infection.

I also cannot stress strongly enough how dangerous I feel it is to do what Kentwood did. Whereas many communities, especially in New York's suburbs, appear to be attacking their youth problem by trying to arrest every kid who's ever been present in the same room with a stick of pot, Kentwood has, in recent years, developed a unique and even more macabre approach: for some strange reason, it seems to have become fashionable in Kentwood to use the in-patient facilities of a nearby state mental hospital to handle adolescents' difficulties whenever possible.

Haverford State Hospital was built in Delaware County, Pennsylvania, in 1962, not because there was great need for it in the immediate area of the Philadelphia Main-Line and other comfortable though less affluent suburbs, but, one would assume, because the available site was the best that could be obtained within the radius the hospital was to serve. There was much controversy about it in Haverford Township and nearby towns, including Kentwood, which is located some miles from the hospital. Local people, naturally, did not think they and theirs would have much use for the place. And though the hospital was to be set deep in the woods, high in the hills, the folk of all the surrounding towns got chills at the thought of escaped loonies. The response of the local gentry to the proposed hospital hardly differed from the reaction one might expect from such quiet conservative communities to the suggestion that a state prison be built on their terrain.

As it turned out, however, there is far greater local utilization of the hospital than there would have been for any hypothetical prison—unless the crime rate had increased by several hundred percent. In the Fifties, suburbanites and their children were not being put away. Their children, at least, were not even going to psychiatrists. Probably most of the kids who went to Kentwood High before 1960 didn't even know anyone who had gone to a psychiatrist. A girl got knocked up once in a while, a guy stole a car once in a while, but they didn't get their heads shrunk ... or if they did it was done with such a shamed secrecy that no one found out about it. And in a small town, there is little that does not get found out sooner or later.

But suddenly, there is a mental hospital near town. Suddenly there are a number of psychiatrists setting up shop in the paneled basements of their new split-levels. And suddenly, Haverford State Hospital is the friendly local loony bin, in which drug abusers, unhappy kids, kids with unhappy parents, and anyone else under 21 who happens to be in someone's way could be dumped, in the following manner:

Concerned parents visit a psychiatrist to consult him about their child. They make a statement, which is then signed by the doctor, who then gets it signed by another doctor— neither of whom need really have ever seen the child in question (although the law does require this)—and the child, or individual under 21, is admitted. Until he reaches the age of 21, he can, of course, be released only into the custody of these same parents or another adult, but even if he happens to reach 21 while an in-patient, release is not easily come by. For more than one or two families in such a small town as Kentwood to feel the need to commit a teenager against his will in such a way, it would seem that the community as a whole would have to be terribly frightened of its kids.

In Kentwood, I interviewed a group of seven people, all friends, three girls and four boys, ranging in age from 16 to 18. They were: Bobby Goldberg, 18; Kenny Carpenter, 18; Laurie White, 16; Peggy French, 16; Kitty Price, 16; Cal Michaels, 17; and Gregory Eisman, 18. Bobby and Kitty were born in Philadelphia and transplanted, Bobby as he was about to enter second grade, and Kitty when she was 12 and going into eighth grade. The others were born in Kentwood or nearby suburbs, and started school in Kentwood. All seven fell into the doper and underachiever categories.

In their degree of intellectual curiosity, they ranged from Bobby, Gregory, and Peggy, who all had genius I.Q.'s and were voracious if sporadic readers, to Laurie whose speech was ungrammatical and whose reading, when she read at all, consisted of the contemporary American equivalent of the penny dreadful.

Bobby, Peggy, and Cal had dropped out of school in the tenth grade. Laurie, Kitty, and Ken had repeated courses or grades or had taken summer courses because of failures. Gregory alone managed to get by.

Their sex lives were also varied. Laurie and Kenny were both virgins, and Laurie intended to remain so until marriage—if she ever got married, which she wasn't sure she would ever want to do. On an acid trip, Kitty had slept with one person, whom she didn't know and didn't particularly like. She feared lesbian tendencies. Peggy had slept with dozens of people. She said she was bisexual. Cal had had one heterosexual affair (with Peggy) and was actively homosexual. Bobby and Greg had moderately active and satisfactory sex lives, and neither considered sex to be a hang-up. It was a matter of great concern to the others. All seven considered themselves basically monogamous, and found serious relationships unquestionably preferable to "free love" or promiscuity.

Bobby, Cal, and Peggy had been hospitalized at Haverford State Hospital within the past two years. Gregory was subsequently committed there.

Besides those of the Kentwood seven who had been hospitalized, all except Ken had been treated at length by psychiatrists. Ken had gone only once, to his father's psychiatrist, and refused to continue. Laurie was the only one under treatment at the time of the interview. None felt they had benefited greatly from their therapy, and none felt that they had benefited at all from hospitalization.

None came from broken homes, though Laurie and Kitty both described critical home situations involving physical brutality on the part of their fathers. All had siblings. Laurie was the middle child and the only girl of five. Kitty had two younger brothers. Gregory was the oldest of four, Cal, the youngest of three, Bobby the younger of two, and Peggy and Ken each the older of two. Laurie was the only one with a working mother, and the only one whose father was a blue collar worker. Incomes of the others ranged from $10,000 to $40,000 a year. About half of the fathers and fewer of the mothers were college educated.

As a social group in relation to the rest of Kentwood High School, these seven boys and girls correspond quite closely to the beat group that emerged in Kentwood in the late

Fifties. In fact, Bobby Goldberg, who could have roughly been called the leader of the dopers, was, as a small boy, acquainted with Barney Katz, who was the major spirit behind the beat group. Bobby had started on the beat group's required reading and listening list when he was about 10, and completed it by the time he was 14—by which time, of course, the beat group no longer existed in Kentwood (all of its members, including Barney and Bobby's sister, Susan, having moved away), and beatniks, the press said, no longer existed anywhere.

11

THE KENTWOOD SEVEN

BOBBY, whose appearance was often drastically altered by a weight gain or loss of as much as twenty-five pounds in a week, depending on his drug intake, always looked older than his age, especially after methedrine began to thin out his straight dark hair. Sometimes he was very thin and hollow-eyed, sometimes pot-bellied fat, with wild, puffy eyes. And we see him at 16 in a very different home environment from the one his older sister, Susan, knew in high school.

The recreation room of the Goldberg house, in which we met Susan and her friends on Christmas Eve in 1959, has changed a lot. The room is Bobby's own room now, and it is beautiful. One of the nicely covered old couches is still there, but his father's desk and books are out, replaced by a large oak worktable, and many shelves of hard back books, including leather-bound sets and first editions, that Bobby has gone to considerable effort to collect. The paneled walls are decorated with a handsome arrangement of Matisse prints, unframed, and the room is lit by electric lanterns hanging from heavy brass chains. There are some small pieces of abstract sculpture, carefully placed. The asphalt tile floor is covered with an old, slightly frayed, but still good-looking

Oriental rug. The big windows are covered with brown bur-
lap drapes made to Bobby's specifications by his mother, as
were the brown velvet pillows on the couch. There is a
decent, though not excellent, set of stereo components, on
which Bobby has done much work himself, and a console
tape recorder that is a fair piece of sound equipment and a
rather attractive piece of furniture. There are also two
guitars and a set of bungo drums.

The room has an entrance through the garden and a private bathroom, and Bobby and his friends are free to come
and go as they choose.

It was in this room that Bobby later came very close to
succeeding in two attempts to take his own life before he
reached his 17th birthday. It was from this room that Bobby
was taken, on the second occasion, to Haverford State
Hospital. There, he was confined, given rough treatment,
and more of the drugs he had already so badly abused. But
during the second month of his two-month stay, he was
often visited by his friends. He was given ground privileges
at the hospital, soon acquired a little pot, and was taken off
the grounds on a number of occasions by his non-drug-using
girl friend for sexual rendezvous.

Bobby dropped out of Kentwood High after hiding behind
the "underachiever" label for years— with a genius I.Q. and
college-freshman-level results on achievement tests taken in
seventh grade. He had started "running away from home" at
the age of 12—in a way that upset his parents, but that
seems like an extended walk around the block compared to
the style of today's runaways. He would hitchike obsessively,
leaving home for 12 to 36 hours, three or four times a week,
usually with no destination in mind. Once he was picked up
by the police several hundred miles and two states away.
Other times, he'd call home around 4 the morning after
his disappearance and his father would pick him up at the

entrance or exit of the turnpike, less than ten miles from the Goldbergs' house. His disappearances were only occasionally prefaced by family disagreements—though he responded to no rules or other attempts at discipline and fought with his parents frequently.

He usually confined his hitching jaunts to summers, but his poor grades at school were largely based on absence— sometimes truancy in the usual sense, but more often psychosomatic, or consciously pretended, illness. He demanded much from his parents and he got it all—whether it was an expensive tape-recorder from his father or deliberate lies to the truant officer from his mother. It was obvious that he didn't want to go to school, and his parents had no idea of what to do. They tried family agencies but got little encouragement about available services. They had too little faith in any form of therapy—or knowledge of what could be expected from it—to seriously consider the investment involved. And Bobby was adverse to any suggestion of help. He just wanted to be left alone.

In tenth grade, he flatly refused to continue going to school.

"I wasn't learning anything. I didn't want to. I wasn't going to school to learn, I was messed up for other reasons. Everyone thought I left Kentwood because I was too smart for the system. Actually, I left out of fear. Fear of the social order. Just a general feeling of 'I don't fit.' I wanted to fit, and in any case, I thought I could find some place where I did fit more easily.

"In a way, I thought I wanted a little more of an academic atmosphere. But I could have had that if I'd changed friends and paid more attention to what was going on academically. But that wasn't what I wanted to do then. I really wanted to kind of follow the establishment. I liked school only when I was successful in doing that.

"If our social system was arranged so that people went to school to learn without ulterior motives, then school would be a better place. As it is, school had half a dozen social functions which are much stronger motivations for going: the draft, parents who want kids to go for whatever reasons —to get a good job, to achieve the social status that an education gives you."

Bobby's friends had similar feelings about Kentwood High. Kenny Carpenter, age 18, had just graduated. He was born and raised in Kentwood and the Kentwood school system. His father is a successful businessman. Ken's friends insisted that, even though he was older than the group I was most interested in, I should talk to him, and I was glad I had.

Neatly dressed in khakis and a clean white shirt, with straight blond hair, a roundish face, and quiet, intent blue eyes, Ken impressed me at first as being quiet, withdrawn, and above all, straight. In a group that included four of his peers and two older young adults, he said little or nothing, answering the few questions put directly to him as briefly as possible. His answers were not given shyly, or with hostility, but simply as if he had nothing he wanted to say. At no time did he actively enter the discussion, and it was not easy to form an opinion of him. When we left the group for the interview, however, I saw quite a different boy. He smiled often as he talked—a warm, open flash of a smile that conveyed a quiet humor and a willingness to communicate honestly and directly.

"No," Kenny said. "I can't say I've been learning anything in school. I never liked Kentwood. I never worked. I just tried to pass. School itself never appealed to me. I liked history and math," he volunteered, "and I liked English, but I did lousy in it. I now regret not working, but since I was accepted in community college, it's okay. I'll work there.

"I'd like to know more about what I missed in school. I didn't get anything out of it. Kentwood is good for a person who is willing to accept rules, about things like hair—no sideburns, it has to be an inch above the collar. They measure it. And no collarless shirts. But they had to change that rule for Nehru shirts and turtlenecks.

"I couldn't have done anything about my situation there until the school gave me certain rights, some way to feel at ease. I always had the feeling that if the vice principal walked into the classroom he'd take me out of school. There's a lot of discrimination in that school. The sports people are allowed to get by with smoking, lateness, longer hair, etc. Otherwise the rules really wouldn't have been so hard to accept."

Kentwood's vice principal is a former boys' physical education teacher who was known among students even in the Fifties for his gross misrepresentation of marijuana and venereal disease. He has been in the Kentwood school system for about fifteen years, during which time he has been the major source of guidance for boys. He had the reputation of a friendly but strong-armed guy who always emphasized athletics and a generally anti-intellectual approach to the high school experience.

"The ideas behind all these rules of his just don't make sense," Ken Carpenter said. "The idea that certain kids are 'distracted' by things like long hair and weird clothes and therefore can't work."

What angered Ken most was his sense that nobody really cared, for instance, whether his hair was long or not, but that the rule and others like it existed for other reasons. He cited the town's attitude toward the community college: "They wanted to build it here, but Kentwood won't let it go through. All the newspapers printed things like, 'Have you ever seen a hippie? Well, you're going to if you let a college be built here. The Republicans are just getting the better of the Democrats by not letting it be here. Nobody really cares if it's here or not."

CAL MICHAELS

Cal Michaels had apparently dropped out of Kentwood in the tenth grade for similar reasons. "It was a hassle, man," he said. "It was really bringing me down. Lots of people are finding it isn't a challenge and it is a hassle and they can go about and achieve their goals without schooling at a place like Kentwood."

I had met Cal several times before, when he was about 15. Over six feet tall, good-looking and well-mannered, he had had light curly hair, brown eyes, and an impish smile. He had been a very pleasant boy and a talented painter. His girl friend at the time was in Haverford State Hospital (she is still there), and he had since been an inmate there himself. Now, at 17, he had a swaggering, almost churlish manner; his smile was more maniacal than impish, and his eyes had flattened to dull buttons in a face that was mannequin-like, pasty in color, and hard in tone. It was difficult to get him to speak specifically about Kentwood High.

"I wouldn't know where to begin to change it. It's so uptight. There are too many people in high places who want certain things; there's no unity. Each is following what they want. The inconsistency was so great that it frightened and upset me to such a degree that I had no recourse but to get out, and I did, and I'm glad. And I think other young people will fix Kentwood's wagon."

LAURIE WHITE

What people Cal was referring to, I don't know, but the kids who are still there seem far less interested in changing the school or "fixing its wagon" than in simply getting out.

Kenny's girl friend, Laurie White, who was going into the twelfth grade, had promised herself she'd try to do better in her last year on principle, but she was rather cynical about the school. She had her own ideas about what she needed to know, regardless of college entrance requirements. And that which, in her opinion, she did not need to know would have to be forced into her with a bulldozer.

"The school's just academic. It's crummy, if you're not academic." By "not academic" she apparently meant "not an intellectual," as opposed to a student following the general or business rather than academic program. "It's my impression that the standards for being an academic student are too high for most of the kids there. The main thing that's wrong is that the kids have no choice in what goes on in the school.

"If you asked me now what I learned last year, I've probably forgotten. I didn't exert myself as much as I should have. In some classes, I just didn't want to learn. Like in geometry, I just sat there and flunked. My use for it is you have to take two maths. So I just decided I'm not going to hassle it."

Wearing blue jeans and a print blouse, with half her shoulder-length, wavy brown hair tied back with a pink ribbon, Laurie looked a lot like Kentwood girls looked ten years ago, except for her sandals and Greek canvas shoulder bag. If I'd passed her on the street, I would have guessed her to be 20. Talking, she seemed more her age. She chewed gum, smoked uneasily, and couldn't keep a cigarette lit. Yet, at the same time, she seemed rather poised.

"I liked school better back in sixth grade, seventh and eighth grades," she said. "In ninth I started not liking it, and in tenth I knew I didn't like it."

I asked her what happened between eighth and ninth grades. She said, "I changed, that's all. I just found school a big drag, the way it was run, like taking subjects I didn't want to take. And it would be better if it wasn't so much on a teacher to student basis, raise your hand and all this. But more like conversation, everyone together. And I personally don't want to be bothered with science, maybe I should be. But I'm not taking physics."

Laurie said that she didn't think she wanted to go to college, but that if she did, she'd want to study languages. But she had to drop her language course for her senior year in order to repeat geometry.

"It's not a hassle if I don't go. If I want to be anything, it would be like a social worker or a stewardess, and you can get training for that. If you have college, you have a better chance, but you can make it with just training.

"Most of the people I know who are going to college are going just to go. I haven't really heard anyone tell me why they're going to college because it's gonna help them. Most people I know are going because their parents prefer them to go or because they don't know what they want to do with themselves yet. So they go to college, wait till they find out, and get a better education, I guess."

Her parents, Laurie says, would like her to go to college, but are willing to go along with her decision. They are, however, concerned about their feeling that she has "nothing in mind" for the future. Laurie insists this isn't so. She has several ideas, the most prominent of which is, at the moment, VISTA.

"All I know about it is that it's helping other people and traveling. I haven't really looked into it, but I'd like to. I think that's why I want to be a stewardess. I want to travel. I haven't even been up in a plane yet. I think I'll like it, though."

Laurie could have gotten more out of school, "If I had gone with the idea that I'm going to learn something, but I didn't. Last year, I was going just because I thought I had to. So I cut a lot. This year, I can't do that. Besides having to, I want to go, because of it's my last year and all. And keeping myself in mid-air isn't too good. Like this geometry is really a hang-up, taking two maths. I don't want to have to go to summer school."

Aside from passing geometry, Laurie's project for senior year was getting onto the yearbook staff and changing the concept of the book "because I think it stinks." She felt that enough people wanted the kinds of changes she had in mind to make them possible, but when I asked her what percentage of Kentwood's students felt pretty much the way she did about the school, her answer surprised me:

"I'd say most of them except the highly intelligent kids. The kids who are doing well are getting what they want because the school is giving it to them."

GREGORY EISMAN

Gregory Eisman was by anyone's standards the most successful student of the seven. He, too, was an "underachiever" in that his grades did not match up with his I.Q. or other test results. But he stuck it out to the end, and his grades were good enough to get him into Columbia.

"I guess I got all I was looking for from Kentwood. I didn't expect more. I set very low standards for myself. My sociology course, for instance, had a lot to offer. But I didn't take it. I just never dug school.

"The kids I know who dropped out seemed to do so because they wanted to and because they were also able to without losing anything. Their parents would let them live at home and procrastinate, vegetate, whatever they wanted to do. My parents literally kept me in school. I might not have dropped out, anyway, but it's difficult to say. I got into lots of trouble at school, but it only affected me in how it affected my status with my parents. They always acted as if I'd affected them adversely.

"All the kids I know who dropped out went to mental hospitals when they dropped out. That's probably most of the dropouts. And they weren't necessarily going there for good reasons. They didn't do much for them, didn't have any positive effects on them. If anything, it's a good excuse."

KITTY PRICE

The parents of Kitty Price, who was entering her senior year, want to give her that very excuse. Kitty is a smallish, very neat looking girl, slender in a tight-looking, nervous, forcibly contained way. When I interviewed her, she was wearing a clean, pretty cotton print Nehru shirt, clean jeans, and sandals. Her short, curly black hair was cut to the shape of her head, rather than in pursuit of a particular fad or style. She looked 14.

Kitty went to a private academy in the city until her parents moved to Kentwood, when she was in the eighth grade.

"I was stuck in an accelerated class in the junior high, but I liked school, and I did well until eleventh grade. Then I just didn't care any more. I started taking drugs. All I did was come to school stoned, and I just wouldn't say anything because I'd be afraid I'd sound strange. So I just sat there.

"I couldn't cut, because I feel better when I'm with people, but not with straight people. I'm afraid they'll take what I say the wrong way. My parents think I'm crazy. They want to send me to Haverford State because of drugs. They sent me to a psychiatrist. I just quit. I was going since January [about eight months]. He wouldn't say anything. He'd just close his eyes, and I wouldn't know if he was asleep or what. What do you say to someone who sits there half-asleep all the time. Finally I just got up and said I didn't have anything to talk about, and I left.

"At first, I did want to learn in school. I liked history and art. But last year when I went to art class, I just didn't feel like doing anything. My teacher asked me why. I don't know why. I wish I did. I'm not interested in too much. Nothing means anything to me. I just want to get out and get rid of my parents."

PEGGY FRENCH

The Kentwood school system may be inadequate to meet the needs of many of its students, but transferring to private schools has failed to provide the "answer" for those Kentwood dropouts who have tried it.

Peggy French, the 16-year-old daughter of a philosophy professor, was one who did try it. She left Kentwood in the ninth grade and attended an excellent private academy for tenth grade and the beginning of eleventh. Out of school for a year and a half, she has had no further formal education except for summer art classes.

"I can't really pinpoint why I stopped. I was bored and restless, and I didn't really feel that I fit in at all. It wasn't a question of grades. My marks were all right. I just didn't adjust to the situation."

Like Laurie, Peggy looked much older than her age, but while Laurie looked perhaps more innocent than she was, Peggy looked more tough. She had shoulder-length, thick, curly blond hair with dark roots in evidence, and she was wearing a tan work-shirt and white jeans. She is pretty, big, and self-confident looking, a little on the buxom side, a little assertive in her movements, but quite feminine. She doesn't smile much, and her tight, opaque brown eyes are at once astute, penetrating, and sullen in expression.

When I asked Peggy if she had been learning anything,

she qualified her "yes" by adding, "as far as the process was concerned.

"I enjoyed biology and parts of math, but I was disappointed with English. I felt that they were really holding me back. Most of the books they assigned, I'd already read. There was no point in going over the stuff."

Peggy had no suggestions for improving the school. "They were already adequate for most of the students. It was me. I really couldn't fit in with that scene. Most of the people were able to cope with it and didn't have complaints. I just didn't feel like going to school for awhile."

Peggy said she got along well with her classmates, and although she said she might have been a little too outspoken and made things difficult for herself with the teachers and administration, that did not seem to be the problem either.

"I really enjoyed the tenth grade. It was still new, and I got really good grades. I made a whole game of getting fantastic grades. I got along well with the kids and I was surprised to have come into a new school and adjusted so well. I was respected for my ideas. I think some of the kids tended to think I was snobbish, but they respected me and didn't make me an outcast or anything like that," Peggy said, as if the role of outcast was what she had been accustomed to.

I asked her what had changed between tenth and eleventh grade.

"The drug scene became more important to me than school for a while. I hate to say it, but that is what happened."

Exactly what is a "drug scene"?

The following pages, written by Bobby Goldberg especially for this book, tell what the drug scene was like one weekend in Kentwood. Cal Michaels's version of the same weekend follows Bobby's story.

BOBBY GOLDBERG—JUNE 28, 1968

A Friday evening. I was with Kenny and Peter. Somebody had given Kenny $50 for Meth, and we all drove down to Jimmie's (after calling, of course) to get this handled. I was, as usual, the negotiator. They parked the car (Peter's $4500 Barracuda), and I got out to go in. Jimmie's apartment, in town, was a royal abomination. The place was littered with parts—parts to almost anything and everything you can imagine. His dog, name of Captain Crunch, then just a puppy, was jumping around, probably stoned. Jimmie was 38, had neither hair nor teeth, and was an eyesore. He was lying on his bed in his underwear, enthusiastic about the weekend. Bart, a good-looking guy of about 20, with starry stoned blue eyes, sat on the couch eating a bowl of Captain Crunch. He looked much healthier than the rest of us. Jimmie was planning an orgy. He invited me. I didn't have any intention of going to it, but I told him I'd think about it. Max, the *Man,* a guy of about 40 who supported a mother, a wife, two kids, and a girl friend by peddling his wares, which he kept in a little black leather bag on the seat of his Lincoln, directly between him and the gun in his glove compartment, had not yet arrived.

Jimmie asked me to call Pat, a 16-year-old fat girl who was in love with me for a while, though I constantly ignored her, and convince her to come up to his apartment so he could molest her. Reluctantly, I consented to do so. Doing favors for Jimmie was a tolerated part of the whole scene. I handled most of that. Jimmie did the same favors for Max. Pat agreed to come, and I left to drive around town with the guys until the stuff arrived.

I called from a phone booth. Max had come and we went back to pick it up. We went back to Kentwood where the guy we were buying for was going to pick it up. It was a good chunk of speed, and we split it directly in half, half for us, half for him. Then I got out my trusty old outfit (a slang word, usually meaning an eyedropper and a pacifier, though mine consisted of the glass part of a tuberculin syringe and a pacifier) and slipped on a #26 or #25g needle and we all did up the rather large cut we took. I wasn't satisfied, though I'd done a lot—about a quarter-spoon.

The guy who put up the money came. He looked at it and said it was awfully small for $50. We told him that was all we scored. He had never shot up before, and I hit him with a good shot. That made him very happy, and he had no more complaints. I wanted more for myself, and I talked him into giving me a dime's worth with my radio as collateral until I could pay him. He still has the radio.

Peter left. Ken and I drove out about five miles and found Laurie, who was refreshing. We drove back to my house where I played the guitar for a while and Ken and I played chess. The game lasted about an hour and a half. I won. It was then 12:30 A.M. Saturday. I took Ken home and Laurie came back to my house with me. She could stay out a bit later, and I asked her to come because I dug her company. But when we got back, I no longer wanted to talk. I was feeling pretty lousy and was angry at the insufficient methedrine and was already coming down. So I played a few notes on the guitar and said some uninteresting things. Laurie talked about her relationship with Ken; she didn't feel good about it. I wanted to screw her, but I didn't let her know it. I drove her home. I was silent all the way.

On the way home, I played the radio; the music annoyed me but silence was worse. When I got in, I hunted around for a while for some postulated pirate dope—maybe something Captain Kidd had long stashed beneath my rug.

In desperation, I called Jimmie, told him I was really strung out, and asked him for meth. He said they had done it all. The sounds from his apartment indicated a good time. Cal and Peggy, together as always, were there. They asked if I would drive into the city and take them to Kentwood. They said they had left people there, and that Cal's parents were away for a few days. I said yes; I had nothing to lose.

I arrived at 3 A.M. A man in the street said, "Captain Crunch is gone in a car." I didn't believe him, so I checked the door. There was a note that read, "The party hath proceeded hither." It was Cal's handwriting. I wondered who had driven them.

I knew they had gone to Cal's, and I chose to follow rather than to go home. I took the expressway, rolled down all the windows and let the air blow in my face. But I still felt pretty rotten.

When I arrived, there was a black Lincoln in the driveway. I didn't place it at first. I went in and walked upstairs. There were some people there I didn't know. The house was maybe twenty years old, in contrast to the much younger look-alike ranch houses a few blocks away. It was tastelessly furnished, and a color portrait of the Nixon family, torn from a newspaper, hung in the living room over the color T.V. The only appealing part of the house was the two rooms that belong to Cal. His bedroom had thick white wall-to-wall carpeting and walls paneled with very good wood. At one end of the room were two beautiful walnut chairs that had been stolen from a church. I noted with surprise that Max (the *Man*) was sitting in one of them. I exchanged hellos with everyone and was filled in on what had happened so far.

They had all been at Jimmie's except for Gene Poletti and his two friends (the strangers) who had stayed at Cal's and were tripping (one of them badly). Pat and another girl had been with the crew at Jimmie's though they had now gone home.

Jimmie had stayed downstairs with the other girl and applied his technique of giving a chick a huge shot of methedrine and tearing off her clothes simultaneously. Note: The initial rush from a good shot of speed is overwhelming. It could be described as vascular orgasm. I observed, having given a lot of people their first shots, that 99 percent of them removed at least one article of clothing as soon as they could get their wits together.

Meanwhile, Bart, Cal, Peggy, Pat, and Judy had gone up to the roof of the three-story apartment building that Jimmie and Bart lived in. They had all shot up. Cal (who is three-quarters queer) was looking to put the make on Bart (who was not queer in the least). Judy (who once told me she liked all kinds of bodies but she wasn't sure about Jimmie's dog) wanted to make Peggy, who wouldn't have resisted. Pat offset the whole thing, and everyone seemed to be disgusted with her. Note:

Jimmie had picked up Judy when she was 14, shot her up, and . . .

Having acknowledged the above, I walked over to Max, told him I had done a good shot of his meth and wasn't satisfied with it at all. I was thinking about asking him for credit. To my surprise, he told me to wait, ran down to his car, came up and poured a *pile* of meth on a piece of paper for me. It must have been close to a spoon. I was ecstatic. I thanked him half a dozen times, and then sought after a set of works. Someone said Jimmie had them, so I sought after Jimmie. He was in bed with Judy in one of the three bedrooms. He opened the door a crack and slipped them to me. I couldn't wait. I found a vial, mixed it up, being nice enough to leave a little for Cal, and I did it. Wow, did I get off. It was one of the best shots I ever did. I felt good.

Cal carelessly cleaned the works and did what I had left him. Meanwhile Max was admiring some of Peggy's drawings. He offered her some dope for them. She decided against it. Cal did his best to convince her, but she wouldn't give in. Then she left the room, and Cal bypassed her entirely, and traded the drawings to Max. He took them happily and left. Peggy returned and didn't say anything about what Cal had done, but I could tell she was angry. Anyway, we mixed it up, and I hit her with about half of it. She fell back on the floor, squirming and panting, incredibly off. Then Cal did some, and I got off again, too.

Jimmie and Judy came out. We went through a spontaneous vaudeville routine. He had cocaine. Bart bought a dime from him, and I talked him into a dime on credit, which I promptly shot up. Cal sought after Gene and got some acid from him, which he mixed with Bart's coke. Bart also had a little meth, and it was added to the mixture. Bart, Cal, and Peggy split it up, and shot it, all enjoying it. Around this time, Jimmie disappeared into the bathroom with Judy, and didn't come out for almost three hours. They did this often.

Meanwhile, I wandered out of the room and ran into a guy who was having a bad trip. I tried to help him. He went outside. I talked him into coming back in, and finally got him to sleep in a quiet room.

I wanted to go for a ride. I went looking for company and wound up with Cal, Peggy, and Bart—I drove well, except I was foolish enough to offer Bart the wheel after he told me he'd really like to learn to drive. Fortunately, he was responsible enough to decline.

We drove to the lakes down Spring Road, where we stood around for a while admiring the scene. A cop appeared. I got very nervous. I was barefoot and could have been busted for driving that way if for nothing else. He asked us where we were from. We said Kentwood and Philadelphia. He said, "Go back to Kentwood and Philadelphia." We left. On our way, the Cream came on the radio singing "Sunshine of Your Love." Everyone was enjoying, and everyone was happy.

Back at Cal's nothing had changed very much. Possibly Gene and his two tripping friends had already left. Jimmie was worried about his dog, and would be needing a ride home. I told him I would be leaving soon so my father could take the car to work, but that Peter was supposed to pick me up at 9:15 and would take them into Philadelphia. That was agreed upon.

So we rapped for a while and listened to the radio, and I went home to confront suspicious parents.

I locked myself in my room, took off my clothes, turned on the fan, and played the guitar for a while. Nine-fifteen came and Peter wasn't there. Twelve o'clock came and Peter wasn't there. I called and Peter wasn't there. I got up my paranoid methedrine guts and decided to hitchhike back to Cal's.

I must have looked very funny. I thought there were hairs in my mouth. Maybe there were, because maybe that's where they went when they fell off my head. Anyway, I was compulsively trying to get them out, and I had to justify this to the guy who picked me up.

When I arrived at Cal's, everyone commented on my appearance, which was terrible. I explained that Peter had not shown up. Jimmie became worried about having to take a bus and a subway. I called Ken and asked him if he knew where Peter was. He didn't, but I invited him over. Meanwhile, Jimmie started considering a cab, but he had no money. I knew he was hoarding a little meth. I pulled out the only three dollars I had and pointed to my arm. He got what I was saying and reluctantly loaded the works for me. I got off. My blood was black and thick and it hardly moved.

Ken arrived. He said Peter was probably with someone whose name I've forgotten, but I remember his blue convertible and annoying mock-up. I thought this was a good indication because "person with blue car" had money and this meant more dope. Nevertheless, neither of them were seen for the rest of that weekend.

Jimmie took out the end of his meth. The needle had clogged irreparably, and all there was was a 3-inch #20, which is wide and hurts. But they used it and Jimmie and Bart finished off the stuff.

The phone rang. Cal picked it up. He turned around and said, "Can anyone cop any grass?" I said I could but I'd have to go to Germantown and get a key and then to central Philadelphia to get the grass. This looked like a good opportunity to get some dope, because all I had to do was go into an empty house, take some grass, and leave some money, making my own prices. Jimmie said that he could probably cop, too. Then he asked Cal if they had a car. Cal repeated the question over the telephone and was answered, "Yes." So Jimmie decided he'd con them into a ride, whether anyone was going to cop or not. Cal told them to stop over, and hung up. We asked him who they were. He said, friends of Poletti's. It was an unexceptional truth at that time that all Poletti's friends were creeps.

They arrived. They were creeps. They were all under 18. They were from Wynnefield, and they drove a bright new station wagon with a stereo tape deck playing The Doors. They were four.

Jimmie, Judy, and I piled into the car. I lay down in the back and hung my head out the tailgate. It was an annoying ride. Jimmie screamed obsenities at 8-year-old girls, and the driver, whose father, it was said, had several million dollars, expressed a uniform hostility toward all forms of matter and life.

We arrived at Jimmie's, he fed the dog, and we began discussing prices and procedures. Jimmie made a few phone calls, probably to nonexistent people, and, of course, came up with nothing. Then we talked about hash. I don't think anybody wanted to be there.

Now it was up to me. I made a call to Germantown and checked on my key. It was there. But another problem arose. Our clientele was pressed for time. We squabbled. Finally, I offered to bypass the key and break into the house for a fee of $5. Jimmie advised against it, and I withdrew the offer. They complained and finally gave up. Judy said she would see us later, and left. The Wynnefield boys hatefully consented to drive me home, with a few unbelievable detours, but I had no say in the matter. So a new cycle of action began, with the previous one still incomplete.

We drove to Wynnefield, stopped for water ice (I had no money so they bought me some), and proceeded to race through a shopping center, where they honked the horn, screamed to everyone they knew, and abruptly stopped a few times to exchange words with bystanders. I didn't want to be there at all.

They began to talk about "Monster"—a stupid name for methedrine if I ever heard one. They would stop and try to get "Monster." I came up to present time; I wanted some. I discreetly inquired about prices and the possibility of a free shot. No conclusions were reached, so we discussed "Monster" in general. Subtopics included: quality of Monster; how much everyone had done; how high everyone had been; how many "knock-out shots" (Stellar Shots, tastes) one should get out of a good spoon; general spoon size. Note: It's difficult to get a true spoon (1/16 oz.) from modern businessmen. Some will give you a gram (approximately 1/28 oz.). Some give you even less. Sometimes you're lucky. I listened to them and laughed inside. I figured I could do more in one shot than the four of them combined. That may or may not have been true. I told them about the time I had an ounce. They were impressed, but they held it back.

We pulled up in front of the "Monster" man's house—actually, mommy and daddy of "Monster" man's house—and one guy, the one I disliked the least, went inside. He emerged quickly, his face expressive of failed purpose.

Soon we were driving again. One guy asked me if I'd ever done "Electric Monster." I asked him what that was, and he told me it was like ordinary Monster, except it makes your ears vibrate. I laughed.

My head was doing mathematics. I told them I could get the speed from Max. I gave the price and finally we made a deal. The stuff had to be inspected and sampled before payment. I said I'd arrange it.

Back at Cal's, I went in alone. People were wandering around in their personal frenzies. I found Bart and spoke to him about the deal, meanwhile convincing him to buy a spoon also. He called Max and worked things out. I was appointed to execute the plans. So I went out to the car and presented the foursome the results, also insisting on a taste for myself out of their spoon. They agreed, but I never actually collected.

First, we drove back to Wynnefield where I was dropped, with one of the four, into another car. The other three went off somewhere. That was a relief. We went to Jimmie's.

Two spoons there awaited us, and the money was turned over. Jimmie grabbed Captain Crunch and a rubber hot-dog that made noise when you squeezed it, and we set out again for Cal's. Both Jimmie and I sat in the back seat.

After five minutes on the road, Jimmie caught sight of a pair of good sandals by my feet. He communicated to me that he wanted me to steal them. I didn't want to, but I complied. It was easy. I opened my shirt to let the cool summer air against my chest. Then I unbuttoned my pants, slowly brought up the sandals, slipped them behind me, tucked them into my pants, and buttoned up. We arrived at Cal's, and said goodbye to the last of the Wynnefielders. They were never seen again.

Jimmie and I walked through the door with the newly acquired sandals and a spoon. I think Bart, Cal, and Peggy were the only ones there at that time. I pulled out the sandals, and Jimmie said, "Look at my latest theft." I cut him off and explained that I personally had committed the crime, which didn't seem to matter to anyone, anyway. But Bart admired the sandals and I insisted they were his on the grounds that he had paid for the spoon. There was a bit of disagreement, but I convinced them that I had the right to give them to anyone I chose.

We went upstairs. Cal asked for the spoon. I pulled it out and handed it to Bart. No one had a needle. I called Kenny. He said he had a 25g and would be over soon. Bart pulled out a clinical 2½-cc glass syringe (we rarely used one) and we waited.

Half an hour passed, while we verbalized our anticipations. We hoped to see Max again, and we were waiting for Judy's call. Primarily, although we had not yet done the dope we had, we were already looking for more.

Kenny arrived with three girls, Laurie, Kitty, and Louise, the latter previously unknown to most of us. Jimmie's eyes rolled when he saw them. Introductions and hellos were exchanged, and everyone seated themselves comfortably around the room.

Bart poured the whole spoon into a vial and added 2½ ccs of water. We figured on five ½-cc shots. There were more than five of us, so some had to be excluded. Surprisingly Peggy managed to talk Cal out of his shot. One would have expected the opposite.

So the needle went around, and five of us were off again, not really wrecked, but comfortable. This was the high point of our lives: watching the crystal dissolve, assembling our outfits, drawing up, tying ourselves down, and finally seeing the blood follow a bubble or two up into the neck of the works. A good hit! Between shots we kept ourselves busy listening to music, making some form of conversation, and some of us had a little sex here and there. But there was always an anticipation present —the next hit, a big one.

Bart was playing with some Imperiale cologne, a fine luxury from Guerlain. Note: Most of us had good taste. Louise, who, along with Kitty, had heretofore been silent and withdrawn, made an appreciative gesture with her nose and asked what the fragrance was. Bart never answered the question as she asked it, but simply rose, said, "Here, smell," and crowded her into a corner, pushing his chest over her face. He wore no shirt. His pants were open. He wore no underwear. For the remainder of the short time she was there, Bart was slyly on the make for her. Jimmie also showered her with lots of affection. He was gentlemanly without ceasing to be vile. He managed to ascertain that she had a boy friend. He thought that was sweet. She gave him her phone number.

The dogs were barking ceaselessly. Kitty and Louise left. Kenny and Laurie went into the bedroom, to do what, I don't know. In any case, their relationship seemed to be pretty much back together by the time they left that night. As soon as they closed the bedroom door, Jimmie began to bother them. He would burst in, observe, and make some not very funny comment. I did my best to hold him off, and finally succeeded. Ken and Laurie were virgins, frustrated, maybe frightened.

The phone rang. It was Judy. Someone would have to go and meet her. We hassled with that for a while, and Bart finally volunteered. He left, and Cal, Peggy, Jimmie, and I went down to the living room.

We sat in comfortable, tasteless furniture, drinking icewater, while Charlie told us about "Judy's cunt." Apparently something was wrong with it this weekend because of something he'd done to it last weekend. He was proud. Cal mentioned that he wanted to make Bart. Jimmie talked about homosexuality. The dogs kept barking. Jimmie talked about nudity.

Bart and Judy arrived with a copy of *Playboy*. Ken and Laurie came downstairs. She turned to me and said, "Thank you. I mean that in more ways than one." I think what she meant was that I had been helpful in mending her relationship with Ken. I don't remember just what I had done. They left. It was 2:00 A.M., late enough for both of them to get trouble from their parents.

Jimmie struck up a conversation. He told us there were these very important prefixes in the English language that we never used. They were para-, meta-, and ortho-. So we all talked about para-, meta-, and ortho-. We went upstairs and continued the conversation, which by this time had already become interspersed with comments like "Where's Max already?" This was a tension point that multiplied its intensity many times over the next few hours.

The prefix conversation was temporarily terminated when Bart began showing us all of *Playboy*'s polished breasts. Jimmie alone showed true enthusiasm over this. I picked up a copy of *Avante-Garde* and looked at the pictures. We began to wonder by this time whether Max was actually going to come or not. We worried like our parents worried about us. "It's 3:00. Where is he?"

Around this time, it occurred to me that the cheap guitar in the corner of the room belonged to me. Although they were borrowed, I had much better instruments than this. I hadn't played it in years. I would trade it to Max for dope . . .

". . . if he ever comes."

Jimmie put on a pair of Cal's bikini cut, pastel blue jockey shorts, and laid his bald head down in Judy's lap. It was a center-ring attraction. There was silence and cigarettes.

Cal and Peggy got involved in doing "speed drawings," intricate .0001 Rapidograph work. I went into the master bedroom and went through all the drawers, enjoying myself looking for anything of interest. After half an hour, I returned with half a dozen innocuous pills that no one could identify.

Where was Max? I was flipped with anxiety.

What would Portnoy do? I retreated again, laid down on what Cal's father once called "The only conjugal bed in this house, fella," and jerked off. I tried to sleep. No good.

So I returned to the group. Jimmie got up and we rekindled the prefix conversation, this time with a dictionary. Jimmie was in the middle of a sentence when the phone rang. He cut off sharply, eyes rolling, and said, "This is important." And he grabbed the phone.

Yes, it was Max. He was right around the corner and on his way. We all jumped for joy, and then sat as if we were waiting for the boss and his wife to come for dinner. Everyone but me talked of methedrine. I had decided many hours before that I wanted to top off this weekend with a shot of heroin (H, scag, smack, horse, as you wish). I had made a postulate and discussed with everyone the possibilities of my obtaining a bag of the wonderful oblivion. No one else seemed to share my desires with much enthusiasm. I certainly wouldn't have minded some speed, but I wanted a shot of smack afterwards. I laid plans. I would have it.

He arrived. We greeted him as if he was a rich uncle with leukemia. Everyone asked about King Meth. He hadn't brought any with him. They were all disappointed. Very disappointed. He pulled out some grass and rolled enough joints so that everyone had two of his own. We smoked. He picked up the guitar and began tapping on it. He handed it to me. I handed it back and said, "For you." He said, "No." I smiled.

"Go ahead. It's yours."

For the generosity I showed him, I think I would have preferred him to drop dead. That would have meant lots of dope.

He opened his satchel and pulled out a bag of H. And handed it to me. It was a big bag. Oh, boy. He warned me not to do more than half. Then he laid a bag on Jimmie for being a good business associate, and gave him the same warning. I thought it would be courteous to wait until Max left before I did it up, so I held off.

Jimmie went down to the kitchen and mixed up a delicious concoction of food containing just about everything, and we all managed to get at least a spoonful from him.

Max left. Jimmie and Judy went into the bedroom and sat down on the bed. Cal and Peggy followed them. I remained in the outer room that comprised the other half of Cal's space. It was light outside once more.

I sat myself comfortably in front of a candle and cooked up three-quarters of my bag. I shot it up and walked into the other room, where Charlie had cooked his whole bag up in a vial where it sat, a brownish gray liquid.

A minute passed. Then it hit me. And wow. The rush passed through my veins like a gift from the god of High. Note: A shot of smack usually takes effect instantly, but I find that after a heavy speed run, the rush may come as much as five minutes after the shot.

Meanwhile, Bart, Judy, Cal, and Peggy shot the vial-full. Jimmie said he could do without it for the good of the group. I was grinning at him. He asked me how much I did, and I told him. He called me a junkie. I reached for the remains of the bowl of food, and he pulled it away from me. I protested. Then he told me I had been selfish, and I should have shared my bag. This hadn't occurred to me. He was right, but I didn't feel bad about it. I offered him the rest of my dope. He declined as I hoped he would.

So I went back to the other room, cooked up the remaining quarter of my bag, and shot it. I felt good. I'd done four times as much as anyone else. Cal and Bart would throw up a number of times. I wouldn't get sick at all. I never did. Knowing that made me feel even better.

The group dispersed. I went into the master bedroom and lay down. I wanted company, so I found a cartoon show on the T.V. and went out to promote some watchers. I found Jimmie and Judy in a sloppy heap sleeping in Cal's bed. Bart, Cal, and Peggy were in another bedroom, air conditioner going full blast, eating a salad and alternately getting sick. Bart had taken off his clothes. Cal had his eyes on him.

They came with me, but only stayed a few minutes. The room was too hot for them. I turned on the air conditioner, but they weren't satisfied. It didn't cool off fast enough. So I took off my clothes, listened to the tube, and enjoyed the peace.

I got lonely again, and I went back after them. The room had cooled off. Cal was after Bart. Bart was after Peggy. Peggy came with me.

We closed the door, took off our clothes, turned off the television and lay down. We looked at each other. We wanted to screw, and were about to, but Peggy became hesitant. Cal might walk in. She said he wouldn't mind if we were just lying there nude, but he'd be very upset if he walked in and found us screwing. So we wound up just lying there and teasing each other.

The phone rang. Cal walked in shortly afterwards, looked us over and said the call was for me. I had to pull myself over Peggy's body to get it. Cal observed and left. The call was unimportant. An hour and a half passed. It was approaching noon. I knew I would want more scag later, and I knew it would be difficult to get. I never got it.

Cal came in again. He said we'd have to get up and start cleaning. Later he would ask Peggy what we did in bed. He closed the door. Peggy looked at me and got up. Then she jumped back on the bed, kissed my prick, and ran out of the room. I lay there.

Soon I got up and dressed. Peggy was in the shower. I had hoped she'd come back. Ken and Laurie were at the door. They came in and we talked. Cal appeared from somewhere. He was very angry at me for having gone through his parents' things. They had told him they wanted no one in that room, and things there were slightly upset.

Peggy left the bathroom and came downstairs. Cal screamed at her. At this point, he was being generally nasty toward everyone. Laurie cleaned, under his supervision. People talked about food, and one by one, everyone left.

The house was clean. Peggy was crying upstairs, and Cal was pacing downstairs. Parents would be there soon. I walked out onto Primrose Avenue. My parents were there to pick me up.

CAL MICHAELS

My parents had gone to the shore for the weekend, and they left me in charge—which was quite a responsibility, but I feel I shouldered it rather well.

I invited some friends over and we sat around and we took a lot of dope. It was a smashingly successful social affair. I enjoyed it immensely, and I can hardly wait for my parents to go away again.

Interestingly enough, so many drugs were taken in the little house where I live that if Kentwood knew about it, they'd be scandalized. It would almost be worth it, just to scandalize Kentwood, to have them know.

There were six or seven main characters and other little people drifting in and out, and other people stoned on acid or whatever they were taking. The whole thing ran alternately like a medieval morality play or modern theater of the absurd—ridiculous at times, pathetic at others, but I think an elevating learning experience with a generally positive effect on myself as well as on the other main characters. The ones that were drifting in and out, I didn't stop long enough to talk to them and find out how they were hanging in there. They were mostly male. People slept over and went out and came back in—it was fun city for a while.

I don't think the other people's parents knew where they were, and if my parents found out, they would get so uptight that I think they know that something did happen, and they are afraid of the enormity of it, so they haven't bothered to pursue it, just to save themselves the anxiety and uptightness.

12

GROWING UP HIGH

WHEN Bobby Goldberg refused to continue going to Kentwood High, his family got busy, and catalogs from all kinds of private schools—none of which Sam Goldberg could afford—began to pour into the house. Sarah felt Bobby just had to get away from the bad influence of his friends, most of whom already had police records involving car theft, minor vandalism, and repeated shoplifting. Bobby had been implicated in one way or another in all these activities, but so far he had escaped without a record. His mother, however, was convinced that a change of environment, the opportunity to make friends who shared his intellectual inclinations, and some individual attention from understanding teachers, were all that was needed to straighten Bobby out.

Unfortunately, things did not work out as she had hoped. She and Sam made long trips, with and without Bobby, to numerous preparatory and "special" schools for "gifted children with adjustment problems," but Bobby would have none of it. Sam began to think that a military academy might do Bobby more good than a progressive school, but he knew it was futile even to bring the subject up. No one could understand why Bobby was so disinterested in good schools that could really meet the challenge of his superior mind. No one was able to see (and Bobby would not tell anyone) that he was scared to death of competition.

Finally, a new prep school in upstate New York, which advertised a program based on the teachings of A. S. Neill, was visited and agreed upon. Bobby was taken there in early September, after having missed nearly an entire year of school. In November he ran away and eventually came home to Kentwood. The school's connection to Neill's philosophy apparently existed only in its literature, and by the beginning of the following semester it had been closed by the New York State Board of Health.

Bobby, now 15, went to a tutoring school, and got a job that paid decently and afforded him some responsibility. He continued to tutor on and off and work on and off, and when the time came for his Kentwood High School class to graduate, he passed a state test and got a diploma. He never did become reinvolved with his delinquent friends. But a new difficulty had been added to the problems of his earlier adolescence. At 14, within hours of his arrival at prep school, he had discovered drugs.

Many parents have expressed the opinion that it was Bobby Goldberg who introduced Kentwood to drugs way back in 1964. A physician who was a panel member at a recent Kentwood meeting on the drug problem firmly believes that this is so, and on a number of occasions had telephoned the Goldberg house threatening Bobby's arrest. Bobby Goldberg had returned from school in New York State with a pound of pot. It was undoubtedly the first pound of pot to appear in Kentwood, at least in the possession of a young teenager. Whether or not it was Bobby who single-handedly turned Kentwood on and started a chain reaction that is affecting hundreds of kids who never even heard of him, it is plainly possible that one child with a pound of pot and a handful of interested friends can initiate the turning on of an entire town.

And why did Bobby himself first turn on? Plainly, he was a disturbed child who, before drugs, had been inclined to use escape as his major weapon against his problems. But the same factors that make it so easy for many "normal" children to experiment with drugs were also at work. He had heard pot discussed in a casual manner by his college-age sister and her friends, and had read about people turning on in novels. He had heard no negative mention of drugs except in health class, where pot was covered in the same two sentences as heroin, morphine, and cocaine. His parents had never felt any need to discuss drugs or alcohol with either of their children. While it may have been Bobby's emotional difficulties that perpetuated his use of drugs and developed it into a problem of life and death magnitude, it was probably only simple curiosity, unhampered by restraining taboos, that prompted him to accept a puff of the first joint that was offered to him.

There are many kinds of non-therapeutic drugs used by countless children in countless communities throughout the United States. There are many styles of drug use as well, as we shall see. Until recently, drug abuse by middle-class children was considered to be at its most dangerous level among runaways and weekend runaways in the highly concentrated and cultified urban disaster areas where so many kids do go to turn on, tune in, and drop out. It is unfortunate that it took us so long to notice the teenagers turning on in our own mahogany-paneled basements, and those teenagers nodding on heroin in the last rows of our best-equipped classrooms, and the kids tripping out on acid in the safest and best-tended of our private local parks.

PEGGY

When Peggy French dropped out of school, she began devoting all her time to drugs. "I was thinking in terms of my existence from one high to the next high." Soon after turning on to pot "for real," she was taking "all sorts of obscure pills, and hash and acid on occasion." Peggy had had pot for the first time at 13, when she ran away to Greenwich Village and met some people who gave her a little. But it wasn't until much later, at home, that she really became involved in drugs.

"Now I take lots of meth, grass, and hash. And scag, but not with any frequency. I stopped taking acid because I was disappointed in my reaction to it. I didn't find it to be any deep, revealing mystical experience. I dug lightshows and things like that. So what. I could turn puppet trips into meaningful things and then they were over. I just didn't think I needed them."

She was reluctant to admit that what she got out of meth was "just a great physical feeling."

"I'm afraid my existence is a little too drug-oriented right now," she said. "I hope this will change. I still think in terms of my next high, from high to high, which is bad, I think, for me. I can't feel as good as I did before. When I'm on meth, I feel like . . . well, I know this is distorted, but this is the way I want to feel all the time, and like I know I felt like that before I started getting high."

Peggy could not remember a time when she had been opposed to the use of drugs in general.

"In health class in fifth grade it was talked about, and I never thought it was bad. I was curious. I associated a certain glamour with taking drugs. Most of the kids in the class agreed they were harmful, but the whole presentation was so unbelievable to me. I didn't know anyone who had tried anything—maybe I had heard of people through other people—but I'd had no real contact with it. I just didn't believe it."

I asked Peggy if there were some drugs she now thought one should not take, and she mentioned meth and scag as having obvious bad effects, without really answering my question. I asked her how she reconciled that opinion with taking them. About meth, she said, "Well, it's had bad effects. I mean sometimes the depression alone is enough to make me think I'll never take it again, but if you're talking about permanent damage, I haven't projected into the future that much. I haven't met up with anything yet. If one of my teeth were to fall out, I'm sure I'd get more serious about it. I wait and get healthy and eat and everything and then I take it. You get the full impact from it that way. Spacing it, I don't think it's bad at all."

Peggy worries occasionally about getting busted, but "I'm not paranoid like I used to be whenever I was high. I feel I can control myself. And what would happen is my parents wouldn't want the law to get into this, or have me in a detention home. It would be a very bad reflection. They'd get me to a psychiatrist and stuff. I think they'd probably commit me to a mental institution."

She seemed quite cheerful about the idea.

GREGORY

Gregory Eisman's drug history was similar to Peggy's. He'd started young with pot, at the time of the interview said he'd tried just about everything, but, like the others, was involved primarily with methedrine.

"I'd like to try heroin, but I haven't yet. I've had coke twice, but I never got off. And acid, well, when I first took it I looked upon it as something that had something to offer. I can't say it has nothing to offer anyone, but in my present situation it has nothing to offer me, with the exception of mere pleasure.

"The way I started smoking pot was a person I'd just met and become very friendly with turned me on to it. At first my reaction was I didn't want to start because I was quite sure that at some time I'd be caught doing it, which I didn't want to happen. As it turned out, I did start, and I was caught.

"This made me stop for a while, at least pot, and I didn't take anything, except very rarely. Then I started taking a lot of amphetamines from my mother, because that was quite safe. It was almost impossible for me to get caught, the way I did it. I don't know why she was taking them. And she never noticed how many were there.

"I got caught because a friend of mine tried to commit suicide or just took too many Nembutol by mistake, I'm not sure which. Anyway, his father [the doctor now on Kentwood's drug-abuse panel] shot him full of Benzedrine, and he rapped and his father found out everything.

"I've been caught quite a few times since by my parents, and they've turned me in to the police, but I've never been confronted with legal punishment. They did it 'for my own good.' At least the first time they thought it was their responsibility to bust someone else. They *said* it as if it was a civic duty. But they also look at it as a way to stop things that are going on, not only with me, but with other kids. It's always gotten into involvements with the entire family, through perhaps my stupidity."

Greg was a slim, quiet boy, polite and well-mannered in such a way that one took note of that fact. His wavy brown hair was short. There was a thoughtful look in his light brown eyes, and a thoughtful, almost solemn timbre in his voice. He wasn't sure how he felt about the fact that his parents had, more than once, placed him at the mercy of the law.

"My parents are really uptight about the whole drug thing," he said, "not only as it will affect me, but as it will affect them. But that's their choice. I have younger brothers and sisters. My father has his business [he is a dentist] in Kentwood, and he feels I am having adverse effects on him and all the areas of his life because of this.

"The situation of establishing some kind of relationship with them is for me one of constantly trying to deceive them to think I'm straight, and them worrying about when I get it, where I get it. Because of the fact that I want the things they have to offer me, in the open I accept their conditions in order to have economic means. But really, I'm just doing as much of what I want to do as I can while getting other things I want as well. They think I'm straight now."

Greg said he was shooting methedrine on weekends. Earlier in the summer he'd been smoking pot every day.

"Meth is something I'll go to trouble to get and look forward to. It is also having about the least desirable effects. I think meth really changes you. Grass, not that much. It gives you slightly different attitudes toward things—perhaps more carefree. Grass is a pleasure drug. But they are all for pleasure. They also limit awareness. They create—what I learned last night, what I never looked at before last night— you react to just about everything that happens to you, and you are hung up in this. A lot of times you don't look at it as being hung up because it's enjoyable. But a lot of times it's not enjoyable, it's paranoid. For me, it's a fascination with what could be looked at perhaps as decadence. And I resent drugs, because I associate them with unpleasant experiences. Like the way things are between my parents and myself. I look at it as more my fault.

"I used to look at myself as above a lot of people because I was into this scene. I don't think this is so. Just about everybody takes drugs. A lot of times I feel the urge to brag about it in a way. I don't like to feel it, I don't like the need to brag about it, as if this is something to pride myself on. It's become the thing to do, in a lot of senses. It might pass, but not until something else comes along. I used to think about looking for an escape. I guess I still look for an escape in drugs, but not in the same way. I look at it more as a very temporary escape, like just relief from something—perhaps a little pressure, or relief from tensions."

At the time of these interviews, everyone in the group appeared to be discovering that the more they used drugs to relieve their tensions, or for whatever reason, the more tensions they were bringing into their lives.

LAURIE

Laurie White, who had been smoking pot for less than a year, and who'd since had a fair amount of acid, methedrine, other amphetamines, as well as hash and other variations on grass, was trying to decide if she was, as she put it, "the right kind of person to take drugs."

"I'm not sure they're for me," she said. "But I always enjoy them. My parents say that this is an escape from the world. That I take dope because I am not a realistic person, and I want to escape realistic things. I don't know if they are right or not. Until I'm convinced one way or the other, I'll just keep going the way I am. I'm not sure that's right either, but it seems like the only thing I can do right now, until I find out for myself. That's what I mostly do. I don't listen to anybody. But people tell me things, and I'm pretty sure they're going to be right, but I go ahead and do what I want anyway, and I get into a lot of trouble and hassling and everything to find out for myself—but at least I found out.

"Taking drugs has changed me a lot. I'm more of a quiet person, more peaceful. I don't lose my temper like I used to. I used to make judgments on people before I even got to know them. Now I don't judge people. I just accept them. I like to get into people, get to know them. It was mainly the grass and the meth. I think they've matured me, and I think they've made my personality better. When I said that to my mother, she said, 'You're crazy, or they'd have them on the market.' I think she's crazy for saying that."

Laurie introduced the subject of drugs into our conversation when we were talking about religion. She said she considered herself to be a religious person, though not necessarily a Presbyterian like the rest of her family.

"All of what I believe is in myself. But I went into a church the other day, and I felt goody as hell being there, so I had to get out. I didn't think I had any right being in there, and I would like to go into a church and not feel that way. But I wouldn't like to change the way I believe."

"Would you have to change the way you believe?"

"No. I'd just have to stop doing things that make me feel guilty. I don't believe in going to church every Sunday, if that's what you have to do to communicate with God, or whatever you believe in—I believe in God, so I'll say communicate with God. If I want to get rid of something that's in me, and ask forgiveness,or something like that, like if it's a problem with myself that I want to forgive myself, I'd just sit down and start talking. But I'd feel guilty as hell now if I started to do something like that. Like before, a couple of years ago, if my conscience was really getting to me, and it hit me I wanted to get rid of it, okay, I'd just sit there, whatever I was doing, and talk about it, think to my mind, and in my mind I'm talking to the Lord. But I feel guilty doing it now."

"Why?"

"I guess it's because my parents say I disappointed them a lot, and I don't feel like a good person, that's all. Like I really didn't feel guilty until I got busted, and everyone charges at you, and that's when I started feeling guilty."

"What happened when you got busted?"

"Gad—I feel guilty when I say that, too, but I say that a lot—pretty much, you know, tears shed, how could you do this, you must be very unhappy, you weren't this way a year ago, stuff like that. When are you going to get on the right road? Don't you care about yourself? A bunch of shit handed to you."

In actual fact, Laurie is not all that unhappy, and considers herself to be much better off than she was a year ago. As for getting on the "right road," it is indeed presumptuous of adults to assume that such a road exists on every teenager's psychic map, to be joyfully and blindly followed as if it were made of yellow brick and led to the Land of Oz. Laurie obviously does care about herself, and her serious consideration of whether drugs are for her or not, and her determination to stick by her own instincts, are a sign of health.

"When I first started smoking pot," Laurie said, "I went into a diner, and I wanted to stand up on a seat and tell everyone what was happening to me and how great it was, and that they should all take it, because I was so much happier and everything was so much smoother for me, and I thought that if they all did, everything in the world would go smoother, and everyone would be together, and not all this prejudism and segregation and all this. I thought that pot would help to get rid of it, and I really wanted to shout it to everyone.

"I don't want to shout it anymore, but if someone came up to me and asked me if they should try it, I'd probably talk to them about it, but I wouldn't tell them yes or no they should do it, and I wouldn't want to be the one to give it to them. I couldn't take that responsibility for another person. But I have to say, I think it's helped me. Like the things I've told you, I might not have told you before. But you're asking me, and I'm telling you."

The incident in which Laurie and a number of other Kentwood High students, including Kenny and Greg, got "busted" did not involve anything as serious as an arrest. In fact, it amounted to little more than being "found out" by their parents. But the idea of arrest seems less real and therefore less threatening to most kids than the actual or psychological punishment that only parents can inflict.

KENNY

"At first I wouldn't touch drugs because of my parents," said Laurie's boy friend, Kenny Carpenter. "I wouldn't let myself want it so I wouldn't hurt them. Then something happened where I just didn't feel that anymore. I'd tried to create a good relationship with them and never got it. Bobby offered me some acid and I took it. I have never listened to them since."

That was two and a half years ago, and Kenny had not taken acid again until two weeks before the interview, though he'd been involved with grass, hash, meth, Demerol, and coke. In the past two weeks, he'd taken acid twice.

"After speed, acid is very frenzied, uncontrollable," he remarked. "It wouldn't be anything to take acid and think. I'd take it again because other people are getting something from it, but I don't like to lose control. I like meth because it helps me to do a lot of thinking. I'm freer to talk, not uptight. I know it's a crutch, but the more I do meth, the easier it is to talk. I know I do it for escape, to get away from reality. But I hope gradually I'll be able to do the same things without it . . . rap, be comfortable."

Kenny stopped to think when I asked if drugs had changed him. He decided that they had. "Instead of just going on, I stopped to look at myself. I straightened out a lot of ways of thinking that I didn't know I was into, but they were making me disgusted with myself. All the changes I've seen in others have been for the better, too. At the very least, they give a person a more rounded personality, knowing what the other side of things is."

But he didn't believe that everyone should take drugs, or, for that matter, could be broadened by the experience.

"I always used to be cut for smoking pot. Now the sports kids and the grease are starting to do it, too, but they go more for scag. And they still criticize meth because they haven't tried it. One of the guys who'd gone on to college just brought some pot back once and turned them all on. But I don't know how much it's changed them. It seems when you're straight, the more you do drugs, the more you continue in a straight state.

"I used to think drugs were bad, too, but when I was fifteen, I changed my mind. It was really changing my mind about how I felt about following my parents wishes, rather than how I felt about drugs. I hadn't thought about them that much. I always thought about not wanting to become an alcoholic. Drugs weren't even that real. We never discussed them in the house. But there were always these best-selling books around on how to stop drinking."

KITTY

The emphasis was on drinking in Kitty Price's house, too.

"My parents have no faith in me," Kitty said repeatedly. "They make me feel young. They've messed up my life. They don't like my attitude. It started when I came home drunk once. They got mad. They said, 'You don't show any sense.' I never drank again. Drinking doesn't interest me. I'm allowed to drink at home, now, but I don't want to.

"I used to think drugs were terrible. I'd see old movies about junkies, and they would really shake me up. And then all of a sudden, it happened, and so what. I stopped caring about anything before drugs. Maybe if my parents would have stopped impressing on me how *important* things were— like school. 'Fuckin' weird,' my father calls me. 'Fuckin' weird. Everyone looks up to me. You'll ruin my reputation. You don't dare walk out of this house unless you look like Jim Price's daughter.' He wants me to be him."

Kitty's appearance seemed acceptable enough. There was such a neatness about her, a compactness in the way she carried herself and the way she wore her clothes, that I couldn't imagine her looking sloppy, or finding sloppy or very far-out clothing even desirable to wear. As for the importance of school, she had been an A student. Why had her parents seen the need to press her to the point where she just didn't care?

"I started drugs when I was sixteen. In school a girl had a joint that she was smoking between classes in the ladies' room. When it was time to go to class, she had half left, and she asked me if I wanted it. I said yes. I didn't think about it. I just did it. I started taking dex in the summer, then speed, acid, grass, and I smoked smack with the grass. I took digitalis once. I took two, and I was up for two days. I came down last period in school. It was really awful.

"I took acid only once, but not enough to get really high. I'll take it again. I'm afraid that flashes on acid might wreck me. Flashes back to my childhood, things I don't remember, maybe being really happy as a little kid. I'm scared, but I want to find out.

"Some of my friends say I've changed for the worse. I

don't think so. Some of my friends haven't changed at all. But now I feel that when I say something, people don't think I mean it. I know I mean it, but I feel that other people don't believe me. I hate that feeling.

"I'm paying for it. I don't want to get busted. It would be a big shock to my parents, lots of trouble. I wouldn't be allowed out. Sometimes I'm not allowed out now, but I run out to get high and come back. It seems like all I ever do is score. I'm high for a couple of days, and then I have to get more. I use my allowance. I once stole from people's pocketbooks in the gym lockers. I've pawned jewelry lots of times, then I save from my allowance to get it out. Last week I pawned a pair of cameo earrings my father gave me.

"If someone is happy, they don't need it. At first I got high out of curiosity, and then because I was unhappy. But if someone is happy as they are, why take drugs?"

Yet, later that afternoon, Kitty said that when she had children she would want to turn them on so that they could experience what she had.

BOBBY

"Up until recently, I took drugs all the time because I felt bad all the time. Since I've felt good, I haven't taken any," said Bobby Goldberg, who had, ironically, gone straight.

"It was very complex," he told me. "I had a chance to see myself. It was partly because of some things I'd been reading, secondly because of drugs themselves, and thirdly by being in a situation where I could objectively watch other people doing the things that I had done.

"This past Friday night, I was locked in a basement over-night with Kenny and Laurie. I was on acid. I watched them all night, and as morning came around I wanted to try to help them, but then I realized that was fairly ridiculous unless they turned around and asked for it, which they were not about to do. They were hassling with each other, and just arguing generally. And I could see everything that was wrong in the situation, and it was so simple and so easy and no one would really listen to anything, and so I watched them fool around with their needles and hassling each other, and I was very suddenly aware of what I'd been doing. And I realized I hadn't been listening to anyone else, and a lot of people had things to say, such as my parents, for instance. Finally, I just sat back and was generally happy watching everyone else be miserable, and they were all sitting there trying to get off, and they couldn't hit a vein, and I told them they could just swallow the meth, and they were complaining about the holes in their arms and how they looked, and it seemed very simple that if they didn't like the holes there they shouldn't put them there, and I looked down at my holes, which I didn't like, and I decided I wouldn't put any more there.

"That afternoon, I went over to Cal's, and he wasn't there, and I spent two hours talking to his parents and I realized that for the first time in my life I went there and could look at one of them and listen to them without having already decided what they were saying or were going to say and what was wrong about it, and I became aware."

13

"BUT I'M BREAKING
MY MOTHER'S DREAMS"

FOR kids on drugs, home life is often a hell of guilt and deceit and suspicion. Children who were unhappy at home to begin with are not the only ones who get involved with drugs. Often a child's drug use is the beginning rather than the result of a tense and hostile relationship with his family. If a child is using drugs frequently, his parents are likely to find out about it sooner or later. If they don't, it's probably because they are afraid to know, rather than because the child has managed to be extraordinarily discreet about his activities.

Some parents who do know or strongly suspect that their child is using drugs are afraid to confront him with this fact. And the child probably suspects the extent to which his parents are aware of his drug activities, and is equally afraid to bring the matter out into the open. This constant withholding by all parties of what is uppermost in all their minds creates a breakdown in communication that is far worse than violent arguments or open resignation to the grim fact of a disagreement that cannot be resolved.

One can hardly expect parents not to be concerned if

they feel that their child is in trouble or heading for it. But too many parents, rather than making an attempt to communicate with their children about drugs, turn their backs on the problem. In the course of my research, I found that many parents, as well as schools and communities, were unwilling to acknowledge the fact that their children were coming in contact with drugs. Not only did they feel that private talks with their own children were unnecessary, but they were unwilling to make available to teenagers any more information about drugs than what the textbooks contained—even in the form of passionately anti-drug speakers or literature.

More enlightened parents, who do want to communicate with their children about the drug problem, often fail because they approach it with too many misunderstandings. For example, many parents who realize that a child's casual use of pot doesn't necessarily mean he is maladjusted, and who may have even considered the possibility that pot is not dangerous, are utterly shocked to discover that the apparently happy child they have raised to be an ethical and responsible person has shown a blatant disregard for the law of the land by smoking a joint.

Usually, however, the first time a child tries pot is by no means the first time he has broken a "law," and from the child's point of view, it may not be nearly as serious as earlier transgressions that the parents may consider minor. He may have made some decision about the safety of jaywalking, or he may have gone through a wave of guilt or fear in breaking a childhood taboo such as stepping on cracks in the sidewalk.

A Catholic child's first omission at confession may have been the first step toward his ability to handle the illegality of turning on. For a Jewish child, it might have been a decision that the dietary laws he has been taught to adhere to are irrelevant and do not apply to him. It is often an awesome step for a Jew to defy the laws he has been taught are the laws of a 2,000-year tradition and bite into a ham sandwich. It is far more awesome than disregarding a law he believes is silly and difficult to enforce, and doing something that, he has heard from sources he considers reliable, may hold great pleasures or insights in store for him. The horrified parents who ask "How could you do that?" have no idea how easy it can be.

And then there are the parents of the hard-core drug abusers—some too hurt and angry to try to understand, others trying very hard, but trying too late. There is little they can do to help once things have gone as far as they have with the Kentwood Seven, and the parents know that. Their sense of helplessness only increases the break in reality and the breakdown in communication between parent and child.

Of the Kentwood Seven, three feel hostility toward their parents, and a sense of hopelessness in reaching a point of real communication with them, while four say they have tried to understand their parents' point of view, and seem to have succeeded in at least giving them credit for their own humanity. The three who were the most troubled by their parents were Laurie, Kitty, and Ken. Of the seven, Kitty was the most lacking in hope for her future and self-esteem in her present. She said repeatedly:

"My parents think I can't handle responsibility, and they're afraid to let me try. They've messed up my life. They have no faith in me. They make me feel young, they won't let me grow up.

"At one point, I guess I really liked them. My father beat me up once, and then after that he tried to make it up by giving me all sorts of material things. I liked it before we moved to Kentwood. We had a good family life, and I loved all the toys I got. But material things don't mean any-thing any more. They were so great.

"I haven't kissed or touched either of my parents since I was a little girl," Kitty volunteered. "I never did talk to them. My mother never told me the facts of life. I was always ashamed and afraid when I was a kid. My father always treated me like a little kid. They didn't want me to grow up, and I was always afraid they'd find out I was grown up.

"They live in the dark ages. They never partake in the world. They never tried to find out what's there. I think they should get divorced. They don't get along. Sometimes I think it's my fault. They fight about me a lot. But they'd be happier if they were separated. When you start caring about what everyone else thinks, happiness goes down the drain."

Laurie White, despite a difficult father and a turbulent family life, seemed to be one of the most able to follow her own way without being diverted too much, even by drugs. From childhood, her life had been tough, and she had been forced to deal with many realities at an early age—including poor food and shelter, and a large family in which everyone's help was needed.

"My father and I don't talk at all. We are just two people living in the same house, trying to avoid each other. I've told him I hate him, and that he disgusts me, and I want nothing to do with him. He tells me he hates me, he tells me he thinks I'm a slut and the lowest thing on earth, and he loves to gos-sip about it to his friends. I've been present when this has occurred, and I calmly tell the truth of exactly what is. I don't even think he believes these things. He's just saying whatever he wants to, whatever sounds the best.

"Also, my parents are prejudiced. Not so much my mother as my father. He's completely against the colored race, and it makes me sick to hear him talk about it. My aunt is, too. We sit there and watch T.V. and "Peyton Place" comes on, and they had a Negro doctor on, and my aunt went, "Ooooh, a nigger," and it made me sick. I left the room. I don't want to hear it. I never believed it, even when I was young and I didn't know any colored people.

"My mother and I aren't as close as we used to be, but we're both trying to get back together, because I've changed in a year, and she didn't want to accept or understand it, and also, starting drugs and trying to keep it a secret. When I'd go into the house under the effect, I'd try to avoid her, and she didn't know what that was about till I got busted. I don't have a good idea of who my mother is. I think she's going down the drain. I told them things until drugs. Then I didn't. And when they found out, well, they found out what they expected. Now it's okay.

"At home, I just sleep, bathe, do the laundry, and do my share of the work generally, and I eat snacks. I never eat at home. My parents aren't happy. I wouldn't like to look back on my life and see it like my mother's. I think I'll be pretty permissive with my own kids. After age 10, there's not much you can do. But I'm breaking my mother's dreams."

Laurie's boy friend, Kenny, said, "My parents live for money. Money has no value for me. Love is more valuable to me, but not to them.

"I like my parents, I guess, pretty much the same as I always have. But we always argue about discipline. I talk to my mother, not to my father."

When I asked Kenny if there was a time when he decided it was better not to talk to his parents, he said, "They decided. I tried to say something, and they said, no, don't go on. My father won't hear about the things I want to say. He's always worrying. He won't allow anything that society doesn't accept. If I tell them something, all they can think of is how their raising me right has been destroyed. I'm trying to raise myself. My parents say, 'He's just a mixed up, stupid kid.'

"When I started drinking, okay, big thing. They would have done anything to stop me from taking drugs. Now they no longer have any real knowledge of what I do. My father is a racist, struggling for money, trying to push on others what he has. They're not happy, but that's the way it is. Their attitude is, 'Well, that's life. It's a hard world. You have to struggle and give up a lot for what you want.' "

The four who showed more tolerance for their parents were not by any means uncritical of them. Cal, for instance, who had no concept of self-improvement or change, had a somewhat condescending attitude toward his parents, though he said he loved them.

"I'd like to know more about them and have them know more about me. Once I get out of the house and stop putting them uptight about the drugs I take and the life I lead, I will be better able to be with them and get to know them as people, objectively. They would be able to better relate to me as an independent being, because my dependence on them is now inhibiting communication."

Cal, who spent most of his time at home, said what he usually did around the house was "lie around, take dope, read, see people, eat."

"My parents have got problems," he said. "Their children have not turned out as they would have wanted them to turn out, which is unfortunate only for my parents. I don't feel guilty about anything concerning them. I'd like to turn them on."

Peggy French lived at Cal's house for more than six months, going home once a week or less. She said her parents were "very good" about the arrangement. They might well accept any arrangement that afforded them a fairly good idea of where Peggy was, since she had been running away or staying away regularly since the age of 12.

"The first time, I just went to a friend's house. But it was a very dramatic runaway. They knew all about it. The purpose was to impress them, get their attention. Then I went to New York, because I was curious about the whole scene there; I was infatuated with beatniks and all that. I wanted to see it. But that was partly to impress them, too. I made it very dramatic, complete with letters and everything. All I was trying to say was, 'Pay more attention to me. Realize that I'm bored.'

"I knew there'd be repercussions, sure. That's part of the reason I did it. Another thing was, I didn't want to be like my parents. They're really introverted. They feel dissatisfied with themselves—and I feel qualified to say this—and they're disliked by most people. They have a difficult time adjusting to people socially, and they don't have many friends. I didn't want to be as unhappy as they are, and as afraid of people. I ran away to get used to people, get to know people, because my parents were so introverted, and I was, too."

Gregory Eisman had perhaps more reason to resent his parents than most kids had, because they had repeatedly turned him in to the police, and he knew that they would do so again. But he took responsibility for much that was wrong with his relationship with them, and tried to see their point of view.

"I resent them," he said, "because they have something I want, but I'm not willing to do what they want me to, to get it. I also resent them because they are uptight about things, and because I am trying to please them a lot of times not merely to please them, but to create some security for myself. But all it creates is uptightness for me—their uptightness.

"They also make me feel very dependent on them because

they feel—which is true—that I'm not controlling things, so they have to control things. I fail to assume control, so they assume control, which I don't like. As far as I can remember, things were harmonious only up until the time when I was in second grade.

"It would be nice to let them know that I feel good sometimes, that I myself feel I've failed myself, and that this isn't the way I want things to be, even if I'm making them that way. But if I discussed things with them, being honest, it wasn't so much that I'd get into trouble for telling them those things. For some reason, it didn't make me feel good. It just seemed like I shouldn't have been discussing things with them."

Gregory decided that the reason for these bad feelings was simply that he wasn't being as honest as he had tried to convince himself he was.

"Both my parents have a strong sense of who they are," he said. "I think I tend to tear that down a lot, though. I can't say they are unreasonable. I mean, all they ask of me is they want me to be responsible in a way they consider responsible. They say, 'Even if you're not living with us, you still can't do certain things because they affect us.' They look at drugs as, no matter what, they are going to have an adverse effect on someone, if I do drugs, even excluding myself. I can see their point in a way. I can see where doing drugs can be bad and is having adverse effects. I should stop talking to you now, I guess, if you don't want it to come back and have an adverse effect on you," he laughed.

"But it's mainly the illegality; even if there's no reason for it to be illegal, it's still wrong. I think they look at just about everything this way. They're always concerned with the law.

"I don't know if they're happy. Sometimes I have trouble judging whether I make them unhappy because I *am* being dishonest, or if I'd make them unhappy even if I was honest. If my dishonesty makes them unhappy, it limits their free choice of things. I'd say they're happy with each other.

"I wish I would be able to just let my kids live and not make them do anything. But then I'd get the feeling that, well, even when you were in your teens, you still didn't know a lot that you should have known, and you could have gotten through some things faster. So I'll want to tell them what they should do, and if they won't do it, I'll make them. But that didn't work for me. But then my parents didn't just offer what they thought was valuable. They did try to force it on me, yes. And yet I wonder, if these ethics weren't imposed on me, against lying, stealing, killing, would I have them?"

"Drugs can't help but change your relationship with your parents," Bobby Goldberg said. "That's one of the reasons you begin to feel they can't understand your generation. Actually, it seems to me that they are willing and trying, and this is something I realized just recently. But our generation is not understanding theirs very well at all. We're unaware of them. We don't look them straight in the eye. We have specified ideas of our freedom and their uptightness, and we decide upon what they're going to say, and before they even say it, we pick out things to relate to our friends to laugh about, and pretty soon we don't care what they are saying at all.

"At some point, perhaps we're afraid to tell them something. We're afraid of them. A parent has a general idea of what he or she expects from a child, and has hopes for his future, and a general identity also that he sees for this child, and I think when it reaches a point where you feel that you have not fulfilled this identity, you are afraid to say this to your parents, and therefore feel you can't relate to them."

Bobby said he liked his own parents, but that he hadn't a few days ago.

"The last time I really liked them consistently was in junior high. Then I became alienated from the school, and I felt ashamed to tell them. I was breaking away from the identity that was set for me, and I didn't feel I could let them know this. I didn't want to be a disappointment. If I'd told them, I think they would have understood. But then, I didn't think anyone would understand. It was a general feeling of persecution, feeling lots of people were against me. I just identified my parents with all other people from the adult world, like the vice principal, whom I deplored."

Bobby looked forward to having kids of his own.

"I'd watch my child and try to bring up anything I thought was bothering him. My parents did this, but they were clouded in seeing me. To prevent that, you have to be careful not to impose a value system. You have to be value-less to see. I'd enjoy seeing myself come out in someone else, and it would please me to watch someone else make the same mistakes, because I know the answers now, and I think I understand enough to see that the kid gets put together on his own."

14

SOME AFTERWORDS

AT THIS writing, about a year has passed since I interviewed these kids in Kentwood, but I have kept track of all of them to one degree or another. All of them except Gregory Eisman had either dropped out or failed enough courses to have had to go to summer school or repeat high school grades. But the failures all persisted through their repeated courses, and the dropouts all got some tutoring and took and passed state equivalency tests at the time they would have graduated.

Most of them had some desire to go to college, almost any college that would have them, and some were admitted. At the time of the interview, Bobby Goldberg had already flunked out after his freshman year at a large university near his home. He had done well the first semester, but massive doses of amphetamines kept him out of most of his second semester classes, kept him from many of his exams, and distorted his thinking on those he took.

Bobby is the only one of the seven who has matriculated at a college to date, but it is very interesting that an extremely apathetic group, so involved in drugs that any venture into the realm of ordinary responsibilities required considerable effort, had such a strong motivation to get that high school degree. It was as if, out of all their dissatisfactions with themselves and with their parents' and teachers' highly critical response to them, they must produce something that the outside, straight, establishment world (whose opinions and point of view they often disdained) would consider worthwhile and would validate.

And what has become of them?

Kitty Price is still struggling through high school. Laurie White has just graduated, and is still uncertain of her plans. She is still going with Ken Carpenter, who has spent the year working at a gas station, rather than going to community college as he had intended. All three are still on the drug trip.

Cal Michaels is still lying around his parents' house, taking dope, reading, seeing people, eating.

Peggy French broke off with Cal not long ago, moved back home, then to New York with Bobby, then home again, and back to Cal and dope, after staying straight for four weeks. She has been accepted by a small college that she plans to attend next semester.

When I interviewed Bobby Goldberg, he was 18 and straight, and considered himself well on the way to being straightened out. He told me he had recently discovered a way of handling his problems—a way called Scientology. At this writing, he is an able, responsible, self-supporting young man, who holds a good job, attends night school, and is first in his class. He has broken completely from the four destructive years of drug abuse that he abandoned when he was only a few shots away from heroin addiction. His future looks bright.

Gregory Eisman, the only one of the seven who had been admitted to a top college, away from home, had really looked forward to that particular change in his life, even though he had no idea what he wanted to do. He saw Bobby change and grow happier, and he looked forward to trying some of the non-drug trips that Bobby had tried.

Despite his lack of vocational or avocational goals, he struck me as unusually aware, with strong and well-articulated personal goals, and I was glad to know he was going away to college, getting away from home, where, hopefully, he might have a chance to be himself. He felt trapped, but he did not really seem trapped to me, because he had a way out. The door was open for him to escape a fantastically confining and confusing world into a new and bigger open space where there was really room for exploration.

A week after I interviewed him, a week before he was scheduled to leave for school, his parents got him up early on a Saturday morning and insisted that he go with them to visit some relatives, even though he had prior plans to meet Bobby and Ken. His parents drove him, instead, to Haverford State Hospital, where he was committed, and where he remained, doing little but working in the canteen, for six months. Somehow, while an inmate at the hospital, he got turned on to heroin. He liked it a lot.

I saw him there one day in early December. He looked worn and haggard and pale. He was apathetic. He told me he'd seen a doctor only a few times. He didn't know when he was getting out and he didn't seem to care a lot. He took his situation totally for granted. They let him go when he had managed to find a job (at a gas station) and an apartment of his own.

Kenny Carpenter found him in that apartment one morning a few months later, unconscious from an overdose of heroin. All his belongings had been stolen. He was rushed to a hospital. He had pneumonia. A week later, he was transferred to Haverford State, where he spent several weeks before he was released. He returned to his apartment and his job. He returned to drugs. He died of an overdose of heroin in August 1969.

15

USERS AND ABUSERS

WHY do kids use pot and other drugs?

How do they start?

And what is the result?

Despite the recent wave of concern for drug-law reform and the gradual emergence of facts in place of myths about marijuana, it still appears to be widely believed that kids start smoking pot for one of the following three reasons:

1. They are maladjusted or unhappy and are seeking escape from reality and responsibility.

2. They are, like kids who drive dangerously for the thrill of it, seeking kicks without any thought of the consequences of their actions.

3. They are pressured into it by a "lower element" in their peer group, or by an older outsider or pusher who is in it for the money, or by the social fact that "everyone is doing it."

I have not found that any of these reasons have very much to do with the average child's initiation to drugs. Most of them try pot because they're curious. But they usually do so on the basis of a decision to which they've given some serious thought. They make the decision after examining data that they find at least potentially valid enough to feel that they can test it out for themselves with little or no risk. They are more than likely to be familiar with the opinion that drugs are a key to self-discovery and increased awareness. And it may well be because of a genuine desire to learn—in other words, because of an innate strength rather than an innate weakness—that a child may wish to make such an experiment.

Like the Kentwood Seven, most of the kids I interviewed throughout the country had heard no mention of drugs in the home—at least not until they had had the opportunity to form some opinions of their own. They had, however, been told a little in their health education classes in the public schools, probably starting around the seventh grade.

Drug Abuse: A Source Book and Guide for Teachers, published in 1967 by the California State Department of Education, states the following in its conclusions about marijuana:

> Marijuana is a potent intoxcant. A person under its influence is irresponsible, and there is considerable possibility that he may inflict harm upon himself and others.
>
> The use of marijuana introduces the young person to a world of "kicks" from which he may find it difficult to extricate himself.
>
> The marijuana user is engaging in a criminal activity punishable as a felony. A crime of this magnitude can scarcely be viewed as an innocent pastime.
>
> The World Health Organization, in a study on cannabis prepared for the United Nations Commission on Narcotic Drugs, pointed up unequivocally the danger of the drug "from every point of view, whether physical, mental, social or criminological." Certainly the experts who made this study would have discovered the values of marijuana if any existed. But since they did not, everyone should accept the information reported as providing the best available advice, and should avoid the use of marijuana.

The above is equivalent to saying, "Don't do it because it is bad. Why is it bad? Because experts say so."

Drug Abuse: A Student's Guide to Narcotics Information, written by Dr. Sidney Birnbach, and used in Westchester County, New York, is another manual that fails to differentiate between pot and other drugs, and associates all sorts of not necessarily related behavior with drug use. It lists the following as some "signs which may indicate narcotics addiction":

1. Injection marks on arms or legs.
2. Disappearance of personal belongings such as watches, radios, golf clubs, etc.
3. The use of odd-looking, odd-smelling cigarettes.
4. Sudden loss of appetite and weight.
5. Spending time alone, locked in bedroom or bathroom.

Many of the kids I interviewed had originally received the impression from manuals like these, or from textbooks, teachers, or in more enlightened communities, from special speakers, that even a small amount of marijuana itself could be fatal, or that one puff of pot made you a drug addict, ready to steal and kill to support a habit, or that anyone who smoked pot was seriously emotionally disturbed and/or a criminal in need of psychiatric help and/or restraint behind bars.

In today's world of mass communication and massive use of marijuana on junior high and high school campuses, a young person would have to be downright stupid if he failed to observe for himself that most people who smoke pot are neither dying nor crazy nor prone to violent criminal acts.

There are as many different styles of drug use among teenagers as there are different kinds of teenagers. As the following chapters will illustrate, the Kentwood Seven represent only one style. Not all kids who experiment with drugs or use them as an integral part of their everyday lives are "dopers." And in dealing with the drug problem and effectively combatting the use of drugs we know to endanger health and sanity, it is important to differentiate between the doper and the casual experimenter, between the drug abuser and the drug user.

My personal feeling is that drug use does not per se constitute drug abuse. I do not use drugs myself, and I feel that all the insights, the heightened perceptions, and even the highs that are obtainable by some individuals through drugs are available to most without drugs. But I do not feel that the casual use of pot, for example, is necessarily harmful, and I have seen it produce positive changes in many people.

I have also observed that heavy users of any drug do not, ultimately, expand their consciousness, but rather become more tightly locked inside their heads. Many cease to have any notion of what the outside world is like. Regardless of the goals with which they may have started using drugs, they eventually spiral deeper and deeper into themselves and their hang-ups as they turn on and on and on for the higher high, the groovier feeling, the new reality. They are groping toward their own inner limits, looking out only upon that which they can hallucinate on top of the real world.

The Kentwood Seven, for example, and others like them, are so deeply trapped in their own problems that, television notwithstanding, events such as assassinations, race riots, even in the war in Vietnam have barely touched their lives. Their answers to the following two questions, taken together, indicate the extent to which they are out of contact with the world outside themselves:

If you could change something about the world, what would it be?

Bobby: The world's okay.

Gregory: I don't know. I see a lot I don't like, but I've been pretty passive in my reactions to it.

Peggy: I don't know.

Laurie: The hang-ups, war, people, the way everything is rush, rush, rush, everything has to be materialized, and it's all moving too fast, progressing too fast, the way they're changing nature and stuff like that, gas stations on every corner, apartments going up, everywhere you look, apartments.

Cal: It's difficult to change anything about the world.

Kitty: Parents. I'd eliminate them. It's an old cliché, I didn't ask to be born. But why do you have to live with them? Why do you have to be a carbon copy? It's the biggest hang-up in the world.

Kenny: I'd like to try to create more open-mindedness. I'm scared of prejudice.

Do you care who wins the November election? *

Bobby: Not at the moment.

Gregory: I guess McCarthy, but I can't say I feel if he does it's going to mean much.

Peggy: McCarthy, yes, yes.

Laurie: No.

Cal: No.

Kitty: I think I want McCarthy to win.

Kenny: Yes. I'd vote for Rockefeller, I think.

All but Gregory and Kitty said they would vote if they were of age, but none felt even moderately well-informed on the issues or the candidates or the current situation. The responses of the Kentwood group matched very closely with those of other drug abusers interviewed after both conventions had taken place, as well as those interviewed after the election. It is plain that the attitude generally expressed by

* Asked shortly before the Republican Convention of 1968.

the group is one of considerable concern for self as affected by self and others in the immediate environment, less concern for the world at large or awareness of problems affecting other groups, or mankind, and almost no awareness of directly affecting or being affected by anything outside of their immediate geographic or psychological area. I've found this to be true everywhere of teenagers who are deeply involved with drugs. Others, with personal problems of comparable magnitude, and who may have used but did not abuse drugs, were able to take a much more active interest in the world around them without being any less interested in the world within them. In other words, they could envision extending their influence beyond the sphere of their own survival and the survival of their immediate peer group.

In fact, many have been led by limited drug experimentation, especially with pot, into new awarenesses that have enabled them to reach beyond themselves in a way that they were previously unable to. Many feel—and demonstrate —that they are better able to think for themselves as a result of their experience with pot, and that they have released themselves from rigid patterns of accepting everything they are told without question. Others became aware for the first time that there are other people out there, and that these others have some relation to themselves. For these people, pot is a step toward new ideas, new possibilities, new abilities . . . as a result of the effect of the drug, or of the impact of the decision to try it. These individuals, far from retreating from society, become considerably more valuable to it.

Yet, it cannot be denied that, for others, pot is a step toward acid and the possibility of insanity, speed and irreversible brain damage, heroin and an agonizing habit, or even death.

It is unfortunate that those well-meaning authorities and so-called narcotics experts who have perpetrated numerous falsehoods about pot have been, virtually in the same breath, expounding truths about the dangers of heroin. One of their primary arguments against the use of marijuana has been that behind every heroin addict there is a joint. This is about as meaningful as saying that behind every murderer there is an incident of jaywalking. Until recently, I think most young pot-smokers could honestly say that they would no sooner try heroin than jump off the Brooklyn Bridge. But I'm afraid this is no longer as true as it once was.

I am convinced that many kids who smoke pot will never do so excessively for any length of time, or become interested in other drugs. Some of those who do progress very rapidly from pot to whatever else they can get their hands on, like the Kentwood Seven, do so because of intense personal anguish; they use drugs almost in a medical way, as it were, to suppress their pain, or keep it suppressed, or perhaps even in some cases at some moments to attempt to locate the source of their difficulties. Others, however, are not troubled before or during their pot experimentation. They enjoy it. They feel they have gained something from it. Their own experience and that of their friends belies all the warnings they have heard or read. So they see no harm in trying other drugs as well, and they do so with perhaps less consideration of available facts than they gave to "facts" about marijuana.

For these kids, the individuals who have taken a strong stand against pot, not altogether unlike the boy who cried wolf, have lost what credence they had. And their statements about heroin, even when made by others without a similar blight on their reputation for accuracy, have lost credence as well.

PART IV

Trippies, Street Kids, and Runaways

16

THE SCENE

KIDS who spend either their most important hours, or most of their hours, on the street fall roughly into three groups: the trippies, the street kids, and the runaways.

I have so named the trippies because they are more or less out for a cultural, emotional, or sensual ride, without commitment to, or even necessarily understanding of, the street scene. Those who experiment with drugs play with drugs rather than use them. They "go tripping" on whatever is available, often with as little thought about potential consequences as they give to the possibility of increased awareness or self-discovery. If they happen on heroin, their chances of surviving the street scene unharmed are vastly reduced.

The trippies are on the streets looking for action, just as past generations hung around corner drugstores looking for action, and as the kids in the isolated country town where I now live spend their evenings perched like crows on a churchyard fence across from the one store in town that stays open at night. The trippies are not very different from those kids whom society has always been trying to keep "off the streets" with all kinds of entertainments devised for that purpose. There seems to be a long-standing consideration

145

of the innate value in keeping the kids off the streets—an assumption that in doing so we are protecting them not merely from the possibility of being kidnapped or run over or contracting measles, but from all manner of psychic and moral germs. Whatever this unidentified something is that kids hope will happen, it is something parents hope won't.

But in most parts of the country today, a kid with some imagination, curiosity, and guts—and young people have always been noted for possessing these qualities in abundance—can find many more places than the corner drugstore to look for action. For some kids, the logical place is three thousand miles from home; for others, it is only three minutes away.

Bleecker Street. It is a cool, cloudy summer afternoon. The old winos are sitting on their stoop in front of the Greenwich Hotel. Two small boys go into the poster shop down the block, and the sound of the Mamas and the Papas' "California Dreaming" drifts out. The poster shop door closes. The street is gray and lonely as a carnival at dawn.

Bleecker Street and St. Mark's Place, Haight Street and the Sunset Strip have often been described as if they were carnivals to which kids run away, attracted by the rides, the good things to eat, the freak shows, the games, and the prizes.

Unlike the carnival, there is nothing at all to do on Bleecker Street during the day but buy souvenirs of what cannot have been a very good time. There is the poster shop, a pizza stand or two, and the spin-painting place—a storefront containing a big wheel full of fingerpaints on which anyone can produce a piece of psychedelic art for the price of $.75 to $2.50, depending on the size of the painting. Not long ago, spin-art was a quarter. But this part of the Village changes fast. If you should visit the Bleecker Street area, don't count on seeing anything you'll read about here, except perhaps the winos in front of the hotel. One by one, the landmarks are being replaced by whatever business may be lucrative enough in any given month to meet the rent.

On the corner of Macdougal and Bleecker, for example, where the Café Figaro stood for the last thirteen years as a kind of tribute to, and last vestige of, the *"real"* bohemia of the Twenties, hero sandwiches and coffee are now sold in a shiny orange, yellow, and chromium structure known as a Blimpie Base. Across Bleecker Street is the Borgia, one old café that has, to date, managed to keep its cool, unhurried (if relatively unhip) tone, its over-twenty clientele, and its rock-free music policy without succumbing to the changing times and rising rents. But around the corner on Macdougal Street, one more old café, the Rienzi, has disappeared between drafts of this chapter.

At any given time, Macdougal Street has six to ten little stores where earrings can be purchased for as little as a dollar a pair (Bleecker Street usually has at least three). It has some dress shops and a handful of button shops. For a while now, it has had a place called the Underground which you have to walk up steps to get into. On this particular day, the Underground still contains a subterranean soda shop (you walk down more steps once you get inside) with Day-Glo walls and an acid rock jukebox. The upstairs is a large, drafty room fitted with a dozen or so stalls where posters, earrings, buttons, sunglasses, rock records, and miscellaneous curios are sold. There is something surprisingly unnasty about the Underground, despite its sleazily psychedelic commercialism. There are no hawkers outside trying to drag you in. There is no charge for visiting the basement. The college-age kids who run the stalls are pleasant, and not nearly as pushy as their counterparts begging for spare change on the streets. They are just doing their thing and trying to make a little bread.*

At all hours, even in middle of the day, there are people standing on the steps that lead up to the Underground. Often these are tourist kids, sometimes even accompanied by grown-ups, who, having been through the Underground and killed a little time and money, are uncertain what to do next and are surveying the scene. Sometimes the people on the steps are older, harder hippies, like the guy I saw one day in a cowboy hat, leaning against the railing and surveying the Head Shop across the street like a bad guy in a Hollywood Western, a-settin' on the porch of the old saloon, watching the stranger ride into town.

A Head Shop is a place where one can buy all manner of accouterments for getting high in all manner of ways, except, of course, "the stuff," whatever the stuff may be. The merchandise, some created for the hip or would-be hip, the rest strictly for the tourist trade, ranges from licorice-flavored cigarette papers for rolling joints to china canisters labeled "Marijuana," "Heroin," "Cocaine," etc. which can also be purchased in the housewares department at Bloomingdale's.

When I wandered into the Head Shop, the young cowboy from across the street was leaning on the counter inside, chatting with the salesgirl. He was still wearing the cowboy hat, and, aside from his English-style bobby-cape, the rest of his clothes might have been conned out of the wardrobe mistress on the set of a Western as well. He said his name was Hash. He spoke with what I thought was a Midwestern twang. Actually, he was from New England. He was very

---

* Now someone else is trying to make a little bread out of the Underground. What it will become when they finish tearing it apart and putting it back together again, I don't know. I suppose I could find out, but it doesn't matter. Whatever it is, it will be gone by the time you read this book.

friendly, but his mouth curled in an unpleasant way, and he looked at no one and at nothing, though he looked around a lot. He had graduated from a big Eastern university. He had been in the Army, in Asia. He had been around. He said he'd been around the Village for ten years.

"These kids have nothing," he said. "When we came down here, we had a lot. We could eat at the Figaro if we wanted. None of these kids could afford to go in there. And we came down here because we wanted to take responsibility for ourselves, because they wouldn't let us do that where we came from."

Of him, personally, I did not believe that.

He prided himself on his income of $600 a month. "I sell things," he said significantly. "And do a little artwork and photography, freelance." He talked about all the money he'd been offered for various jobs before he'd even started college, when he was just out of high school. He said the only people he'd known who'd really made a lot had never been to school at all.

I asked him if he didn't think it was harder to exile oneself to the Village ten years ago, when people tended to do their thing alone, and were perhaps less dependent on groups.

He didn't understand the question. He said it was harder to be a beatnik, because it was harder to be accepted by a serious group. But anyone could be a hippie.

We talked some more about the little pre-hippies who had been congregating in the neighborhood for the past few summers. The girl expressed difficulty in keeping them out of the shop, which no one under 18 was permitted to enter at that time. I could tell that she treated them gently, but it was hard to say if Hash liked the kids or held them in contempt. Most likely, he simply needed them—if they were customers for what he sold.

Hash said there was a completely different group every three months, and he never knew what became of any one of the kids. He'd obviously known many of them, but he didn't seem to care much. Their comings and goings were merely a change in his environment. They either went back home, got married, got jobs, or lived with someone—any of which put them out of circulation. Being in "circulation" apparently meant having nothing better to do than stand on corners and look for action.

17

ANYTHING IS BETTER THAN HOME

BACK on Bleecker Street, where at 3:00 in the afternoon the sun had still not come out, I saw the two small boys emerge from the poster shop. One had dark hair, and was about five feet two. The other had light brown hair, and was considerably smaller. Both wore short-sleeved cotton shirts and good corduroy jeans. Their arms were skinny and lightly tanned. They were walking slowly, but they weren't looking around. They looked at the ground mainly, and the smaller one kicked a popsicle stick a couple of yards. They didn't walk any faster when they came to the Greenwich Hotel and had to pass the winos. They shook their heads without looking up as the old men hassled them for change. Having made it safely to the corner, they stopped and leaned against a car that was parked on Sullivan Street.

One of the winos staggered up to the boys and asked them if they wanted to buy some acid. They shook their heads and stared at the ground, blushing a little. The old man was not very interested in their answer. He continued to try to sell them acid, which he probably had never seen. The boys backed off a few steps down Sullivan Street. The old man moved on down Bleecker, in search of other prey.

Jimmy, the small light-haired one, turned out to be 12 years old. His friend, Craig, was 14. They were from Yonkers, a nearby suburb in lower Westchester County, and their mothers thought they were spending the afternoon at a local movie. They were bored, they said, more disgruntled than apathetic. There was nothing to do in their town. They had come to the Village looking for action. In my opinion, they found none. But in theirs—well, anything was better than home.

"Around here, there's a lot of stores and stuff," Jimmy said. "And just things you wouldn't do at home."

Jimmy was the oldest of three brothers. His father was a low-ranking executive. His mother did not work, and Jimmy felt she knew him better than his father did. Jimmy's comments about the infrequency of his father's presence at home would have drawn knowing nods from the many opinion-makers who had blamed everything from pre-teen pot smoking to the Yippie movement on the fact that Mom has taken on the dominant role in the family, while Dad works so hard keeping up the payments on the two cars and the three T.V. sets that he has no time to keep up with his kids.

"He doesn't come until late at night. Then he goes to bed because he has to get up early in the morning, and I mostly come in after he's asleep. I see him almost every night, but my mother is home all day. He's off Saturdays and Sundays, but Saturdays he goes to work for a different place. On Sundays sometimes we go out."

Craig, demonstrating another popular cliché of generation-gap commentary, was an only child, living with his mother and grandparents. His parents had been divorced shortly after his birth, and his father, whom he saw at regular intervals, was remarried and living in Chicago. Craig, more apathetic and less articulate then Jimmy, though older, had little to say about either of his parents, except that his mother "thinks she knows more than she does. She talks about a lot of things, and she's so positive she knows where it's at, but she doesn't."

Very likely, Jimmy and Craig, and the other kids you'll meet in this chapter, could benefit from more communication with their fathers, a few of whom were described to me as ogres, while the rest were apparently sensitive and intelligent men who were loved and respected by their children. But the notion that the kids would be "off the streets" if their fathers paid more attention to them was not borne out by the rest of this study.

Neither Jimmy nor Craig had major complaints about their parents, but both expressed much dissatisfaction with life in their suburban town. However, when I asked them which they would rather change, Yonkers or their family life, if given a choice, both quickly opted for a change within the home.

"Nobody trusts anybody," Jimmy said, and Craig agreed.

One of Jimmy's main gripes about life in Yonkers—and almost everything he and Craig had to say was by way of gripe—was that he hated school. His average was about 80-85, he said, but what he was really interested in learning more about was girls. He said things would be better ". . . if they could give you more time to understand it. We got hour periods. You rush into one thing while you're still trying to understand the other thing, and I just forget everything. It's no use. If you learn one thing, it's better than learning nothing."

Jimmy said the last time he could remember liking school was in kindergarten, because there was no work then, and you only had to go for half a day. But it was not only the work that was giving Jimmy trouble.

"I just recently got busted. Pills and everything. And—I

don't know—I'm getting out of this school. When you walk down the hall, teachers look at you like 'don't walk past him, or he'll jab you with a needle or something.' Like I'm all alone in my school except for Craig and he's getting out, going to a different school—just a different school with different kids. Like he's going, if he passes. But I'm passing, and they just won't let me out of the district."

Craig said he wasn't passing because he wasn't studying.

"The big hassle of learning anything with me is just waking up in the morning, and sometimes I'm too numb to learn anything. I'm so tired I just sit there and sleep at my desk all day."

Craig couldn't tell me why he was so tired. It probably wasn't drugs. He just said he'd stopped liking school somewhere around the second grade, when he suddenly no longer felt like "waking up so early in the morning and wasting the whole day." I asked him how he would prefer to live, what he would like to do every day, but he couldn't really say. "What I want to do," was his answer. "Just not to have to do the same thing every day."

He said he wanted to continue with school and go to college so he could get a job, but he didn't know what he wanted to study, or what kind of job he wanted to get.

Jimmy was more outspoken about his dissatisfactions. "I don't know what a school is supposed to do. Like, if you're learning something now, say you're learning something about fractions, when you're old, say forty, you're not going to remember the exact thing. Why can't you just get away with not going to school?"

I asked him why he went.

"My mother makes me. I'd cut, but I'd get caught. I cut every time there's something going on—if somebody's got grass or something. But I don't cut much anymore. When a lot of kids are cutting, we all get together and cut, and we all get caught together."

"What happens to you when you get caught?"

"I gotta stay in. I always gotta stay in." Jimmy mentioned some other punishments, including beatings, and withdrawal of funds, but having to stay in seemed to be the only one that bothered him. "They gotta know where I'm going all the time. Like right now, I'm at the movies."

I asked Jimmy and Craig, what they would wish for if they had three wishes. Their answers were brief, almost identical, enthusiastic, and to the point:

1. Stop the war.
2. Be a millionaire.
3. Be free, like going out at night and stuff like that.

Jimmy was, he told me, allowed out every night, but only until 10 o'clock. "And I can't go places. We finish eating at seven. I've only got three hours. There's nothing to do but hang around the drugstore."

To both Jimmy and Craig, a free person was someone who was allowed to stay out as late as he wanted: i.e., one might conclude, any adult.

"Any person in this country is free," Jimmy said. "But if you mean his whole life and everything, being allowed to do what you want to do. Like when they tell you how to wear your hair and everything at school, and like when my parents say I can't go out, that's not being free. It's just that they don't trust me or something. I know that they care, but I still want them to let me out. But I'd want them to care, too. Like if they didn't care, I wouldn't even go home."

The two boys' ideas about changing themselves were about as literal as their ideas about freedom. Craig said he wanted to be taller, Jimmy wanted to change his clothes.

"I want to wear slob-clothes, bell-bottoms, all painted up and everything. . . an undershirt and a vest . . . and long hair. No beads or things like that. I don't like them. They look girlish."

But despite their generally materialistic orientation, both boys volunteered the information that they believe in God, and that they pray, though neither considered himself a religious person—by their definitions, someone who not only believes in God but "thinks about Him a lot," and "tries to find out more about Him."

Neither was seeking any form of spiritual freedom, a quest I have come to associate with both the bravest and the weakest of the runaway generation. Among both brave and weak, this quest is often used as a justification for taking drugs. But Jimmy and Craig offered no such explanation for their pharmacological experiments.

Jimmy said he wasn't particularly *interested* in drugs, but took them "just to see what it was all about. I could do without it." He started smoking grass at the age of 11, and moved on to speed six months later. "But I wasn't really doing nothing," he insisted. He snorted speed or took a milder version in amphetamine tablets . . . plus an assortment of other pills, uppers or downers. He said he'd never taken acid, didn't know if he would. I asked him if he was worried about the chromosome damage that many researchers now believe may be caused by L.S.D., and he said:

"Yeah, I guess I believe them, but the only think I'm really worried about is shooting up with the needle and everything, and if I'm really going to get addicted to anything."

He didn't think drugs had changed his personality, even though he said his personality changes completely *while* he's high. He thought drugs had changed others more. "Like I used to have friends and they used to talk and everything, but now when you ask them for something, they kind of bash in your head. They just don't want to be bothered."

Jimmy was shocked when I asked him if he thought every-body should turn on. Aside from his feeling that it was "more fun" getting the stuff illegally, the idea of everyone in the world turning on was as inconceivable as everyone in the world spending their spare time building anti-gravity machines, or whatever 12-year-old boys did before they discovered grass.

And if he could walk into any drugstore and buy a nickel ($5) bag of grass over the counter, he said he wouldn't be interested in nickel bags very long. "You figure, what's that? I could do that any time. You want to try something else, so then you try something else, and if that becomes legal, you'd try something else, until you died.

"I used to think if you take pot then you were a drug addict and everything, and then you die immediately. Until I changed the kids I hang around with. They all took it, so I figure, you know . . . and it didn't do nothing to me yet, so . . . but I wouldn't want to be high all the time. I like to be straight sometimes, like when I'm near important people and stuff. But when there's nothing else to do, I like to be high."

Jimmy said he'd heard from his parents and from friends that pot would kill him and that he'd be a drug addict if he smoked it. Later, after he'd tried pot, he'd heard a lecture about drugs in a special assembly at school.

"Some guy came, and he talked about all kinds of people dying and then he showed us films of people who were high, and they were all skinny and couldn't afford food or nothing, and they had to rob to get their money. He was a policeman, and he had two sons who'd been arrested for drugs."

"What did you think of his talk?" I asked.

"It was scary."

"Did it change your attitude toward drugs in any way?"

"Yeh. Now I know they are more dangerous."

But despite this, and despite the fact that Jimmy made a point of telling me how adversely his drug adventures have affected his relationships with other kids at school ("since I got caught, they think I'm a drug addict. A really evil guy ..."), with girls ("If you've got a girl friend who's against drugs ... like what do you want? The girl or the drugs?"), and with his parents ("When I was straight they never used to bug me ... Now they're always on me about all the big kids they don't want me to talk to—and I don't even talk to those kids anyway ..."), giving up pot and pills did not seem to occur to him as a solution to his difficulties. He seemed to regard other people's failure to accept his drug use more as their problem than his.

His school seemed to think it was his problem. They tried to solve it by sending him to the school psychiatrist when he and six other kids were caught with downers and amphetamine pills. "They made all of us go three times. He took three of us at once. We missed our classes, but that was the only thing that was good about it."

Craig had started taking drugs about the same time as Jimmy, though he was 13 at the time, and Jimmy was 11. Craig started with Tuinol, a downer, and quickly graduated to grass, amphetamine pills, a heavy tranquilizer called Stellazene, and speed.

He criticized friends who "don't do anything any more but just sit and take their drugs," and mentioned with implied regret that he himself had done more things than he did now, like taking part in sports, before drugs.

"Two years ago, I thought dope was really bad. I still think it's bad except for grass. Like my mother is always telling me how bad it is, and now I know that sometimes she exaggerates. Some of what she says is right, and some she just exaggerates from what she hears."

Craig's mother found out about his drug activities when a

number of local kids ended up in the hospital from mild overdoses of Stellazene stolen by one of Craig's friends from her own medicine chest.

"She knows a lot about me, but she thinks she knows more than she does. She's so positive I do things I don't do. Like since the Stellazene, every time she sees the screen out of my window, she thinks I'm giving somebody pills, and she always thinks I'm robbing her of cigarettes, and I don't do that. She thinks I take a lot of drugs and do a lot of things that I don't."

Just what *do* Jimmy and Craig do on a summer day when they're not sneaking off to Greenwich Village, or really taking in a matinee at a Yonkers movie house?

"In Yonkers," Jimmy said, "all you can do is go play basketball, or sit around the drugstore and rot with the rest of the guys. Like you wake up 10 o'clock in the morning and say you go out around 11. You sit in front of the drugstore till about 6 o'clock, and if you got no money, all you do, you grub money, and you grub cigarettes, and that's it . . . the whole adventure.

"The only laughs we ever have is if somebody burns himself with a cigarette."

18

WILD IN THE STREETS

BLEECKER STREET. Five o'clock. The beginning of night. The sun has finally come out, and so have some more people. There is something almost aglow about the street, as if it has just rained. A boy who works in one of the earring shops comes out in his T-shirt and beads, leans against the wall, and looks up at the sky. The pizza shop's business is overflowing onto the street, and spin-painting is doing all right, too.

Out of Spin-Art saunter two girls who, I know, are pretty well into the scene. I don't know how I know. One is carrying a small shopping bag from one of the clothing stores on Macdougal Street, which of course means nothing. Perhaps it is just the way they walked out of Spin-Art, as if they had been there before, and they would be back, and they never had made, nor would they ever make, a spin-painting. It certainly isn't their clothes that give them away. Both are wearing slacks and sandals. Both are 15. Eileen, who is very thin, wears a white blouse and a black cardigan over black slacks. Judy, who is chubby but well put together, wears a striped Ban-Lon jersey. Her make-up lies thick on her cheeks. Eileen has no make-up on. Neither is wearing any jewelry or buttons. Both have long but not very long hair, Eileen's black, falling unevenly in damp strands around her thin face, Judy's strawberry blond, thick and straight. Like probably millions of other teenage girls, both have their hair chopped short on the sides, a haircut "in" months ago, now awkwardly growing out.

Near the corner of Macdougal and Third, on their way to Washington Square Park, they meet a friend named Susie. The three girls run into traffic to greet each other in the middle of the street.

"Did you read that book?" Susie wants to know.

Eileen and Judy giggle. Yes, they have.

"Isn't it dynamite?"

They both agree that it was pretty good, but neither seems to feel that it was really dynamite.

"Well," Susie says. "Maybe you didn't identify with it like I did, I really saw myself in that chick lying nude in the bathroom screaming, 'Where's my spike?' "

The name of the book is *Panic in Needle Park*. They are giggling over it, and talking about "identifying with" it like we used to talk in high school about identifying with romantic heroines—at best, Edna St. Vincent Millay, at worst, the girls in *Peyton Place* when *Peyton Place* was still only a book and not a soap opera. They are giggling over *Panic in Needle Park* the way we used to giggle over boy friends and pubescent sensuality.

Susie is 17, older than Eileen and Judy. She seems to have been through something and come out the other end. She talks about "when I was a speed freak." She has her own apartment on Twelfth Street, but she says her home is in Brooklyn. She is wearing a floppy gray T-shirt she bought in Paris, no bra, tight pants, attractive make-up, and rose-tinted shades. Her sleeves are short. I don't even glance at her arms, but I guess that her needle marks are a thing of the past. She says she has started to write her novel.

Though it is a very hot afternoon, Eileen and Judy both wear long sleeves. Unlike their friend Louie, a boy who will join them later, in the park, they do not roll up their sleeves to display their needle marks proudly.

Both girls came from Queens. Judy was stocky and hard-looking. Her parents were divorced when she was 3, and both remarried. She said she frequently saw her real father, who lived around the corner with his new family, for whom she babysat. But when asked about her mother and step-father she said, "She knows I come down here. She knows I can take care of myself," as if her parents consisted of her mother only. She said her parents knew nothing about her, but "must suspect something." She was a blank, unreachable chick.

Eileen was openly unhappy, nervous, confused. She expressed a great sense of failure. She wanted help, but her mother said a psychiatrist was too expensive. Eileen said she hated her parents. "They should take two death pills." Both girls were much more reluctant to talk about their relationships with their parents than anything else. When asked any questions that required them to look back into their childhood, or even a few years back, both expressed an inability to recall much, and neither was much interested in trying.

Eileen said she'd been kicked out of the private school she went to—which was pretty difficult, since you weren't really required to attend classes, but she never went at all. "I just couldn't sit still," she said. "And it was only two and a half hours a day. It wasn't the school, it was me. I just couldn't take discipline. Not that they really disciplined me . . . I just couldn't take sitting still. I was a nervous wreck. I guess if they had art . . . if it was an art school, I would have liked it."

Eileen said she had finished tenth grade "in a way," and that she would start her junior year at the School of Fashion Industries, "if I can make it." She wanted to go to college so she could become a fashion designer, "if I make it." Sitting on the grass in Washington Square Park, she picked at the ground with bitten fingernails. Her pale face was sullen and cloudy.

Judy's ruddy, pancake-makeup-covered face was massy and solid as a chunk of cheese. She said she wouldn't mind school ". . . if I just had the courses I needed to graduate, not just extra courses to keep me in school for the whole six or eight hours." Judy was taking the "professional course," and she wanted to graduate, ". . . so I can get a job, as a secretary or typist or whatever, and I'm saving my money to get an apartment, and my goal in life," she volunteered, "is to get my apartment furnished the way I want—even if it's a one-room studio—that's what my money is going to go to. Just furnish it the way I want. That's why I want to get out of school, so I can get my own apartment and furnish it the way I want."

Meanwhile, Judy and Eileen were spending a lot of time in the Village.

They said that these days they were usually going home at night, though they used to come down and stay for weeks at a time. They would stay over at friends' apartments, and move in groups from one apartment to another.

Judy, who was so anxious to furnish her own apartment, said she liked living at home. "I don't have any restrictions. My parents don't bother me. I can do what I want. I just have to be home by two, or one-thirty. And I can have most of the things that I want, cause I don't want much—besides a few million dollars. And I have my own room, so I have everything I want, really, at my house, and I'm happy there."

Dark-haired Eileen, looking darker every minute as her thin body seemed to sink deeper into her thin black cardigan, said she didn't like living at home. "My parents hassle me too much. I have problems. The schools I go to, just everything. I start fights with them, or they start fights with me. We just don't get along. I can't wait till I move out."

She said she'd move out when she was 18, if she had money, and would work as a freelance artist while going to college, she thought.

"What's the nicest thing that happened to you in the last month?" I asked. The response was an unexpected wave of giggling that lasted a minute.

"I couldn't answer that," Eileen said. "I don't know."

"I don't know, neither," Judy said.

"Well, what was it?"

"This is something we're going to have to decide, because it happened to both of us."

Giggles.

"We consider it a pretty nice thing," Eileen said.

"But nobody else would," Judy said.

Eileen said, "What do we have to lose?"

"That's true," Judy said. Eileen invited her to "do the honors."

"Thanks loads," Judy said, and then began, "Well, we got into . . ." and then they both giggled and then they were practically rolling around in the grass with laughter, and then she got out the words, "a different drug . . ." and then they laughed some more.

I asked them what the drug was.

"What do you think it was?" Judy asked me, and I said I didn't know, because there seemed to be so many new drugs I'd never even heard of before, which was true.

Judy assured me I had heard of this one.

"I'll whisper it," she said.

"Don't say it," Eileen giggled.

"We'll get busted."

"But we're clean now."

"Yeah."

They discussed it some more and giggled some more and asked me was I sure I wasn't a cop, and quieted down a little.

Judy said, "I don't know. Like it's not a *new* drug. It's a very old drug."

"Is it heroin?" I asked quietly.

"Yeah." There were giggles of relief.

They had taken it quite a number of times, they told me between giggles. They didn't say how many. Judy said they had decided to stop about two days ago.

"But you never know," Eileen smiled.

"It wouldn't be for good," Judy said. "It's like even if I wanted to, I couldn't. It's too nice."

They talked for a while about other nice things that had happened to them in the past year. They had both gone with the same boy, at different times.

"He was nice," Eileen said.

"And just having fun was nice. But lately it's been dull because so many people went away."

"You know what was really nice? That day we were in Central Park with Alice in Wonderland," Judy said.

"Oh yeah."

"Yeah, that was really beautiful. It was at night, and we were tripping, and we met all these people who were tripping, too. And we were just running around the park at night, and then we went to the Alice in Wonderland statue, and we had a lot of fun, and that was it. But it was really nice, though."

"Yeah," Eileen said.

"And then, I was going to say, this other guy," Judy went on, "this other guy that I liked and I wasn't *seeing* him or anything, but like I was going to his house every day, and just being friends with him, because I really liked him a lot, and I was just happy doing that."

"And I met this guy I liked also," Eileen said, "and I was really happy, and I was with him for a while."

They giggled some more. I changed the subject and learned that Judy had participated in an international student strike for peace by attending a rally in the park. She also said she'd taken around various petitions "for civil rights" and that one of her girl friends was getting signatures for something, and that she was going to help her. She said she thought it was good to do this sort of thing and "learn more about what's going on in the world," but when I asked her what she thought about the state of things, she said she didn't think about it much.

Eileen said she hadn't participated in anything. "If it's going to happen, it's going to happen, and I can't do anything about it."

I asked them if they had seen a movie called *Wild in the Streets,* in which 14-year-olds win the vote, and a psychedelic younger generation, led by rock star Max Frost (Christopher Jones) takes over the world, and eventually relegates everyone over 30 to an L.S.D.-cure at a funny-farm-like old-age home.

They both said they'd liked the movie a lot, but they were concerned about the validity of "putting all the old people away like that."

"It made me feel very bad," Eileen said, "because when I get old, like I wouldn't want them to do that to me. Like we all have to get old some time. I figured, well, they should just let the people do their own thing, as long as they don't bother the kids."

"I don't know," Judy said. "If that's the way the teenagers all wanted it, to put everybody away, well—if they were ruling, and they voted to do it—well, I don't know. I guess it's not really right, as long as the older people did leave them alone to do their thing. I guess they shouldn't really do that. Because they're part of the world, I mean, they lived here also, and just because they're old, it's no reason to put them away."

Neither thought the movie portrayed their generation accurately, in that they didn't believe anyone as young as "Max Frost," who became President at 25, could be so rich and powerful and have such a nice house. Nor did they feel that all teenagers would vote to put *all* the old people away. "A lot of kids love their parents and they just wouldn't."

"Maybe it represents the ultimate possibilities of a younger generation, like two generations to come," Eileen said. "Like, if it keeps up like it is. And it's getting really bad. I mean, like if I'm 15, and I'm doing junk, what will the next generation be doing? But we're not like the kids in the movie."

"You're full of shit," said their 19-year-old friend Louie, who until now had been sitting relatively quietly at the edge of our circle, smoking Judy's cigarettes and rolling the sleeves of his striped jersey up and down.

"What do you mean?" Eileen demanded. "They're too rich."

"What do you mean?" Louie retorted. "Half these people down here who are dressed like pigs and bums are from some of the richest families around."

"You didn't see the movie," Eileen insisted. "The kids are saying they're nonconformists. They wouldn't follow. Well, maybe they would. But I don't think they'd be able to accomplish a thing like that, outrule the whole government and everything."

Louie seemed satisfied. July said she didn't go to the movies much or remember movies she saw. She said she read a lot, and liked Poe and Bradbury. "If somebody tells me a book is good, I'll read it." Eileen said she didn't read much . . . "*Panic in Needle Park* was meaningful in a way, but not really . . ."

We got to talking some more about drugs.

Eileen had gotten into drugs by sniffing glue when she was 12. A few months later, she got hold of some grass at a party.

"I was quite young, and they didn't want to turn me on, and I said, 'Oh, turn me on, turn me on, I want to try some . . .' oh, I'll be a big deal, a big shot . . . and so I tried it. Big deal."

Eileen said she liked grass at the time, but I got the impression that she only smoked it now when there was nothing better to turn on to.

"Grass makes you too hungry, and I can't afford to gain weight," said Judy, whose first high, when she was 13, had come from diet pills (amphetamines) taken as prescribed by her doctor, in the extraordinary dosage of 25 milligrams ten times a day, enough to pep up a small elephant, let alone a chubby little girl.

Eileen said she'd taken just about everything except for peyote, psilocybin (a shorter-lasting relative of L.S.D., known as "magic mushroom," that to my knowledge has never been abundantly available in the United States for any length of time), and pure cocaine, or "coke."

Judy said she'd taken just about everything except peyote, psilocybin, and pure coke, though she'd taken coke mixed with other things.

"They nabbed some woman today with two million dollars worth of pure cocaine," Louie said.

"Heroin," Judy said.

"Cocaine," Louie shouted. "Today."

"Heroin," Eileen said.

"No, *today,*" Louie insisted.

"In Yonkers," Judy said.

"No. They got fifteen pounds of heroin in Yonkers maybe, in an apartment. But they got two million dollars worth of pure cocaine in this lady's girdle, coming off a plane."

"They got some heroin also," Eileen insisted.

"They grabbed her," Louie said. "It must have been fifteen tons. Wow. But that's all right. They say it was for uptown New York anyway."

"So, it eventually comes down here," Eileen said.

"Yeah," Judy said. "That's right. It eventually gets . . . where do you think it comes from?"

"Harlem," Eileen said.

"What, junk? Down here? It does not," Louie said.

"It does, too," Eileen insisted.

"Wanna bet?"

"Does too," Judy said.

"Nah," Louie scoffed. "They go downtown New York, they go uptown, they go all over."

"Well, of course," Eileen admitted.

"They go to big guys, too," Louie said, satisfied he'd made his point. "Just like the guys from Harlem."

Eileen said that she didn't have any conscience, because if she did, she'd stop taking drugs, because she wanted to. She said she took them because she liked "the state, the peace, like just to be in my own world."

I asked her if she would prefer to get that feeling or just to have it, without drugs. She said she didn't know.

"She likes drugs," Judy said. Everybody giggled.

"What I want from drugs," Judy went on, "is I just like them. Like if I'm in a good mood, I'd take acid. It makes you laugh."

"Spoiled rotten," Louie said.

I asked her if she took drugs usually when she was feeling good. She said yes.

"You don't feel good until you take them," Louie said.

"I just like to take them when somebody gives them to me," Judy said. "Except for speed and junk." Her eyes lit up.

I asked her how she paid for the speed and junk.

Louie said, "They're filthy rich. They're spoiled, rotten kids."

"I use my allowance," Judy said.

"Your allowance!" Louie admonished. "Come on. You beat somebody."

Judy had forgotten about that, but she had to admit that Louie was right. She had done that for speed. "Beating" people for drugs meant making arrangements to buy for someone ("A-heads," Judy said, meaning amphetamine addicts, or speed freaks), collecting the money, buying, and keeping the goods instead of delivering. Judy said she hadn't beaten anyone for junk.

I asked Eileen how she paid, and after hedging through several questions, she reluctantly admitted that she used her allowance. That seemed hard for her to confront. She giggled but looked miserable.

"Why don't you ask us," Judy said, "why do we like heroin? Because I'd really like to know."

"Yeah," Eileen said. "How is it possible for such a drug, for any drug, to do something like that to people? To take a person over. Really take them over. That's what it does. Like we're not junkies or anything, but junkies, like what they do is . . ."

"They dedicate their lives to it," Louie said.

"It's worth it," Eileen said. "But I can't understand how one little—it's just like powder. And it can rule their whole lives, make them steal, go to jail, become prostitutes, just for . . . like powder! I can't understand that."

"Does it scare you?" I asked.

"No."

Neither Eileen nor Judy were scared of getting busted for drugs, either, though they believed if they did, they would be put in jail. Louie tried futilely to convince them that this was nonsense, since he had been arrested eight times, but had never been held in jail. The three of them were getting restless, ready to move out of the park, onto the streets, before dark, while there was still standing room.

A new round of giggles started when I asked the girls about sex.

"We never did it," Judy said.

"We must seem strange," Eileen laughed. "We're into junk, and we've never had sex."

"Sole survivors," Judy quipped.

"I guess when I do it I'll enjoy it, and I won't regret it, because I haven't regretted anything I ever did," Eileen reasoned.

"That sounds like Susie," Louie said, referring to the girl we'd run into on Macdougal Street. "That's what she said. And look at her now. Ha ha ha."

19

AND MORE TRIPPIES

NOT all trippies look for action in places as notorious as Sunset Strip or the East Village. There is an underground almost everywhere—in western Idaho, in Florence, Alabama, in Des Moines, Iowa, in the many private schools clustered in New England and scattered down the East Coast, in the public high schools of Seattle and Miami. The underground may be anything from an old-fashioned beatnik-style coffee house scene, like the one in Sandusky, Ohio, to the more contemporary teenybopper-style parking lot scene one reads about so often in California newspapers under headlines labeling suburban housewives fearful of the kids who overrun the shopping-center parking lots at night. These parking lot trippies are threatening not only because there are such overwhelming numbers of them, but because they appear to be doing nothing, and have no easily discernible purpose in their presence.

Even in the Los Angeles area, not everyone goes to the Strip. Not long ago, there was a weekend scene, now legendary, at a large, respectable, relatively expensive delicatessen in Hollywood. And on Saturdays in many big cities and large suburban areas, there is the shopping center or department store scene, especially popular among young teen-agers and preteens who may have trouble getting out of the house in the evening. One such place, in L.A.'s San Fernando Valley, is the multi-level Topanga Canyon Shopping Center, a veritable Disneyland of merchandise to which 11-year-old girls hitchhike from their suburban homes to pick up 13-year-old boys.

At Topanga Canyon, I met Ricky and Kip, two such boys who were not being picked up. They had hitched more than ten miles to the shopping center. Each had bought a Beatles album. Now they were sitting on a bench on one of the upper levels of the plaza, just looking down, just watching the people pass on the level below, as they did every Saturday afternoon.

"It's dull, there's nothing to do," Ricky said about his home in the Santa Susanna Mountains. "Everything that's out there, you could do it in a week. All they're doing is building new houses."

Ricky said he'd considered running away, but didn't think he'd do it because, "My parents are all right. They don't bother me any. I don't really talk to them that much. I don't go to them and tell them my problems—it's not like that. It's just somebody I see in the evening and in the morning. They give me what I need and stuff. They don't give me any problem."

Ricky's 16-year-old brother had worked for Nixon in 1968, and Ricky was pretty enthusiastic about that. "I wanted Nixon from the very beginning. I thought (John) Kennedy was the ideal man then, but I think he was a nobody now. I think Nixon is a much better President. I didn't really know much about him before he was nominated, so I decided to go to the library. I looked up his official biography and read it and saw what he did and I decided he'd had more experience than anybody. Humphrey was so boring. I read about him for two hours, and then that was it. He was a nobody."

Both Ricky and his friend Kip were unhappy at school, especially Kip, who'd had enough difficulties to warrant a transfer, but was doing no better in his new school than he'd done in the first one.

"You can't do anything about it. They say you can, but you can't. At school they say if you want something done, get a lot of people together and you can do it. But then they just give you a bummer. They put you down and call your parents and stuff."

Kip said he'd been getting D's and C's since the seventh grade, when, "I started thinking for myself, and I didn't like what they were doing, and if I don't like what they are doing, then they don't like what I'm doing."

He pushed a wavy lock of yellow hair out of his eyes.

"I got kicked out of school until I got my hair cut. I took four days to do it. My parents were pretty mad. My mom likes my hair. But they didn't try to do anything about it. They say they will, but they never get around to it."

Both Ricky and Kip smoked pot. "My mom can't say too much about it," Kip said, " 'cause she smoked when she was a kid. My dad thinks he knows about it, but he doesn't. He drinks."

"Kip used to go to the same school I did," Ricky said, "but everyone at our school thinks he's really bad. Our school is the really good school, 'cause it's at the newer end of the Valley, and only good kids are supposed to go to our school. People are moving in there with more expensive houses, higher income. Everybody jumps to conclusions. Kip comes over every week, and they give us a lot of bullshit all the time, and so it's fun to give them a story. They just fall for anything. They think he turns on all the time. At our school, there's not that many people that do. There's a crowd there that would if they could, but it's a little harder to get down where we live. It would be easy down here, but I just don't know the kids who have it."

Ricky looked a little wistfully down at the crowds moving slowly back and forth below. Who had it? Someone must have it. Ricky and Kip were waiting to get up enough nerve to go down and ask.

20

THE STREET KIDS

ONE major difference between the trippies and the other two groups of street folk is that, whatever their trip, whether it's heroin or just a quest for something less boring than home, trippies almost always go home at night to their own warm beds, and are fairly careful to stay out of situations where they might lack food or clothing or other comforts to which they are accustomed.

The second, and smallest, of the three groups has deliberately cast off these comforts. They are very literally street kids in that they go home seldom if at all, and live more or less in the streets, panhandling for their livelihood as if they were either penniless orphans or archetypal wanderers. Unlike the trippies and the runaways, they differ from the older street folk—the people who have created whatever scene the younger kids find on the streets—in age alone.

They are often known to police and other local tracers of runaways, who have given up trying to do anything about them, as have their parents, with whom they are usually in touch and from whom they are not necessarily physically distant. They are, of course, school dropouts, and may be in trouble with truant officers, but in general they do not have to dart around corners or into doorways to avoid anyone but personal enemies.

Pedro was a street kid. He carried a guitar, troubador-style, slung over his shoulder on an embroidered strap. He said he'd been traveling. He was dark, barefoot, sun-blistered, long-haired, dressed in ragged, brightly colored clothing. He had limpid brown eyes and a sad smile. He was 14.

I met him on a doorstep on Macdougal Street and walked east with him. We were interrupted at every other corner by some older person who wanted to make a drug transaction. Clearly, Pedro was well known, not only as a street person of long standing, but as someone likely to know someone who was in possession of a tradeworthy quantity of most drugs other than heroin, or to be able to assist in rounding up a group of customers for same. For the right sum (in one case, a dollar to a girl who was desperate to unload some kind of pills in order to get money for speed), and without making a single overture, he could have bought or sold anything from grass to cocaine in that twenty-minute walk. But he handled each approach with the same disinterest. Dope deals might have been his bag last week, but they weren't at the moment.

He was on his way to the East Side, it seemed, simply because he'd spent enough time that day, or that week, on the West Side, and it was time to move along.

"Even right here in the Village, where they preach so much love and everything," he said, "it's really crummy because they have their little groups. There's so much hate here, it's incredible. Like I hang in the East Village, and I hang in the West Village. But kids from the East Village don't like to hang in the West Village because it's too plastic, and the kids from the West Village say the same thing about the East Village.

"When I came back from Texas, the kids on Macdougal Street, they look at me like—well, I go up to somebody and say, hello, my name is Pedro, what's yours, and so on, but they look at me like I was a narco or something. Everyone suspects everyone else of something. They're out to get what they can, whatever way they can get it."

Pedro got what he could by panhandling.

"They have so much—especially the tourists. They come down here, and they look at us and then take pictures, and then they go back to where they're from and talk about us, and we give them sort of something to do. So why not pay for what they're looking at?"

He came from an upper-class Latin American family. He'd been raised by his young grandmother, a painter, with whom he'd moved to Connecticut five years ago. He'd been in and out of school for a while. When last enrolled, he'd been in the ninth grade. For the past two years, he'd been living on the streets of New York, in between side trips home, and had hitchhiked as far away as Texas.

Like a wandering minstrel, he strummed on his guitar and told me of his life, with an attempt at a minstrel's philosophical distance from his experiences that was more like defensiveness and self-doubt. He had apparently been told so often that he was stupid and/or crazy that he had gotten into the habit of qualifying almost everything he said with this information.

"I'd go straight," he said, not meaning it, "but I know I can't make it so I'd just forget about it. I'd like to make it big some day. I don't mean having a lot of money—I mean just having my own pad and enough bread so I won't starve. Maybe I would like to be a musician, something like that. But everybody puts me down so much that I don't care. Maybe I'll be a garbage man, or one day you'll see me on the Bowery."

I found him neither stupid nor crazy. And while he mouthed many of the most anti-establishment, anti-materialistic clichés of the love generation, he had a few ideas of his own.

"I guess I would like to be kind of a preacher, you might say. I don't know. But when I get into one of my deep moods and start talking deep, people look at me like 'this kid is crazy or something.' "

Pedro's "crazy" talk had to do with the Bible, and he said that the Salvation Army people, who ran a sort of runaway refuge called The Answer in a Bleecker Street storefront, had tried to get him committed to a mental institution on the basis of such talk, and had insisted he was on drugs when he was not.

Pedro saw his life style as a valid, if not necessarily permanent, alternative to what the indoor world had to offer. He saw himself as both a melodramatic figure and a visionary—a sort of rogue hero and St. Francis of Assisi in one.

"Nobody in the Village knows me. They know my face, they know my name. But nobody knows who I am, and nobody knows what I am. Nobody really knows where to get me, where I'm going to be, what I do, what I'm going to do."

I left Pedro on St. Mark's Place, not knowing where he was going or what he was going to do. About six months later, I was talking to police officer James Burns, who had a night beat in the West Village, and I asked him if he knew a boy named Pedro.

"Wears a poncho?" Burns asked. "Carries a guitar? Says he lives with his grandmother. Oh, he's a real sharpy, that kid, a very sharp individual. Good-looking boy? Speaks exceptionally well? You'd never know he was 14. You could see how much more intelligence he has, or at least logic and knowledge, than most of the other kids his age." Burns laughed. "He beat a girl up and got $80 and took off for some place. I guess he's back by now."

21

ON AND OFF THE STRIP

LOS ANGELES. Sunset Strip is a wide, wide open space, wider than any other space where young people gather to grow free. And it's noisier even than narrow St. Mark's Place in New York's East Village on a hot summer night when the Electric Circus is open, and the street people are gathered outside somebody's basement flat with drums and booze and tambourines.

The noise of the Strip is a Super-Noise. The live music crashes out of every discothèque at an illegal decibel; just about every tinny joint that sells a hot dog or a cup of coffee has a juke box. Then there are the cars and the motorcycles filling the road, and the airplanes crossing the sky, all revving it up together in one big celestial hum now rising to a buzz, now falling to a whisper, but persistent, alive, and vibrating, like an electric guitar string plugged into the ultimate amplifier, until dawn.

All the lights are bright; the sky is black. And there aren't many spaces. There are spaces between buildings, and there are spaces between the palm trees, and the buildings are low and flat, so there is lots of black sky, and there are spaces in the parking lots behind the buildings and between them. But there are no spaces in the street. It seems to stay as full of cars as if they were all parked. And there are no spaces on the sidewalk. It seems to stay as full of kids as if they were all lined up there, waiting, watching a parade.

The smoggy air smells good to my New York nose. And the hop-headed kids look happier to me than the New York kids. They are smiling more, and moving more and talking to each other more—despite the desperate way the ones who have no false I.D.s are clustered outside the discothèques where you have to be 17, 18, or 21 to go in and dance; despite the panhandlers with their blind man's tincups, the crazies in their attic trunk costumes, and the runaways with their cracking, blistered feet; despite the hungry and the just plain high.

I like L.A. It is so easy here to stand still and smile at strangers.

Down on Fairfax Avenue, where the Free Clinic competently and not too chaotically serves a grateful underground population from all over the sprawling city, the atmosphere is different. There is a big drugstore on this corner, a Jewish old people's home on that corner, The Free Press here, another hip bookstore there, a bead and earring place even duller and more tacky than the ones on Bleecker Street, a supermarket, a dry cleaner's, and on and on in an endless mixed bag of people and places at the edge of a bare, gray, empty sidewalk that is somehow neither cold nor forbidding nor depressing but simply some place to stand while you are waiting for the traffic light to change.

It is on this sidewalk that I meet Mickey, Bruno, and Joan. They get out of a funny little closed-up white truck in front of the Free Clinic. Bruno is tall, with a lot of brown curly hair. He is wearing a T-shirt and white jeans and some brownish beads, and he is barefoot. Joan is also barefoot. She is wearing white jeans and has some kind of blanket wrapped around her shoulders, and her light curly hair is in two bunches tied with cowhide, falling over her breasts. Like Bruno, she is tall and lean. Mickey is little and thin, and has short, yellow hair, a narrow face, and a slow, resonant, recently deepened voice. He is a straight-looking little kid, with tanned skinny arms sticking awkwardly out of his white short shirtsleeves. He could be Jimmy from Yonkers.

Bruno and Joan and some other people live commune-style in a rented house somewhere in Hollywood. They and all the others at the commune have bad colds. They have come to the clinic for pills. Mickey has come along for the ride. He is 14. He lives at home with his father. His parents are divorced. He is in the ninth grade at Sepulveda Junior High School, where, he says, "They just keep piling it on. Stuff you know already. They just keep driving it in there, more and more. I'm not really trying too hard. School is such a bummer, just wasting away the day. They ought to have interesting classes, like law and stuff."

He said his parents' divorce had interested him in law, and added gratuitously, "It's just weird."

He used the words "weird" and "strange" over and over again to describe all manner of phenomena. But he didn't say school was weird. He said it was good, except for wasting so much time. "A little knowledge never hurt us. I'm picking up on a few things. However, it's not like necessary to go to school, because life is so groovy."

Mickey liked to think about dropping out, but he felt that even if he did it, which he wasn't sure he would, he'd better wait two years until he was of legal age, which was apparently 16. "It's got a lot to do with the future, and jobs. I'd *like* to drop out; however, I don't know if I'd benefit from it. I'd like to get some money up to do things that I want to do. But that involves getting a job, and that involves education."

One of the things Mickey wanted to do was to start, or at least become a part of, a commune, "up in the hills somewhere, with all the people I'm associated with. This is going to happen, I know. I've been thinking on it. We're going. I am. We're going to start a commune, and like any commune, it's just so easy to do. It's like everybody pays a little part of the rent, and part of the food thing and gas and electricity, and that's kind of groovy, because it makes it a little easier on everyone . . ."

The longer Mickey talked, the more resonant his voice became, the more inspired he seemed to be with his own feelings and desires.

"I just can't see war. I'd take all the people and get them all together, and they'd become like in a godhead—everybody would get together, and they would worship God, and just stop fighting, and obey the Ten Commandments. That's what I'd do.

"I was following the election. It's kind of strange, the way it turned out, because back early in the summer it was yeah, Bobby Kennedy and everybody sat there and rooted and then somebody had to go and shoot him down. McCarthy was a bummer, when he dropped out—but he was kind of pushed out. Now Nixon's in office, and that's kind of weird, because he's had about eight years of planning what he's going to do, and as soon as he gets in there, he's going to do it. I wonder what it is."

He said he would have voted for Pat Paulsen if he had had a vote—but he didn't think that he was old enough to rate one. "Right now it just seems like, don't get involved yet. Wait a while." But he thought he wanted to join the Peace and Freedom Party. He wasn't sure why. And he was about to join another organization, called the Self-Realization Fellowship.

"It's a really trippy thing. You go to church, and you sit down and meditate and all this. It's really groovy. It's like everybody should just drop everything, and find God, through whatever means they use. If you go to meditate, you go in and sit down for forty-five minutes, and meditate and chant, and then some cat gets up and lectures on different subjects, like why God does not end wars, and how to find God through Yoga. A religious person is not one who believes in God, but one who knows there is a God. I get up in the morning and meditate before I go to school. I come home and meditate before I go to bed . . . I really couldn't say what is a free person, because there is a lot of freedom going on . . . Like I was hassled by my old man for a long time about church. 'This is a weird church, son, you can't go there.' But I said fuck it, and I went. My parents aren't religious. They don't go to church. I am a believer, that's that."

Mickey said the biggest lie he ever believed was that hippies were bad, "that you should treat them like a bunch of ogres out there, beat them with clubs and things like that. I was brainwashed by T.V. and radio and newspapers and things like that, and I just decided, well, maybe some of this is not true, you know. I have a few friends here who think differently. Then I went out and discovered that it wasn't true. This was about two years ago. I went out with my friends. I met Bruno and Joan and all those folks, and like they're really groovy. I was continually surrounded with, 'Look at them rioting out there, those punks,' and it didn't seem like they were the ones causing the riots, but that the police were out there trying to beat them up. So I got out and got to know them and got acquainted with their customs. I experimented with dope, and I said, okay, that's good. Now I know a lot of people, and people are putting me down for the people I hang around with, and I don't like that too much. It's kind of strange how people have gotten it into their heads, 'Oooh, long hair, how horrible.' "

"How come your hair is short?"

"I go to school. In junior high, there's a lot of restrictions on that. I got slapped with a paddle. But my parents kind of go along with the school's attitude, like 'we don't want any longhairs in this society,' and 'a little discipline is necessary,' and that it is within the school's authority. I try to keep cool and not blow it."

Mickey spent a lot of time reading. "I'm fascinated by Tolkien. *The Hobbit* is a really trippy book, if you really get it into your mind what's happening, and kind of let the book take over your mind. All of Tolkien, and a lot of science fiction, is just based on the idea of some guy going out and slaying a bunch of people for the good of everybody. And I pick up and read books on astrology, Hinduism, Islam, and Moslem things. A little more about God never hurt anybody."

Unlike most kids today, Mickey was into jazz, "the old stuff, when the people didn't have anything to read but they just got together and played." He said the highest form of communication is "like coming in contact, not speech or writing, but with the mind, in meditation or E.S.P. That's kind of strange," he said, using his favorite phrase again.

Mickey dabbled in drugs—mainly pot, hash, and downers—pills he called yellows, reds, and rainbows. He said he'd sniffed glue on occasion. "It's still kind of a trip, hallucinations, etc., if you really put your mind to it. But some of the glue they're putting out now is really horrible.

"In the eyes of some people I was like a really good kid before I turned on to drugs. In the eyes of other people, I was like a fuck-up, a strange little kid. Now it's kind of reversed—but not so much that I don't really have the same relationships with most folks. However, being in school, I can't really be around with all the people I want to. In my own eyes, well, I think, now you're a little cooler. But that's neither here nor there, because I was pretty cool before. But it's made some kind of change. I can go right out and make a friend if I want to. If nobody's around, I can just go make a new friend, which is groovy. Before, I'd just stay around the same crowd, where the same old thing was happening. Now there's something new going on every day. And I never just take up sides. I sit back and I listen and I form my own opinion. Before, I'd decide without even knowing what things are about, and I'd say a thing is bad just because it was taught to me as bad."

What Mickey wanted this book to say was, "Folks should go out and find God and be with God, and become really religious, because that's the only way they are going to get out of this place."

Bruno and Joan were in and out of their funny white truck, and finally their turn came at the clinic, and I was still talking to Mickey in the cab of the truck when they came out, with their cold pills and penicillin shots. I sat on the floor in the back then, talking to Bruno for a while.

Bruno, as it turned out, was a runaway, but a runaway of a rather special kind.

Like the trippies, who can be seen as timeless children seeking the new, and the street kids, who, like their older counterparts, often see themselves as part of a tradition that links them to the mendicant friars, the runaways, too, have roots in the past.

Children have been running away, in escape from the dreary boundaries of life at home, and in search of adventure, since long before the oft-cited days of Tom Sawyer,

Becky Thatcher, and Huck Finn. The heroes of some of the earliest prose works we know as novels, dating back as far as sixteenth-century Spain, were runaway sons of the bourgeoisie who, in seeking their fortunes alone in the great world, met with a series of bizarre adventures, involving, at their very mildest, some drinking, some fast living, lots of narrow escapes, and voluntary or involuntary participation in various illegal, immoral, or otherwise dubious activities— all of which had to be handled with sharp wits and dauntless spirits.

Today's children have not only the sharp wits and daunt-less spirits of their ancestors, but they have a contemporary precedent set by hundreds of thousands.

As we have seen, the trippies are not particularly on the run. They are, perhaps, on a scamper, at most, a gambol. The street kids, while they may carry on their backs all or most of the possessions to which they care to claim owner-ship, are generally not going anywhere. Many, like Pedro, never run away from home, but rather drift off, staying out nights, staying away more and more days, coming and going erratically and with increasing infrequency, until home becomes a last resort for shelter in bad weather.

Real runaways, however, are people who have decided to leave and then left—on the spur of the moment, on the half-serious suggestion of a friend, after weeks or months or years of misery over a home or school situation, after frustration, irritation, torture, boredom, depression, whim. Few runaways start out as either trippies or street people. They have made an independent decision, perhaps one of the first and most important of their lives. They are running either to something or away from something, or they are running for some other very specific reason. While trippies usually have no philosophical commitment to anything, and street people have a commitment only to a scene or a life style, runaways are usually acting out of some very basic commitments to themselves and their own needs or desires, or, in some cases, desperations.

Bruno was a 16-year-old runaway from Seattle on a road trip. But he was a runaway with a difference. He carried with him his parents' written permission to be away from home. Bruno kept his mother and his stepfather, an aircraft engineer, well informed of his adventures, except perhaps his involvement with drugs. He said his parents had been "very good" about his leaving, and that he'd seen them three times since, and talked to them on the phone.

"My stepfather's cool. If you can argue with him long enough to make him use some reason, then he will agree. I wouldn't change a thing about him. Even though he messes me up sometimes, he has a sense of innocence about him, and a strong sense of justice. Mixed together, those are very good. My mother, though, I think is typical of a lot of mothers in that she creates her own problems and she is a little bit weird. She keeps saying please come home, but my dad is cool and knows it just won't work. But it's kind of a bummer. Like I call home and I have to tell my mother three or four times, stop nagging me, I want to talk to you, how are you?"

His mother, he said, was very unhappy when he left, but nonetheless at the end of the summer, had allowed him to obtain the notarized paper saying he had permission to travel.

By permitting Bruno to carry this piece of paper, his parents were raising his status from that of fugitive to the same that any adult would enjoy in traveling around the country. Without such a piece of paper, or some well-organized, well-falsified, and thoroughly memorized identification cards indicating an age over 18, a minor on the run can travel in his own country with only about as much peace of mind as an alien trying to cross borders without a passport.

In hard-core runaway areas, any young-looking person may be stopped by police and asked for identification at any hour. If his papers indicate he is a minor who does not live in the neighborhood, he can be taken to the station house and booked as a transient. In California such an individual is generally defined as "a person under eighteen who is sans legal guardian, and has no visible means of subsistence or has no residence," which by law is all that is required to land him in juvenile hall.

During the summer, it's often difficult for police to tell the runaways from the trippies, and they may round up hundreds at a time on bad nights, or leave well enough alone unless they spot a kid who looks too filthy to be living anywhere, or whose face looks like one they've seen in the missing persons files. But during the school year, the summer runaways who have really committed themselves to staying away are still around, and new runaways continue to appear on the streets in the worst of weather. These are the kids who are really determined to make it on their own through what may be very hard times. These are the kids who are really risking something by a) dropping out of school, b) having to contend with mediocre to wretched weather, fewer people on the streets for hand-outs, general aid, or just companionship, and c) standing out as an open target for routine police questioning during the hours when school is in session.

Most runaways try to keep themselves off the streets during these hours. If they don't live anywhere—and most of them don't most of the time—this is a feat that, after a few days, may provide an even greater challenge to the imagination than the daily search for new sources of food and shelter.

If the parents of a minor report his disappearance to police, who subsequently find him, he can legally be forced to return home. While this may be altogether inappropriate, especially in the case of some older runaways, it is at least practical from the law's point of view. However, an individual under 18 years of age who leaves home without his parents' permission is not merely behaving in a manner unacceptable to society at large, he is guilty of a crime. It is a crime that only individuals under 18 can commit. It is the only crime other than curfew violation that only a juvenile can commit. It is also, oddly enough, the only crime listed in the "offenses charged" columns of the F.B.I.'s *Uniform Crime Reports* which describes the offender and not the offense. In other words, "runaways" appears in a list that includes not "prostitutes" but "prostitution," not car thieves, but "auto theft." The offense, it seems is *being* a runaway, not the act of running away or having run away.

After completing the eleventh grade, nearly five months ago, Bruno told me, he had left home with ten dollars and a pack on his back. He said he'd been in L.A. for about a month, and was now a legal resident of California.

"I had three partners, and we'd been on the road together since June, and this was our second trip down here. We slept in a vacant lot under some trees, and then I met these people—they were really good to me, and then one morning they went to jail. They got busted for two kilos [of marijuana]. So I got them out on bail. That's how I got down here, and that's why I'm going to stay here, because I owe a lot of money."

He was also staying because he liked L.A., and "because my people are here." When Bruno used the phrase "my people" it took on Biblical sanctity. He used it not, of course, in reference to his family, but to his "partners" and his new-found friends, who were, at least by virtue of the communal home they provided for each other, actually filling the role of family.

Bruno answered many of my questions as if his life had begun when he went on the road ("I don't feel qualified to even talk about religion because, being on the road, there were so many things I wanted to get into that I just couldn't get into . . ."). He'd been reading a lot of Kerouac, he said, along with some Huxley and some William James; the influence of Kerouac showed. Bruno's many expressions of contentment with his present "simple life" ("I work hard, and when my body needs it I go to sleep, and then when I get up it's a new day and I start all over again . . .") were somewhat colored by statements like:

"This is the longest I've stayed any place for a while. I get the itch, I want to go on the move." He wanted "to go everywhere," especially to "a country where a lot of dope grows . . . where life is simple and you can do something."

But Bruno was not untroubled by the fact that he did not know what he wanted to do, or even whether he preferred a life that was basically easy-going and pacifistic, if not passive, to the active pursuit of goals. As we talked, he was quick to recognize that he was contradicting himself frequently, and toward the end of the interview, he admitted good-humoredly that he was in a dilemma or two.

"I may be kind of a pessimist—I've kind of given up on the world. I want to let it do its thing, and I'm just going to get as far away from it as I can. It's a big thing to tackle, to change it. And I've seen it, from sleeping in ditches and sleeping under trees, and sometimes I get a little bit bitter at people because they're so—well, they're sick. I just got tired of fighting them, I fought them for so long—although I know that no matter what I say, I will fight them further. But if I had my way, I'd let them just do their thing and destroy themselves."

Yet, Bruno was aware that he might be changing something by what he called, "working at just living."

"I kind of feel that this is a part of a revolution in a way,
and although it might only be the beginning and I might
not profit by it, my children will profit by it, or my grand-
children—and then I could say to myself, well, I had a hand
in this, and that I helped make it come about that the world
is better.

"I'd like to get into the legislature and rip it apart. I'd
like to change the ways of the government. I really fear
right wing and conservative people with a passion, to the
point where I could get even violent . . .

"It's a thing that kind of fluctuates with me. Every time
it gets like I don't want to do anything, a while later, it
will make it an even stronger passion that I do want to do
something . . . I'm free in the sense that I can go anywhere
in the world I want and do anything I want to do, and
there's no place I can't see. But still there are things I
want to do that keep me bound. Future plans, ambitions.
Things like that."

An A student who liked school—the learning part, at
least—Bruno had dropped out when he needed only five
more credits for his diploma.

"I figure in night school I can do that within a few months,
four or five days a week, four hours a night. Yeah, I want
to finish, and after that, I want to go on, but right now I
just can't do it.

"It was cool last year, because I had my own identity.
People didn't hassle me. I had no problems at all. But being
there in the school among what were to me all these sick
kids, it was just too much for me, and I got really down. It's
kind of a society hang-up they have even in the schools. Like
they start out with school societies, and already people are

hating each other and knifing each other in the back over nothing, and it's not cool at all."

Far from being a loner, Bruno had been part of an underground of about twenty students in an academically superior public high school. By the end of that year, however, he was one of only three who had remained to see the term through. All the others had finished by now, he said, or were in night school, and a few had started college.

Bruno, too, wanted to go to college "someplace, just a place that will give me this piece of paper that says I'm just as good as those people out there, so that I can fight on their level. A diploma or a degree—to me it doesn't matter. I don't believe in going to school for a diploma or a degree. But if I can just be at least where they're at, if they can at least understand that I got that, then it's cool. Cause that's too often the hitch of it—look what I got, look what I got, this and that, and this and that . . ."

Bruno's voice faded in a soft hiss into the night. The inside of the truck was so dark we could hardly see each other between the passing of cars. But I could feel him smiling at me, and I knew, from the enthusiasm in his voice whenever he talked of school, that he wanted to go to college at least partly because he dug learning.

Meanwhile, Bruno was working to pay back the bail money he'd borrowed "just selling dope and things." He'd tried every kind of drug except cocaine, starting with acid at 15 and progressing up through heroin before he'd ever left Seattle.

"That was a bad time, before there was an underground, when it was mostly syndicate. I kind of have a thing about needles, it's just too easy to get hung up on, 'cause it's beautiful . . .

"So I kind of quit except now—I kind of don't like to talk about it—no, I do use it once in a while."

After what he guessed to be about sixty acid trips, Bruno hadn't taken any acid in over a year. "That wasn't where it was at. Acid shows you the way, and that's about all it does."

He seemed ambivalent about all drugs except pot, which he said he loved and would never give up. But when I asked him if there was a time when he thought dope was bad, he said,

"Oh, yeah. Dope is bad. There's no doubt about it. DOPE IS BAD. You have to be able to limit things to some extent. Dope can really be bad. Even pot. You have to be careful, and know what you are doing."

22

THE DIGGERS—ONE LITTLE ARMY

VARIOUS underground communities across the nation maintain a strong sensitivity to the injustices of the "establishment" world. In some, this sensitivity manifests itself as paranoia, which is likely to be intensified by certain patterns of drug use. In others, it results in a sincere and often skillful attempt to take responsibility for the welfare of the group—whether that group be a commune of a dozen young adults and their children, or, as in the case of the Los Angeles Free Clinic, all of the sprawling and diverse undergrounds of a vast metropolis. And the fact that most runaways are subject not only to all the dangers their parents can conjure in the widest imaginings of their sleepless nights, but to legal action which is in itself, as many police officials have agreed, usually inappropriate to the situation, has drawn many undergrounders above ground.

Over the past few years, the runaway problem has given rise to an increasing number of underground professionals in New York, Los Angeles, San Francisco, Boston, Washington, and other cities. Some of these individuals had professional credentials in the social sciences before dropping out; some of the best of them are simply gifted human beings. Almost all of them decided that somebody had better help these kids, and in order to help the kids as effectively as possible, established their own legitimacy as a source of community service, usually either by gaining church affiliation, or by careful, patient, and persistent work in establishing communication lines with police and other agencies in local officialdom.

"A kid of fourteen can't cope with the streets," said Tom Cox of the Diggers Creative Society in Los Angeles. "Even if they wanted to fool with the illegal part of it, they just can't make it. They are going to get busted, or they are going to get into some very bad situations where the people who are sheltering them have nothing to lose. In one case, there's a guy who collects fourteen-year-old boys and sends them out to earn money for him. I've dubbed him the Faggot Fagin. A fellow named Caesar, runs around town with a red cape and red toga sort of thing—obviously an ex-actor— and he has his great spiel and he's always got three or four young boys trailing after him. It's really a very bad scene. Same thing happens with a chick, different way around. She balls a different guy every night to find a place to sleep. That is not exactly the life for a fourteen-year-old kid."

Like most of the other runaway services, the Diggers are attempting "to form a bridge between the kids and the adult world."

"We know how the kids think, and a lot of us around here are old enough to know how the parents think, too. We may sympathize with the kids, but still we have some idea of what's making the parents tick as well. A lot of times a kid will sit in front of me and say, 'Well, my father is an old fogey . . .' 'Well, how old is he?' 'He's thirty-eight.' Well, I'm thirty-nine."

Thirty-nine, and not trying to look any younger, Tom Cox is kind of a dropout himself, having recently left an advertising career in New York for the wide open spaces of the West. A big man with thick brown hair, a walrus mustache, and a radio announcer's voice, Cox was no aging bohemian. Obviously at home behind an executive-sized desk, he wore a blue oxford cloth shirt with loosened tie, and related to his telephone as if were part of his arm. I spent two afternoons with him in his office, while he handled a 21-year-old T.V. repairman coming down from a bad acid trip, a county social worker officially checking out the Diggers, a 13-year-old runaway boy from Brooklyn who had to be kept clear of any trouble while legal arrangements were finalized for his permanent stay in Los Angeles, the boy's mother, the mother of a local runaway girl who'd gone home via the Diggers that day, a public school administrator about school for the Brooklyn boy, and a gentleman who was offering shelter to runaway girls, but reputedly demanded a high price for his help.

Firm yet gentle and easy-going with the kids, hard-hitting with the bureaucrats, tough yet understanding with the parents, almost breathless by the end of the day, Cox was doing a hell of a good job.

I was turned on to the Diggers on Hollywood Boulevard by a couple of panhandlers in their late 20s who were passing out little green pieces of paper announcing "Green Power" and soliciting funds for a mass Thanksgiving feed-in in the park, to be "sponsored" jointly by all the underground groups in the city. I asked for the Diggers' phone number. Green Power said I'd better not call and gave me the address instead.

I did not expect much from a place which, I was told, would probably deny me an interview if I did something as straight as call in advance for an appointment, but I was pleasantly surprised. I felt something known as "good vibrations" the moment I walked into the dim waiting room on

Selma Avenue, a few blocks from Hollywood and Vine. Selma Avenue is a uniformly dingy street lined with small, low-slung factories, and even inside, the Digger quarters, which were temporary, were, unlike most hip houses, not very bright. Little attempt had been made to psychedelicize the place in order to make the hip and would-be hip feel at home.

Directly facing the door, a bulletin board announced the rules of the house (the most important of which was no drugs), held letters sent to transients c/o the Diggers, and like the walls of the Free Clinic, proclaimed love for all. The main waiting room, the size of a smallish living room, had dusky bare floors and walls and shabby, puffily upholstered chairs and couches. A few paperbacks and some newspapers that were a few days out of date lay on a scratched coffee table.

Behind a desk, a long-haired, granny-gowned receptionist pleasantly manned a busy phone while keeping a cool but careful eye on the little boy who was lounging in a chair across the room.

His name was Freddie, and I got the distinct feeling that he wasn't waiting for anything, but had come here for a place to sit, and would get up and leave at any moment. On the other hand, he looked like he'd been sitting in that chair for hours, maybe days—and would be there again as long. In any case, he showed none of the impatience of one who was waiting. When he learned I was from New York, he struck up a conversation with me.

He was from Brooklyn. He was 13. In one way or another, he'd been on the run for a good three years. He'd been in and out of reform schools, both private and public, in and out of the homes of two sets of parents, and his next step was jail. He'd made it from Brooklyn to L.A. on his own steam three times. He didn't want to go home. He didn't want to go to jail. He was here for help. He'd been here before. He was pretty sure he was going to get what he wanted. The Diggers had found a couple to put him up for a while. The couple were willing to become his foster parents. Freddie's mother was willing to let him live in a foster home. All that had to be done now was to make it legal. The Diggers had been working at it for three days. Meanwhile, Freddie ran small errands for them—going out for cigarettes or coffee, delivering some documents in the immediate neighborhood, never straying far.

While we were talking, almost unnoticed by me and perhaps by Freddie as well, a tall girl had appeared in the chair between us. I hadn't seen her arrive. She was just suddenly there as if she had sprung out of a cushion. She wanted a match. I gave her one. She couldn't keep her cigarette lit. I kept giving her matches. Her name was Isabelle. She was wearing bermudas and a white sleeveless sweater and sandals, carrying a shawl and a canvas bag.

She told us where she was from—a small town about thirty miles away—and that she had left home this morning. She had been on her way to Big Sur, but had ended up here instead. "But Big Sur is in the other direction," protested Freddie, who obviously prided himself on the fact that he would never make such a mistake. The poor girl, who, as it turned out, was only 14, though she looked much older than Freddie, could offer no explanation for what had occurred, nor did she seem to find anything illogical in setting out for someplace and ending up some thirty miles farther away from it than where she had started. This was obviously more than Freddie could tolerate, but he decided to try. As the three of us waited for Tom Cox, both Freddie and I tried several times to engage her in conversation, but failed. Occasionally, though, when we were talking, she'd interrupt with some brief, irrelevant remark. Otherwise, she just sat there between us, staring straight ahead of her, smoking, using up pack after pack of my matches.

Tom Cox told me later that Isabelle had climbed out her window at six that morning. Around eleven, someone who knew about the Diggers had seen her wandering on the Strip in an undrug-like daze and had brought her in. And there she was, in worse shape, Tom said, than any kid he'd ever seen. You didn't just come down from a trip like the one she was on.

The Diggers arranged for her to spend the night with her married sister. She went home the next day, after the Diggers had conferred with her mother, her father, and the psychiatrist she saw irregularly.

"The father turned out not to be the gentlest soul in the world," Cox said. "He'd been spanking her—now you don't spank fourteen-year-old girls—even normal ones, let alone one that's got her problems. So something's got to be done about him. One of the things we suggested is that he come down here on Saturdays and do a little work here, see what the kids are like. He's going to see a lot of bad things—but he's also going to see kind of a cross-section of where it's at. This is important, even if it just crystallizes his hostilities and makes him even more hostile—at least it changes what's going on."

The Diggers had never had anyone in who was as disturbed as Isabelle was, Tom Cox told me. Nor were most runaways being spanked at home. However, the communication gap between Isabelle and her parents was typical, he said.

"It's almost always a total lack of communication. It isn't just minor. The parents have absolutely no idea what's going through the kids' minds."

The reverse, he said, was also true. "These kids don't even read newspapers. They just aren't interested. I left a copy of *The New York Times* out there for two days. Maybe 50 kids were in and out of here in that time, and no one touched it. No one even picked it up and moved it. You'd think, a strange newspaper, someone would at least have the curiosity to see what it was."

In counseling the runaways who came to them for help, Tom and his co-worker, Digger Paul Johnson, who'd been at it longer, did not necessarily try to get kids to go home, but rather to take a look around them and see for themselves what they were doing.

"Kids are not really running away," Tom said. "They are running to something they think is there which isn't there. They think it's just groovy street scene, oh, boy, all these fascinating, you know, hip types, they don't have to go to school, they live in these groovy communes—which of course isn't true. There's nothing more revolting than the street scene, but they don't really know it. They think it's really an exciting thing. It's complete freedom, but they don't realize that it's kind of hard to have freedom if you're out panhandling for food, or selling the *Free Press* to pay your rent. Now that's not exactly the way to do your thing."

"I guess I'm somewhat of a person that if I see something that has to be done, I can walk around it for a while but I can't just completely ignore it. I'll try to do something to change it," said Paul Johnson, black, over 30, a one-time National Guardsman, and chief coordinator of the L.A. Diggers.

What he saw, Paul said, was "a little girl, strung out on methedrine, who was hungry and had no place to stay, and the only people that she could talk to were the speed freaks, the people who were in the same bag that she was in."

In the past nineteen months, Paul and other Diggers, with expenditures of $1,200 in cash, not including donations of food and clothing, had helped provide 80,000 meals, 20,000 nights of shelter, and 1,500 jobs. Nine hundred runaways who'd been to see the Diggers had gone home, 49 pregnant girls had found living arrangements for the duration of their pregnancy, 42 mothers with children had found homes. These were the Diggers' statistics, not counting, of course, thousands of casual referrals, the outcome of which they never learned.

"I see the Diggers as one little army that you cannot destroy," said Paul. "When you don't need them, they're the dirtiest, rottenest, lousiest bums in the world, but when you need them, they're God. I went through that same thing in the Army. I used to take more shit from civilians than anybody in the world, cause they couldn't understand why I was in that thing. But the minute there was talk about Watts exploding and the ghettos blowing up—'Call the National Guard!' And that black cat who's sitting over there saying, 'I'm not going to fight in the war,'—You let 5,000 Ku Klux Klan come into his neighborhood—'Call out the National Guard!' And that's what's happening with the Diggers. When the police have a little problem that they don't want to set five hundred men at, or they want to find out about something, they come to the Diggers. And this is just a small army. About seven people that have withstood a hell of a lot of things."

23

HUCKLEBERRY HOUSE

UNLIKE the Diggers in Los Angeles, Huckleberry House in San Francisco exists for the sole purpose of aiding runaways. While the Diggers' quarters were hectic, Huckleberry's, when I visited them a few days later, were relatively quiet, and staff member Steve Lieberman told me they were seeing only about five runaways a week at the time. They had moved from their legendary Victorian house on Broderick Street near the Haight to the second floor of a Presbyterian church-owned building at some distance from the scene . . . or what was left of it. L.A.'s eternal summer does not exist in San Francisco. It was bleak and rainy and cold and, nearly a year and a half after the legendary love and acid summer of 1967, the streets of Haight-Ashbury were deserted except for angry Black Panthers and crazed amphetamine heads with half their brains worn out by speed. Also on the streets were pushers, killers, and pimps. There were some forty murders in Haight-Ashbury during the first six months of 1969. Few stores were open. More than half the buildings in each street were boarded up. The sidewalks echoed, and fear hung, tingling, on the impassive wind. The runaways who persisted in coming—and they are coming still—were having a rough time.

With a larger staff, foundation money, and fewer people to handle, it would seem that Huckleberry House would have had the time and money to do more with those who did come than the Diggers. Not so, however. It seemed that Huckleberry's, like the Haight, had nearly had it. Its older staff members had gone, leaving the care of the place to a group of 25-year-olds who, dedicated as they might have been, were additionally motivated by the fact that Huckleberry's indirect church affiliation made work there acceptable alternate service for C.O. draft status. The dorm and kitchen facilities that the Broderick Street house had provided for those kids who were able to get parental permission to stay a while were gone, too. And here was a 15-year-old runaway burning the hot chocolate he'd cooked in a tin cup. The physical quarters were not nearly as crowded and sun-faded-shabby as those occupied by the Diggers, but the place lacked vibrations, and the people, though full of proud statistics and pretty good philosophy about the care and handling of runaways, lacked the ear-to-the-ground, fingers-on-the-pulse-of-the-community feeling that was evident in even the physical movements of Tom Cox and Paul Johnson and the rest of the Diggers' staff. Outside of L.A., though, not too many people knew about the Diggers, while Huckleberry House was famous. It had become both a legend and a science, and it was all very well organized on paper, but there was a 15-year-old boy there who had no place to sleep that rainy night nor had he had a place in the months past— and Huckleberry's had done all it could do for him.

Charles was a tall, attractive young man with shortish, softly curling reddish-blond hair. He looked older than 15; if he had not introduced himself to me as a runaway, he would have blended in with Huckleberry's staff members. His home was in Smithtown, New York, a big, semi-rural town on Long Island. It was nearly Thanksgiving. Charles had left home in March. He said he'd thought about running away since he was 7, and had taken shorter "trips" before— to Philadelphia, New York City, other parts of Long Island, staying away six days, three days, four days.

"I came home and it was cool for a while, and then it came back to the same old scene—my father smacking me around, doing my thinking for me . . ."

Charles had been kicked out of public school for "just being generally rotten," whatever that meant, and the school had arranged to have him tutored at home.

"Like the way they put it—don't get me wrong, I'm not bragging or anything—they said I had a high I.Q. and it would be a shame to quit school, and so they sent tutors to the house, and one thing I didn't know about—they were going to graduate me in the eleventh grade and send me to college in my twelfth year. They didn't let me know about this until after I came back from California the first time."

Charles said he would have split anyway, but I doubted it. "It would have been nice to know," he said. "It might have swayed my decision a little. I might have put up with it for another three or four months . . . but I felt like I had a hell of a long time to wait."

Charles described himself as one of the straightest kids in a pretty straight town before he left home: "self-conscious," "paranoid," the kind of kid, as he put it, that, if a bunch of guys were doing something wild, they wouldn't want him to know about it. At the age of 10, he said, he'd changed his mind about a lot of things. The biggest lie he'd ever believed was "that the best thing you could do was grow up to become a well-adjusted good citizen. I think that's about the worst thing you could do. I just looked at a lot of things, and saw how screwed up the world was, and how hung up people were in each other's lives, and in their own lives—my parents, stuff I saw on the news, stuff just fit

together. I looked at attitudes toward sex, politics, econom-
ics. I always felt that sex was something to be open about,
even though my parents and my friends didn't."

Five years later, though, at 15, Charles still believed that
all drugs were fatally dangerous. He had had no contact
with them at all, and thought he would soon die if he smoked
marijuana. Then he left home.

"First I just wandered around in the area for three or
four days, then me and two other kids skipped out of school
one day—that is, *they* skipped school—and went to New
York, and we met this hippie guy and he said he was going
to California, and we said we'd come along."

The four of them hitched together to North Carolina,
where they split up to meet again in Jacksonville, Florida.
But when Charles got to Jacksonville, he failed to find his
friends, and he had been more or less alone ever since. For
a month and a half, he hitched, explored, and visited ("I
didn't know anybody, but I visited people anyway") his
way to San Francisco.

"I really felt best when I was in the middle of nowhere,
hitching by myself. I got this universal feeling of being a
part of the flow of life—you're not the whole machine,
you're just a minor cog—it was really a great feeling. I was
no longer caught up in my minor hassles."

Unfortunately, the feeling didn't last. By the end of July,
he'd been sent home by San Francisco's juvenile authorities,
after a freak arrest when a car in which he and a 14-year-old
girl had hitched a ride was stopped and its driver busted for
drugs. He'd had a phoney I.D. but, "It wasn't too valid—
just an application for a duplicate driver's license from
Ohio."

Between March and the end of July, though, except for
two weeks spent in Huckleberry House, and some days in
juvenile hall, Charles made it on his own—finding food

and shelter, and even, for a short while, having a job and his own apartment. In New Orleans, on his way to the coast, Charles had been turned on to grass, and between March and July, he'd tried acid, hash, peyote, and mescaline.

"I'm much more easy-going now, more open. I used to be very concealed. I still am, maybe in my feelings, but not in my thoughts."

He had no doubt that drugs had changed his relationships with others for the better. In the time he was away, he felt he had become a leader instead of a follower among his friends.

"When I got home, they more or less respected me because I had gone across the U.S. by myself, and they felt maybe they couldn't—or at least they hadn't—and they kind of looked up to me."

So, when things went sour once more with his parents two months later, Charles didn't hesitate to leave again.

Within less than three weeks, San Francisco's juvenile authorities were again putting him on a plane to New York. "But I got off the plane. Then I called my parents. It's two hours to the airport from Smithtown, then the waiting, then two hours back—so I just thought I'd save them the trouble. Then my father got uptight and said he had a warrant out for my arrest for breaking and entering into my own house and taking my own clothes, and I hung up on him. Half the clothes he bought, the other half I bought. I climbed into a window in my house, took my clothes and split, and he has a warrant out for breaking and entering and theft. I figure if he's going to be like that I don't even want to know him."

Since that phone call, some three or four weeks earlier, Charles said he'd "just been wandering around." He described his typical day as follows:

"I get up usually around seven or so, and go out and get

something for breakfast. I can usually make a little money either selling papers or spare-changing [panhandling]. Then I go over to the research project—that's a project where they want to find out about drug addicts. They pay you a dollar an hour and you tell about your drug experiences, and you take shrink tests, and have interviews with psychiatrists. After I get back from the research project I usually wander over here, or I just scoot around the city. I usually end up here at night, almost every day. I stay here until around ten, then I go out and I just ask people for a place to stay, and if I can't find a place to stay, I just wander around all night, which is really bad, because if you know what the Haight is like—you can pretty much get killed or busted or beat up—and this is in the daytime—I had my jacket stolen twice last week in three days, and I was chased through the park last night, so it's not getting too good. All of a sudden all these things started happening to me.

"Since March until now, this has been the only time I've been hassled by anybody. Even hitchhiking across the country, I've never been hassled, and then all of a sudden it hits me, three incidents within a week. I've been pretty damn lucky up till now, I guess. But the thing that gets me is that even though I was lucky, I was just about surviving, and now it's like how bad is it going to get? I mean if that was good luck, I don't want to be around for the bad."

"What are you going to do?" I asked.

"I dunno. Kill myself maybe." He laughed. "I'd like to get a job, but getting a job when you're under age is really a hassle. Like everybody tells me I could pass for nineteen or twenty, but you still need that little piece of paper in your pocket that says you're nineteen or twenty before you do anything legally."

Charles had had a job at a Kentucky fried chicken place, but had been fired for a combination of coming in stoned too often, and getting so stoned that he forgot he had to go to work. He didn't care much for the job, he said, and hadn't really minded losing it.

"It seemed pretty close to falling into a rut—getting up, going to work, coming home, eating dinner, going to bed, getting up, going to work—nothing left but what you're doing for a living. Even getting chased through the park last night, that was something different. It was a really bad scene, but the thing I liked about it was it was different and unplanned and it was a surprise, and I love to be surprised by life. Just sitting down and planning things ahead of time and worrying about tomorrow before you worry about right now is a waste."

Charles' talk had become enthusiastic, and I asked him if he had, in general, been having a good time in his wanderings. I was somehow surprised that his answer was almost an unqualified no.

"I get stoned once in a while, and that's fun, but it hasn't really been a great time. Like the one thing I really do miss is my home life. Like I don't know if runaways really think about this, but sooner or later, they're going to miss their home life. They're going to miss not being able to grow up with their brothers and sisters, and like leave the house more or less with their parents' consent or their parents' blessing, whatever you want to call it, and that's one thing that plays in the back of your head, that when you left home your parents weren't with it one hundred percent, and you know there's always going to be that on your back. I don't know— a lot of kids either realize that now or are going to realize it sooner or later—like that's one thing I really miss—having my childhood swiped more or less."

"Do you feel like someone swiped it," I asked, "or that you gave it up?"

"It was swiped," Charles said without hesitation, yet not

bitterly. "Like even if I'd stayed home—I'm not saying staying home would have given me everything. Like I left home because it was really just so bad, like I wasn't really having a childhood at home either. Here it's worse in a way, but it wasn't anything close to being good at home, and this is the lesser of the two evils."

Charles said that if he could change something about himself, it would be his age. "If I were eighteen, I wouldn't have to worry about ducking around corners when cops come, or wondering where I am going to stay—'cause the way I see it, I could get a job, and wouldn't have to worry about where or when I'm going to eat, and wouldn't have to worry about the legal hassles. I've looked for other jobs, but you have to be eighteen for almost all of them, and you have to have identification, and I'm neither."

I left Charles sitting alone next to a big old-fashioned radio with gentle Simon and Garfunkle turned up to a roar, in a small, proper living room in the part of the house that the Presbyterian church used for lonelyhearts-type socials. It was dark outside. It was dinnertime. It had just begun to rain.

The next morning, I read an item in the San Francisco *Chronicle* about an unidentified young man, believed to be about 17, who had been found dead in the park that night. He wore neither coat nor shoes; there were no signs of violence; cause of death was unknown. He had dark hair. He was not Charles. But he could have been.

24

THE FRIENDLY LOCAL STATION HOUSE

IN New York City, where the winter is longer, the summer hotter, and the scene more concentrated and inbred than it is in California, few runaways even attempt to sleep in the parks. Those who can't find shelter with new friends turn next to crash pads or communal living quarters. But most communes, where no older person seeking a place to spend the night would be turned away, must for their own security observe the law that forbids anyone to provide overnight shelter for a runaway minor without his parents' permission. So the kids are left to rooftops, alleys, and tenement hallways.

Whether or not this law discourages kids from leaving home, or encourages those who have left to go back, it certainly makes the street scene tougher than it might otherwise be. It also makes it impossible for agencies other than police to offer a runaway much practical help if he refuses to call home. Even when a runaway has been picked up by police, he still has a choice about calling. But then, he almost always calls.

For N.Y.P.D.'s Lieutenant Jim Burns, a handsome, curly-haired cop whose beat has included the Macdougal and

Bleecker "Kiddy Korner" for the past nine years, runaways are all in a night's work. But Burns makes no attempt to underestimate the problem. On the bitter winter night I interviewed him, there were eight hundred teenagers on record as missing from Long Island's Nassau and Suffolk Counties alone. When I asked him a question that amounted to, "What if your kid ran away?" he found it difficult to answer, but he said, "No one is immune. It could happen to anyone. It's pretty much of an upper-middle-class problem. Most of these kids come from good homes—that is their parents own their own home, or at least have a very good apartment."

Burns, who at first modestly said that his major qualification for dealing with runaways was that he had a good memory for faces, later admitted that he liked the kids and generally had a good rapport with them.

"A lot of the times I'll talk to the parents if I happen to be here, or, say, if we don't have any men here in the station house at the time, of course I'll have to sit here and wait for the parents to come. And of course then is when you try to find out if you can help, and say anything to the parents that might help them understand their child a little bit. 'Cause, don't forget, most of these parents just don't even understand why the kid left. They have no idea. They don't leave because of fights or trouble in school. They just say, 'I don't even know why he went. He used to like to wear these kind of clothes, and used to have the money to buy them. And all of a sudden, one day, he went.' "

Burns blamed the problem not on the generation gap, but on the mass media—the newspapers, magazines, and T.V. reports that created a situation in which "it suddenly became fashionable to live in the slums." As he saw it, running away was one of the best things a young teenager could do to gain status among his friends, and those who were picked up after only a few days—too short a time for the run to really count—were, for the most part, the only ones who were really disappointed at being picked up and sent home. Others, he thought, were relieved to be able to get back without having to take responsibility for a decision to return. A pick-up by the cops helped a kid save face with his friends.

"The smart ones will come and take a look around in one or two days, and decide that dirty living is not for them," Burns said, opening an envelope and taking out a color photograph of a flat-chested little girl in a frilly formal gown. "They think something is really going on here, which it is not. There's nothing here but to walk around." He ripped open another envelope. Another faded Kodachrome print. Another prepubescent face, this one with freckles and pig-tails.

On the bulletin board behind us there were dozens like it—Bar Mitzvah pictures, Confirmation pictures, Sweet Sixteen pictures, family-portrait snapshots with the dog included, junior high school yearbook pictures, school I.D. card mugshots—pictures in which every kid looked homely, and every kid looked straight.

In the old days, Burns said, the young people who came to the Village at least *thought* they had come to do some-thing creative. Whether he had talent or not, each one was at least pretending to try to make it—as a folk singer, a writer, something. "Today, not many of them come here with even a guitar. They have no idea why they are coming here. Kids come from the West and from the South. They think they're going to find original ideas here. There's no original ideas here. There's only kids."

And yet, the scene on New York's Lower East Side, made up of little kids and older kids, continues to thrive like a scrubby but stubbornly hearty tree in depleted, but not yet barren, soil. Before, during, and after the hippie flowering, the Lower East Side has consisted of street after street of grimy, six-story walk-up buildings, urine-drenched hallways, overturned garbage cans, ravaged automobiles, rapidly multiplying cockroaches, and probably double the Manhattan average of two rats per person. It would take a lot more than middle-class love and the vitality of inspired youth to clear the streets of generations of immigrant poverty, squalor, violence, ignorance, and fear.

For a while, they really tried. Early in the hippie movement, one of the original groups of Diggers (no connection to the Diggers in L.A.) obtained equipment from the city and actually went to work as volunteer street cleaners. But the neighborhood neither understood nor appreciated nor responded. While the front of an occasional building is brightened by a wall-to-wall coat of psychedelic art, and an occasional block has gained a degree of class and considerable profit from shops that seem to have a much higher rate of survival than those in the West Village, the Puerto Ricans and Poles and Ukrainians hate the underground, the undergrounders resent the all-American English-speaking straights, the panhandlers are ubiquitous, the revolutionists respond erratically toward the rest of the world at large, and the speed freaks and the junkies and the pushers of all races, creeds, and socio-cultural persuasions continue to rape and rob and kill. For a runaway, the street scene is as tough and murderous and lonely as it has ever been for any immigrant kid who ever grew up in any ghetto, including this one, and who, unlike so many of the kids who make their homes on the Lower East Side today, had no choice.

25

ST. MARK'S PLACE AND POINTS EAST

KICKS, drugs, search for kindred spirits, and quest for that mythical piece of action aside, why do kids choose the Lower East Side? Not merely, as the well-meaning Lieutenant Burns insists, "because it has become fashionable to live in the slums." Not merely, as Burns believes, because they are not "smart" enough to realize after a day or two that "dirty living is not for them." Those kids in need of quarters constantly attended by Mr. Clean stay home in the first place. Maybe the sanitary conditions are too much for some. The neighborhood isn't beautiful; it's probably the dirtiest, most run-down neighborhood most of the kids have seen. It doesn't always smell good; in fact, it often reeks, not because of poverty, but because of apathy and carelessness and bitterly abandoned hope. And yet it is alive. It assaults the senses with sounds and smells and multi-level vibrations and unharmonious sights that, over the years, have come to make sense together—The Electric Circus, mod clothing, Puerto Rican grocery stores, head shops, Pentecostal churches in storefronts, in streets lined with shops where you can buy everything you need to join the underground at a price only someone with a very good

job or a very rich father could afford, streets lined with overflowing garbage cans and paved with broken glass, streets
lined with fruit and vegetable vendors who arrive early in
the morning with their wares on open pushcarts and pack
up and go home after dark. Open windows from which one
might hear Spanish, English, Yiddish, Polish, Russian,
Ukrainian, or music, often live, often good, always loud,
from marimbas or electric guitars or jazz horns.

The appeal of such a neighborhood is not so difficult to
understand in contrast to the very silence of the suburbs,
where everyday human events have less impact, somehow, on
both the senses and the spirit. To a middle-class child from
Pennsylvania or Connecticut, a place where old women in
babushkas actually sell vegetables from carts on the streets
is mythical. And it represents a contact with the basic needs
of survival, which we have striven so hard to put aside in
order that we and the generations to come might have time
to explore the "finer" things, but without which we often tend
to lose contact with ourselves. It represents a level of realness
and of relevance to the streams of life that many young
people seek, and find unattainable in a split-level house with
no history, no past, no intimation of a yesterday or a tomorrow.

Not far from St. Mark's Place, and two short blocks from
each other, Louis Abolafia, 26, and Robert Benedetto, 33,
operating from their respective tenement apartments on East
Fourth Street, seek to aid runaways and their parents.
Neither has met the other, and each is skeptical of the other's
methods and motives, though both admitted to knowing
virtually nothing about these.

Abolafia, whom the *New York Post* and other straight
papers have called a "hippie leader," was more like a self-
styled underground megalomanic—especially since by now
there were no more hippies, and as far as I could tell,

Abolafia had no followers—except for the several young ladies (all of legal age, I believe) who bared their breasts under his auspices at various nude-ins, including at least one at Wall Street on lunch hour. Abolafia also ran for President of the United States in 1968, and did some prelimary campaigning for the New York mayoralty election in 1969, on some sort of nudity ticket that billed him as "the only man with nothing to hide." He was the only person who refused to speak into my tape recorder in over a year of interviewing.

Abolafia's quarters consisted of a single long, narrow, storefront room that, its windows boarded up, served as election headquarters, painting studio, and public relations office from which Lou was constantly telephoning contacts for movie roles, magazine publicity, book contracts, or T.V. appearances as any or all of his many identities. It was also his living space and a runaway contact and counseling center. Photographs identical to those Jim Burns had showed me in the Charles Street station house were taped up all over the walls, in between newspaper clippings about both runaways and nude-ins, semi-nude and completely non-erotic photographs of Abolafia and friends, and several of his large, abstract oil canvases. Attached to many of the photos, or scattered on the battered, paint-can littered couch and on the big desk that was nearly buried in papers were letters like the following:

Dear Mr. Abolafia:

I'm sorry I didn't write before, but I had to arrange to get a picture back for you to have one. There is another problem. We spent so much on the private detective that right now I do not have the money to send you. My husband was to have been home today, but did not come. I will send the check as soon as possible and more if you find her. If this is alright with you, it will be greatly appreciated, if not possible, I will understand.

Her name is Carol Lynne Ottling, born February 4, 1955, dark brown hair and eyes, 5 ft. 2 in. and weighs about 105. Her complexion is pale and she has acne. Her teeth are good and we love her very much.

This picture is about a year old. I do believe her hair is straight now and about shoulder length. She had on a green, brown and yellow tweed coat with a brown fur collar, and a black or dark brown furry hat. A green corduroy pocketbook. She has a brown skirt, a green plaid skirt, and blue slacks with her. White knee socks and brown loafers.

She is most likely getting back at me, but there are so many others that she is hurting by doing this.

She left here between 8 & 9 A.M. Nov 21st and has not contacted anyone since.

If you can explain to her that we all love her dearly and want her home with us. As far as being yelled at or punished, we don't have to, she has done so much damage to herself and I will do everything to help her. She is a very good girl, stubborn but who isn't.

Last summer she spent her whole vacation helping to teach deaf children. She has a wonderful personality and is liked well by all.

Please find her and ask her to call me. She had about $20.00 with her, two watches, and pierced earrings.

Thanking you in advance.

> I remain
> Very sincerely,
> Lucy Ottling

Good Luck!

Abolafia told me that he tells any kid who comes to him to go back home, that pot may be okay for some people, but in general he is down on drugs and doesn't use any himself, that kids should stay in school and study history, and that he was no longer searching out runaways at parents' requests without some sort of retainer (he considered $30 a minimum

contribution), and that if he didn't meet the parents and
sense a real interest or involvement on their part with the
kid and his welfare, he wouldn't bother unless there was
considerably more in it for him—and not in promises, but
before the fact.

Benedetto, on the other hand, is a Paulist Father,
known to the community as Father B. His only publicity
was an occasional article in the *Village Voice* and an ad in
that paper at Christmas time that read:

Catholic Priest (not unsympathetic to Village causes) will
act as Go-Between for any teenager wishing to negotiate
peace treaty with family for Christmas. Will also do what I
can for any pregnant teenager wondering what to do now
in regard to family, etc. No sermonizing and confidences
will be kept.

"If I were a runaway kid," Father B. said, "and somebody
like Abolafia told me to go home because there was nothing
down here, I would right away want to know what he was
doing here if the place is so lousy. I wouldn't tell a kid to
do that. I figure if a kid's fifteen years old, he can make up
his mind, perhaps, and whatever he wants to do at this
time—it may be the worst thing for the kid psychologically
at this moment to send him back home—and as I said, I
am of the opinion that some people have to drop out."

Father Benedetto's sixth-floor walk-up apartment was
brightened by a touch of psychedelica and flowers—
posters with slogans such as "Be a Prophet," and cheerfully
framed quotes from Nietzsche and other secular folk. He wore
blue jeans and a plaid wool shirt, and spoke with a heavy
New York accent. He'd had thirty-five responses to his ad
this season, and it was still, in January, keeping him pretty

busy. He was not, however, having too much luck in permanently reestablishing runaways in their families.

"The younger ones, they may go home. But others, they weren't ready. They came because they wanted someone older than they were who would listen to them and wouldn't pass judgment, and would give them a little security in the decision which they had made. Some wanted contact, some wanted to go home maybe for a while . . . like a weekend, or Christmas maybe."

He laughed. "But that doesn't always work out. Because sometimes this is where the big fight comes. You work out the whole thing, and then they go home, and the first thing they do when they get home is start in with the kid, so by the time they get back, they're pretty sure reinforced without me that they just can't live at home."

"The big thing with the parents is to get them away from this tremendous guilt that they feel that it's all their fault. When the kids run away, it's not necessarily anybody's fault," he laughed. "The poor parents. You bring your kid up to the age of—they're leaving now at about eleven and a half. You give them—all right, they may have made mistakes. You give them love, and maybe it was misled. Maybe there were a lot of hang-ups in the family. But there was a basic love here. I mean they don't basically hate the kids, usually speaking, you know.

"I was walking by a city project the other day, and I looked up at all the buildings and apartments—and I've lived in New York City and Brooklyn all my life—and I said to myself, if I was a kid and I lived in one of these apartments, I'd run away. I felt like running away right then. Because I just felt completely insignificant, completely dehumanized. It was a shattering experience. I have lived all my life in apartment houses, and I never realized till lately how many thousands of people there are, and how insignificant the human being becomes. And if it scares me, what does it do to the kids?

"The emotional thing that must have gone through his mind in making that decision to uproot himself from everything that he is, is quite traumatic, it's unbelievable. So he gets down here, he has nothing. First thing he says is, at least I'm free. I don't have them any more. It's the first time they've been face to face with personal responsibility, even to the point where they have the option to suffer and maybe even die if they want. It seems to me that some people at some time in their life—it might be when they are very young —have to go through some terrifying experiences in order to learn to live. They might come out better for it. They may have to mix up their lives for a couple of years in order for them to really go through the growing process.

"We are a country of immigrants, a country of restless people who pulled up stakes all over the world and said let's go to a new country. Their parents and grandparents. This is a generation whose whole background is moving, moving, moving. The seed is there. Even the Puritans wanting to get away from the establishment. And the stranglehold lack of freedom we all have is very much present. Kids can see this affecting their parents even if it isn't affecting them. You see them coming from New Jersey down here on the weekend. Busloads of them. It's like 'I can make believe now . . .' "

Or is it "I can touch reality now"?

Is it "I can be free now"?

Or "I can be responsible for myself now"?

26

A MATTER OF CHOICE

GLANCING through an old diary from my high school days, I was astonished to see how often I mentioned the desire to run away. I had had no recollection of having considered it. It seemed that the urge rose out of such incidents as a fight with my mother about clothes, or an upset with a boy friend, combined with an overwhelming sense of the tedium of Latin and algebra, topped off by the awareness that there was an enormous world out there about which I knew practically nothing, and to which I had no access. On one occasion, I went as far as to work out a plan of action on paper, but I never packed a suitcase, nor did I leave the house without knowing I'd be back at the appointed time. However, had the act of running away been part of the culture of a whole generation as it is today, an act with several years of precedents set by hundreds of thousands of kids, I probably would have joined their ranks.

Adolescents as a group, not only in recent years, but for generations past, have often been accused of conformity. Parents are very quick to berate a child, whose behavior they find disturbing, for not having the sense to think for himself, for following the crowd. Yet at the same moment, these very parents are looking at mental pictures of other children whose behavior or development does meet the standards they have knowingly or unknowingly accepted or set. My mother did this; I believe my grandmother did it with her children, and very likely her grandmother did it, too. I cannot emphasize how strongly I feel, after spending so many hours talking with so many kids who have been, in my opinion, so erroneously lumped together, that teenagers deserve much more credit than they generally receive for their own individuality. Yet there are ways in which they do function as a group, as a generation.

Teenagers identify with, and are loyal to, each other because, like other minority groups, they are in the same plight. Whether they are spoiled or deprived, brilliant or dull, spaced out or straight, they are bound together by the fact of their age.

This is not to say that teenagers don't put each other down. They are rabidly critical and demanding of one another. As we have seen in the preceding chapters, they have their rigid social strata. The thirty kids sitting together in any given junior high or high school classroom do not necessarily even say hello to each other. But in the long run, at the gut level of survival, they are together, and it is, in a sense, Them against Us.

"Being a part of the subculture I'm in, I don't believe a lot of what's going around," a crew-cut 16-year-old chemistry whiz told me on his way to a Rotary Club meeting.

"What subculture?" I asked.

"Oh, teenagers. Our little subculture."

"Is there anyone your age whom you would exclude from that?"

"Oh, probably not," he said, as if the idea were naïve. "You can't help but be in it."

Most of the kids I talked to reluctantly, as if they felt

obliged to say it, mentioned the breach between the generations that exists in their own minds, though many of them were a bit sheepish about giving credence to a phenomenon surrounded by so much publicity that publicity itself seems to have created it. And they were quick to say, though not always convincingly, that the dichotomy isn't as sharply defined as the mass media insist.

In general, however, kids are not *against* grown-ups, though an astonishing number of parents seem to feel as if they are the victims of some enormous juvenile conspiracy. In my opinion, young against old was a much more prevalent attitude in the beat generation; even the hippies didn't seem to feel as out-and-out persecuted by the whole establishment as the beats did, nor were they as intolerant of their elders.

However, more and more kids have less and less faith that the grown-ups can get the world out of the mess it is in, even though they are aware that many adults genuinely want to do just that. Kids have no patience with good intentions; adults, as kids see them, aren't all dead, or numb, or stupid— they just don't know what to do. They are too tired, too trapped.

Nor does it seem that adults, individually, are *against* youth, much as their fears and misunderstandings may cause them to berate a runaway generation. Institutions and attitudes, however, passed on from generation to generation, unexamined by individuals and perpetuated by authorities, have done much damage. As Eda LeShan so simply and accurately puts it in *The Conspiracy Against Childhood,* "We seem to have two entirely separate sets of criteria for judging children and adults." She goes on:

> We do things for them that they should be doing for themselves, such as driving them to school when they ought to walk or apologizing to Grandma about how busy they

are when they should have written a thank-you note for the birthday present. On the other hand, we make them do things for which they are totally unready. . . . We can be far more demanding of our children than of ourselves.

We come home at the end of a day's work, take off our shoes, have a drink, and spend the evening talking, reading, or watching TV; our children arrive home after a six to eight hour day at school and put in four more hours on homework. . . . We are far more tolerant of our friends, relatives and co-workers when it comes to an appreciation of their worth as individuals. As adults, we admire each other for whatever narrow range of talents each of us may have, but are quite insistent that our children should excel in everything. . . . In our adult world, we accept and enjoy differences—but when we see exactly the same human qualities in our children, we are unnerved.

Most children of the middle class are denied the opportunity to take responsibility for themselves; they are forbidden to experience anything beyond a certain set of experiences, forbidden to think beyond the sphere of certain ideas, denied mobility, and, whether they take it upon themselves—literally steal it for themselves—or not, they are denied the right to be as they are. And who, indeed, has the right to be as he is? Everyone. Most kids know this; too many adults have forgotten it. And too many adults have turned their own refusal to allow children responsibility into the notion that kids prefer to be irresponsible.

I quote from *Normal Adolescence,* written by the Group for the Advancement of Psychiatry (GAP), and endorsed by the U.S. Department of Health, Education, and Welfare:

At present in prosperous North America, adolescents are given many of the economic privileges which in the past were earned through years of hard work. Their privileges exist without accompanying responsibilities, and they are in the position of young princes with a world of pleasure created for them. Nowadays it would seem that it is not the adolescent who envies the adult, but the adult who envies the adolescent. The adult may wish to join the colorful, vital, and potent world of the adolescent with its freedom from responsibility. The advertising man knows this very well and everything from soft drinks to automobiles is sold in an aura of adolescent gaiety and sexuality.*

Happily, GAP also tells us that "in spite of the stresses of adolescence . . ." (not the least of which may be trying to live up to this colorful, vital, potent, irresponsible, and pleasure-seeking image of themselves that the T.V. thrusts at them daily as if from a mirror), "the vast majority of young people ultimately make an adequate adjustment."

It seems that GAP, too, has bought the ad man's "aura of adolescent gaiety and sexuality" as the truth. Unfortunately, however, these "young princes with a world of pleasure created for them" are slaves to the system, slaves to the dictates of society, as much as the middle-class man is a slave to his job. With the difference that the man chose to have the job, whether he really wanted it or not; regardless of his circumstances, he did have a choice. The teenager does not. He is bound not only by the conventions of society, but by the law of the land to do as he is told regarding where he lives and how he spends most of his time—just for a start.

But now, the teenager has begun to challenge such laws— set up generations ago for his protection, today often functioning toward his destruction. He has turned off his T.V. set and closed his magazines and denied the role of "young prince" that society has chosen for him. He has said, "Yes, I do have a choice, and this is what I will do." Perhaps he

* Group for the Advancement of Psychiatry, *Normal Adolescence* (New York: Scribner's, 1968).

chooses not to go to school any more, not to live at home any more, in a sense to relinquish the remaining years of his childhood. Or perhaps he examines the alternative of running away or dropping out—an alternative that grows more and more real for the majority with every kid who does choose it—and says, "No, not now. Staying in school is better. Staying at home is better. There is something that I want *here*," or, "For now, I'd better stay cool in order to have something I'll want later."

We have no way of knowing how many of the "good" kids have chosen, just as the runaways and dropouts have chosen. They have simply chosen something more palatable to the adult world—maintaining the status quo instead of changing it. But they are finding alternatives to examine, not in the adult world—adults seem to them to have no alternatives even for themselves—but in the actions of other teenagers. And the fact that they are still around, apparently behaving as they should, doesn't mean they haven't stored these alternatives in the back of their minds, connecting them to actuality by a brief list of ifs regarding tomorrow or next week or next summer.

PART V

The Children of Marx and Coca-Cola

Los Angeles, California— Westchester County, New York

"... The suburban kid, of course, is the victim of so many things over which he had no control. The fact that he lives here, and the reason he lives here, why his parents moved to a suburb in the first place. Ninety percent of the time they moved to avoid the black people. They moved to frustrate integration, and it didn't work. Whether this was conscious or unconscious is to me frankly unimportant. The fact is, it happened. It was done by design. Maybe unconscious design, but design nonetheless. Have you ever noticed how difficult it is to travel in the suburbs, waiting for buses, etc.? When whitey decided to keep the black man out of his nice little suburbs, he figured out a series of subtle ways to do this, and one of these was transportation. So to live in the suburbs, you not only need one car, you need two. Which right off the bat means you have to be a person who can afford two cars, which means a certain income level, which precludes a certain portion of the black population. What has happened, however, is that, as the old saying goes, he who spits up in the air best watch it, because it is going to come down and hit him in the eye some day. Well, it has come down and hit him in the eye, because as a result of keeping transportation a very unimportant part of suburban life, 1) their kids can't travel so they are stuck in their immediate neighborhood, and they are bored to tears because there is nothing to do, and 2) as soon as they are old enough they have to have a car ... and those of them who cannot afford cars are really angry people, even if they're living in a $35,000 house, if their family can't afford a third car, they're frustrated, they're poor, they're unhappy about their existence, and they steal cars and cause all kinds of difficulties over automobiles.

"Finally, the white suburban kid who either just graduates from high school or doesn't want to go to college or perhaps even drops out of high school and has to go to work is stuck with an inability to get to work. Hoisted by their own petard. They've really jounced themselves, they honestly have. And this is again part of the problem. They over-extended themselves financially, buying houses they couldn't afford, but they bought them because the city was changing, the neighborhood was changing, when Junior got into trouble it wasn't because he was a sick kid or because you had loused up in some way, shape or form, it was because the neighborhood was changing.

"There were Puerto Ricans moving in, Italians moving in, or Jews moving in . . . whoever it was that you weren't, moving in to louse up your neighborhood. And so they moved and what happened was everybody took their sick little kids and ran to the suburbs and overcrowded the schools and taxed the facilities of the local school systems, as well as the police. Take a look at New Rochelle. We have close to 80,000 people, and we have less than 160 men on our police force. It's ridiculous. Because they had over-extended themselves financially, they are very, very tightfisted now, don't want their taxes to go up so a lot of the auxiliary services are not provided and the whole little system is festering and rotting around their ears . . . the end result being that the kid is being hurt. The teenager grows up in an angry home. Youngsters and parents never talk except in angry exchange. Kids who have houses that would knock your eyes out are never in them. If they are, they are down in the finished basement either screwing or smoking pot. And television and the multiplication of television sets! They reproduce themselves, they honestly do. Everybody has their own little machine. They don't even do that together anymore. It's really sad. I think suburban youngsters are the ultimate victims of so many things that went wrong . . . and I don't go for this breast-beating I AM A GUILTY PARENT routine, because I don't blame the parents individually. It's not parents, it's society. But parents are part of society and kids are part of it, too, and they've done their share. I'm not saying they're blameless. They've done more than their share.

"I try to tell kids it doesn't matter if your parents are hypocrites; it doesn't matter if the world stinks. It honestly and truthfully doesn't. I say this even to minority kids. Sure we can go back and say that the black person has been oppressed. Of course they have. But nonetheless, some black people have made it—against great odds—but if a handful of black kids, ten, fifteen, twenty years ago could have had enough guts, enough determination to say that despite all that militates against it, I am going to make it—and make it—then certainly today's average white middle-class kid who sees a world of hypocrisy, a world full of disorder, a world full of unhappiness, can make it. Because they can change it. They really don't believe they can, but they can. They certainly can. But you don't change it by running for a stick of marijuana. You don't change it by letting your hair grow down to your backside and looking dirty and saying the hell with it I don't need it. When I worked with poor kids, it was so easy. You knew what the roots of his problem were—poverty, ignorance, prejudice, the whole thing. And if you did, in the individual case, a little something about some of those, you changed the kid. Not so today. The whole sociology of the country has to be changed. It must be. It will be. Or it will blow up. One way or the other.

"I think it will change the way the situation of the black man is changing today. We whites for years talked about 'we really ought to do something about those black kids. We really should.' And we had our token Negroes, and we each had our little black man digging dirt for us or doing other menial tasks. But then they burned Watts County and they burned Newark and they burned Detroit, and people got frightened. And I think the same thing is happening with our kids. It was all right when Nick Romano wound up in jail or wound up on drugs or wound up a bum. He was just a bad kid. But when for instance we have a narcotics raid and the daughter of a county health director and the son of a mayor are involved . . . when the Establishment sees this happen, and when you see the influentials getting hit, then the Establishment gets concerned.

"With all these political revolutions, people will have to concede that somewhere something is wrong. Of course you've got your conservatives, who say, 'Let's go back to the way we were. Twenty years ago we didn't have all these problems.' That's a

232

lot of crap. We had 'em. We just didn't acknowledge them. Sure, some people are going to say get your guns out and shoot 'em. But the good people, the intelligent people will realize that something's wrong, that we can't afford to lose a whole generation of kids."

Joe Tortelli
Executive Director, Youth Bureau
Executive Director, Human Rights Commission
New Rochelle, New York

27

THE ALL-AMERICAN BOY

A FEW months ago I received a letter from Roger which said, in part:

> My "Marxism" (if one wishes to call it that) is material-
> izing in the general direction of Leninism, to use exceed-
> ingly vague terms. Materialism and dialectical materialism
> are leading me to the conclusions that capitalism does
> have definite historical contradictions, but that the change
> of state power from one class to another can only be by a
> violent conflict. Well, whatever, my hopes for American
> Revolution #2 are quite low at this point; the contradic-
> tions are being smothered, as an earthquake fault by the
> city. The crisis is inevitable, so it seems, yet the compliant
> nature of the working class makes me wonder.

The letter also included an ecstatic paean to Zefferelli's film *Romeo and Juliet,* and a charming poem that was extraordinary for its freshness and lack of sentimentality, if not for its literary merits.

Roger is 15 years old. He is a high school sophomore in Hollywood, California, and he looks like an ad-man's version of the all-American high school boy. He is tall and strong looking, fresh-cheeked and rosy as an apple. He has

234

shiny, honest hazel eyes; his wavy light brown hair is neatly cut; his clothing is conservative, immaculate, well pressed. Any mother would be proud to be seen sending him off to school in the morning. He has the kind of look that is exploited by breakfast cereal companies to advertise an All-American, vitamin-packed, muscle-building product.

Roger is one of a large group of young students in public schools all over the country (only some of whom are united under the letters S.D.S.) who are working toward radical political goals as actively as their collegiate brothers and sisters. Any estimate of their actual numbers would be guesswork.

How does a high school become radicalized?

While we've heard much about S.D.S. and other political organizations disrupting the status quo at colleges and universities all over the country, the activities of the high school S.D.S. have received less publicity. And there seem to be as many different approaches to student power on the high school level as there are on the college level.

A wild-eyed 15-year old who called himself Moon, and who practically accosted my tape recorder at the Topanga Canyon Shopping Center in California's San Fernando Valley one Saturday afternoon, had this to say (after an hour and a half of other remarks, all of which may have been induced by speed):

"Your book should express the views of people, the views of teenagers, how they really feel about life. Because what they've been doing, they've been messing us all up. We can't talk, we can't go out and have a public thing without a per*mit,* ya know, and do you know how much a per*mit* would run for all the teenagers getting their say out? Something like a thousand dollars. We can't afford that. I was trying to get a per*mit* to hold a public speaking of all the teenagers, I was going to get the press, ya know, this was after Kennedy died, I was going to get everything happening. I was going to get the teenagers before the press, get them up in an organized thing, ya know, so that thousands and thousands of them could say their ways and how they really felt, so it would be on T.V., and so everybody would see how they felt, before they hit them over their heads with clubs and things like that, see how teenagers felt, and the way they really are—calm and nice, and they don't like to hurt people—they'd just see them the way they are, as people . . ."

Moon gave up his plan, which he had undertaken single-handedly ("After I got the per*mit*, I was going to tell everybody about it, and like I know they would come . . .") when he found out what it would cost. But he had something else up his sleeve.

"Right now, I'm in an organization, I don't know what it's called, but I'm going to become the leader of that thing, whether they know it or not. They don't know me, but I've just been observing them, and they believe in peace and all that. And I think I'm going to follow them, and I'm going to become their leader, whether they know it or not. I'm going to go there, and I'm going to say, I feel that we should get a per*mit*, and we're going to earn money to do that, from the kids. I know the kids would be willing to pitch in and work, and that's what I'm going to do, whether they know it or not. I'm going to be *in there*, and I'm going to get them to think about it, instead of just sitting there with their stupid ideas, saying come to the Social Democratic Society, or whatever it is, over the loudspeaker in school. It'll be come to the thing, get out your say, whatever it is. I mean, we could earn a lot of money for a per*mit*, if each kid pitched in a dime in the school. We'd get it all right."

I didn't meet any of the S.D.S. members at Moon's school, but the ones I did meet would have been shocked at the naïveté of his approach. Some radical high school groups have the same goals as their collegiate counterparts, which at their simplest level can be summed up as more intelligent attention to the needs of non-white students, and more say in the curriculum and other policies of the school in general. However, a board of education is a bit bigger to contend with than a board of trustees, and high school radicals have probably met with less success in effecting major academic changes than in reforming dress codes, and in standing up for certain principles or Constitutional rights that high school students have not made much fuss about before. The latter range from refusing to follow arbitrary procedures of rote patriotism in holiday assemblies to refusing to salute the flag.

In one L.A. school, these activities, for which individual students had received severe disciplinary action, got so little publicity that the relatively hip, relatively young (under 40) guidance counselor I spoke to there knew nothing about them. Nor had he heard of S.D.S., which had staged a small walkout in his school only a few days earlier. He and I were both shocked to discover how much more I knew about the goings on in the school after spending 72 hours in the company of some of its students, than he had managed to learn in his day-to-day work with them. Had some of his paperwork been put in the hands of a clerk, where it belonged, he might have had time to discover some surprising things about the young people he'd been hired to help.

Roger, for example, describes himself as "a third-generation radical." His parents met "in the movement," and his father was a union organizer in his youth. But, Roger says, in the past few years, his parents have become less and less radical. Like so many ex-leftists, "their allegiance was with Russia, and they saw what happened with Russia and

Czechoslovakia, with Russia and Israel, and they became very disillusioned.

"They also became very disillusioned in the New Left," Roger went on. "And my father now describes himself as a pragmatic dissenter. Which means, when you come down to it, he's a liberal. But, like the night Johnson announced he wasn't running, my father ran around the house shouting, 'It's the kids that did it, the students did it.' And he was really enthused about that. When he saw anyone who looked remotely like he'd ever been in a demonstration, he would shake their hand."

Roger started his own radical group one summer, when he was 14. His interest in S.D.S. had been aroused by his older brother, who was in college and had recently become a regional organizer. The group Roger organized was not exactly affiliated with S.D.S., but was "a study group, among the peace kids I had known in junior high. It fell through right away, but out of this group formed a nucleus. It was the nucleus of high school S.D.S. which involved about fifty to a hundred people all around L.A., including San Diego and San Fernando Valley, and the city itself.

"The first study group was just for political education. It was a kind of anarchist and Fidel Castro–Ho Chi Minh combination," he said cheerfully. "We presented films on Cuba and North Vietnam. And we read *The Quotations of Chairman Mao,* for whatever that helped us." He laughed. "Reading quotations doesn't do anything.

"I tried to pick out the brightest kids I could, who would respond to this type of thing, and present them with a certain historical analysis from *not* the school's point of view, and leaning toward Marx, definitely. Basically, it comes down to opinions on political history. I feel that history runs in certain ways, and I feel it has a certain organization.

What they talk about in school is Washington fought at Yorktown, Washington was at Valley Forge, the French helped us, Lafayette came, we had a couple of battles at Gettysburg and at Bull Run, battles were won here and there, but reasons for the conflict and necessities for the conflict are ignored, and I feel that's the most important part of history. They say let's use history so we don't have wars. I say good, okay. We fought the Revolution. Why? We fought the Civil War. Why? The books have their reasons, but there are certain economic things happening, I think, that are never talked about in school. And also there's Toynbee. They totally ignore him in school. It's unbelievable. Toynbee is like one of the major historians, and they just say, 'Well, it's not like that.' "

How did Roger get into a position where he knew that he wasn't being taught the whole truth in school? He attributes his political awareness in part to his radical heritage, and in part to his own efforts to educate himself politically. But it would hardly seem that he was spoon-fed Marx with his pablum. Roger is the youngest of three children, who describes his 22-year-old sister as "the straightest person in the world. She lives up to my parents' image of her exactly," and his 19-year-old brother as "below me in political education until he got to college and met a teacher who led him into a political type of thing. When I was 12 and he was 16, I ignored him. He had faith in American democracy."

At 12, Roger was already a member of a Zionist/socialist youth group. "I got a good political education from them. They talked about the meaning of socialism, the necessity of socialism. They introduced Marxism on a very elementary level, a very interesting level. There was indoctrination definitely, but it was an alternative—it was not what school indoctrinated you with."

At 13, Roger quit the youth group because of conflict

with another leading member, partly over a girl and partly over politics. "Within the youth group, I represented the status quo, and the hippies were becoming the thing at that point, and this other guy was aligning himself with their form of cultural radicalism. He smoked dope, cigarettes, stuff like that. And I couldn't have that, because I was the establishment there," Roger smiled. "But he was the one who was influencing the rest of the group; I felt totally ostracized and I left. By this time, I was getting pretty sick of their Israeli nationalism, too. My political education pretty much finished there. I was very much on my own."

Roger, a ninth grader rapidly approaching his 14th birthday, now started his "first organizing thing." He and two others, including the rival mentioned above, joined in putting together the first junior high school underground newspaper in Los Angeles. They succeeded in reforming the codes of dress in their school. But Roger was disappointed. He said his rival saw the newspaper as "just a reform type of thing," while he envisioned it as "an educational media."

The following year, Roger was similarly disappointed with S.D.S., but for different reasons. During all the tenth grade, Roger was *the* organizer in his school, and the mainstay of S.D.S. there. "When we had our first rally, it was kind of successful, and we organized a study group out of that, involving twenty to thirty people. It had a couple of united moments when it was attacked by the football team, but during the summer (1968) and after that, the group disintegrated. What happens is, people have a certain political education, but they don't carry it all the way through. They were in conflict with the non-S.D.S. people (peace kids) within the study group, and they literally tore the group apart. The same happened at another school. They started out with a hundred twenty-five kids, who eventually managed to organize a rally of seven hundred. But they ended up this year with fifteen kids walking out in the strike on election day. It was kind of frustrating."

How did S.D.S. deteriorate?

"A lot of the S.D.S. kids were infatuated with Marxism, Marxist-Leninism, and Nihilism, and they started talking about, well, let's do the working class thing. Let's talk about working class revolution. I left because of this thing of turning on working class kids, getting kids aligned with the working class, let's make everything relevant . . . talk about codes of dress, let's get the narcotics officers off campus, let's get the teachers off campus, let's get the kids off campus, let's blow up the school, let's make Molotov cocktails and throw them into the cafeteria and get some good food . . ." Roger laughed.

"There aren't any working class kids for us to organize. And I grew up with working class kids, and I know there isn't going to be any class revolution until they realize they really have a place in this society. I told this to S.D.S., and they said no, what we have to do is make everything relevant. They were going to hold a rally on election day; so instead of holding a rally about how come there's no difference between Nixon, Humphrey, and Wallace, they said no, let's talk about codes of dress. So everyone backed out of it, and they had about two people left to run the rally.

"They view action from a different position than I do. They would like us to walk out. Let's be active, let's disrupt. Which has its place. I think it was kind of important to disrupt at Columbia, because they were infringing on other people's rights, and with everyone accepting it, how were they going to stop it? But at our school, disruption would have proved nothing. It would have made no point. It would have just alienated kids."

And how do you arouse the political interest of complacent, middle-class high school students who, rather than being third-generation radicals like Roger, are first-generation liberals? Roger says you educate them, and this is the form of political action to which he has devoted himself since leaving the S.D.S. ranks.

"There are maybe fifteen kids at our school willing to work with S.D.S., because they have common goals in mind —they want to see radical, drastic change in everything as soon as possible—which I do, too. But I don't think S.D.S. has the means or the education. The main hang-up of S.D.S. is their own lack of political education.

"I'd like to educate the people en masse, and also organize cadres, really hard core, like Lenin did. It's a perfect example. He organized a hard-core group to lead discontented people. But the discontent situation came of itself.

"It doesn't compare with starting from codes of dress. That's absurd. But, even to educate kids, I still feel you have to talk about the cadre situation. You have to be picayune. You have to weed out people. You need people who have a certain amount of intelligence, who are willing to listen. They don't have to be discontent, because when they see what the political situation is, a discontent will arise. But, to a certain degree, they must be frustrated. The first people you are likely to get are going to be discontented, frustrated kids, who may or may not be intelligent. But this is all right. You don't talk to the kids who smoke dope. If they're intelligent enough to listen, they may come to you.

"One of the major hassles with the study group I started was that the kids were intelligent, but not frustrated. They were discontented to an extent because McCarthy wasn't getting elected, but they weren't frustrated. Because they still had a place. They still had something to work for, some relationship with the society. They were going to be the scientists, the chemists, the people who could do it and not feel they were selling out any more than anyone else. The people who could very easily rationalize situations like theVietnam War, and people who are also very concerned with themselves.

"In the movement, you'll find two kinds of ego-trippers: those who are concerned with themselves, and those who want to make a name. Those who want to make a name stay in the movement, and those who want to be safe join the Y.A.F. [Young Americans for Freedom, a conservative group]."

Roger couldn't say exactly what kind of kid was likely to have the right combination of discontent, frustration, and intelligence to make a cadre member, nor was he able to say whether it could be possible for middle-class high school and junior high school students to identify with the working class fully enough to go about "educating" them realistically.

"Even talking about organizing a cadre is kind of absurd," he finally said. "Cadres won't be meaningful until a revolutionary situation is created, and that won't happen until we get our asses kicked out of Vietnam and Guatemala and a couple of other places, and the economic situation just starts crashing around our heads. When the working class realizes what its economic situation really is. We had a lot of people voting for Wallace in this last election, because they just got something, for the first time. And my feeling is that when they first see themselves losing it, first they are going to become really fascist and blame the radicals, the Commies, the hippies, the Negroes, and eventually they will realize that it was their own inherent condition. When they see this happen, when you've distributed enough agitative literature . . ."

Meanwhile, Roger, when last heard from, was biding his time. "I'm educating myself to a higher degree. I'm doing a lot of reading. A friend of mine has been talking about organizing a study group I've been wanting to get into. She puts her father up as a kind of knower of Marxism, and I'm enthused about that. I want to hear what he has to say. And then there are these other kids, just some friends of mine. I've been talking to them, talking about where the scene's at. They're discothèquers and dopers, but they're radicals, too, in a sense. They just don't have the education. They're talking about imperialism, so I ask them, 'Do you know what it means?' They think so, but they'd like to be sure. So I talk to them for twenty minutes about that. I'm good at talking for a long time."

Roger himself hardly presents a picture of a frustrated individual in any aspect of his life. He is dissatisfied with many things—with school, with the world as he sees it, with the Left as he sees it. Yet, unlike many of his contemporaries, radical or otherwise, he seems to experience a sense of fulfillment in his day-to-day life. He relates well to his family, is happy about where his own head is at, and is functioning in his world on several different levels.

28

DAUGHTER OF THE OLD LEFT

IN contrast, Carol, who of all the radical students I've spoken to has the most profound psychological commitment to the Left, is deeply unhappy. Despite her unusually adult preoccupations, she displays many of the classic insecurities of adolescence, the effect of which is heightened by her strong sense of the dramatic.

Carol, an eleventh grader just turned 16, is a slender, freckled, blue-eyed girl, with a small, sweet voice, who wears her black hair in tight little natural curls all over her head. She looks her age, wears sweaters and miniskirts and knee-socks and blushes easily. She gives the appearance of smallness without being particularly small. Her heart-shaped face and delicate features are pretty. Her eyes look as if they are about to laugh or fill with tears, and they are quite likely to do either at any given moment.

Carol is the older of two teenaged daughters of a former Communist Party member.

When I asked her what she would change about the world, she giggled at the question. "Turn off the tape recorder and I'll tell you," she said. Then, "No, why not reveal it for all time. The eventual dictatorship of the proletariat. International Communism.

"Those are powerful words, but I've been doing some studying and some talking and some listening—since seventh grade. That was my big awakening. It sounds very hack for someone—to anyone, I suppose. I don't know how many more 16-year-old Communists you are going to meet, but I can tell you that as far as it affects my life, it makes things harder. But I wouldn't give up my ideals.

"The seventh grade was the very very beginning of it, when I came to my father and said, in effect, teach me about these things. I want to know why I am here—and Rockefeller is there. And he taught me. It was like the fairy tale. He was waiting for me to ask. He wasn't about to push it on me. It's a difficult thing to give your children, because it will set them apart for the rest of their lives. Wrongly accepted, it can wreck your life."

"What in particular struck home to you?" I asked.

"At that time, little things. Like why do they want to suppress things I want to print in the school newspaper, when this is the way I think? Who is doing it? And the answer would come back and I'd ask more, and then he would teach me other things, which made me look around and I'd say, hey. . . ! It was like opening a golden, golden door, until I got to the point where I was learning it was not just a matter of knowing about class structure and the class struggle, but that discipline had a lot to do with it. Self-discipline and group organization.

"I want to make something plain. Although I'm far from the Junior Achievers, and the clubs sponsored by the Rotary people, and the teenyboppers, I am also very much against groups like S.D.S. It impresses me as being futile. The kids in it are very uptight about what is happening—the war, the draft, problems with the administration, lack of freedom of speech for the minorities as well as the majorities of people—but their means of expressing themselves are very poor. They're trying to teach the repressed masses," she said sarcastically, "by example. And what they are doing is going out and asking for trouble, inviting violence . . . and then they say, 'Look what they are doing to us. *Wake up.'*

"And when they're leafletting for a rally—I've read some of these leaflets, and they can't possibly appeal to anyone except sympathizers because they come on so strong and from such a bad angle. It's all, 'crush the ruling class, defeat the imperialist war-mongers.' If you said that to some poor kid from Podunk, Missouri, who had never been out of his home town—no. Not even that. Just the kids who go to this school. The average high school student—it's like 'What ruling class? What war-mongers?' Before you read Shakespeare, you've got to learn the alphabet."

Carol went on to talk bitterly about the revolutionary movement and its role in the lives of those students actively participating in it. She felt that it was destructive to the anti-war movement, in that it was swallowing up and ultimately damaging a lot of students who were valuable to "the cause."

"They are letting their emotions get the better of them to the point where they will be destroyed, if not physically, emotionally, to the point where they just can't operate. The groups that are being organized to educate people about class consciousness and what's happening in America are a very good idea. They teach the ABC's of political action, and that's the beginning. But as far as hurling yourself into a demonstration against a group of cops eight feet deep— eight cops deep—which I saw at Century City—and which impressed me with the power of the police, it's not the way to go about it.

"It's not even a matter of following prescribed stages. Since Marxism is based on the laws of nature, dialectical materialism, there are certain patterns. You can predict the development of something from these laws, that have been adapted from nature's own laws. It's nothing mystical, and it's nothing religious. It's just that way. It wasn't my father that pointed this out to me, it was I who first noticed the S.D.S. temperament—very intense, very dogmatic, and in their own way, crazy. It just bothered me to have something thrust on me. Like, 'You shouldn't be doing this! You're on our side, not theirs.' What makes you think I'm with you people?

"Now, donating time and labor to a movement is a really big thing, which unfortunately a lot of my friends don't realize. And they give of themselves so long and so much that it bothers me. It's hard to talk to them. I never argue with them. These kids are beating their heads against a wall in so many ways. They're constantly calling some kind of rally or meeting, and nothing—speaking as an outsider—seems to get done. I see friends of mine every day with another pamphlet, another leaflet, another project. And over such petty things. I'd rather see them go to class and get their grades. This will have a greater effect on what happens to them in the future than this meeting or that. I'll go that far, even though I'm against the war and against—well, a lot of things—and *for* a lot of things."

Carol was also cynical about the motives of some of her fellow students for joining S.D.S., as were some of the S.D.S. leaders I spoke to. "There's a lot of glamour to it," she said, "in the idea of being the vanguard of the pro-letariat. *We're going to save the world.* They take themselves even more seriously than a drill team. There is a sense of false self-importance and prestige. They have a clique, like the beatniks at one time. It's just very attractive to dissatisfied people."

Carol, of course, shared most of the S.D.S.er's dissatisfactions. She felt the difference in her means of expressing them was a result of her family background. Like Roger, she lived in a home situation where she was able to agree with much of what was going on, which, as she said, wasn't true of a lot of Hollywoodians.

"It doesn't even matter so much if the parents are politically aware or not," she said. "You can have two ex-members of the Communist Party who have culminated or degenerated to the state where one will encourage or influence his kids to join S.D.S. because he feels it is a thoroughly constructive movement, correctly oriented. And the other one, as in my case, will encourage their kid to find the movement that's best for him or cool it for a while. That's one of my difficulties. I have to cool it. I can't commit myself to any organization around. There are enough ideological differences between them and me to discourage me from joining any of them."

Politics seems to be a source of deeper personal frustration to Carol, who has not really gotten her feet wet in it, even though she has saturated her mind with it, than to Roger and some of the other kids like those I spoke to on the East Coast, who are "dropping out" of the political scene with no less *angst* than dropping out of school has caused their classmates. And although Carol's frustrations seem more peculiar to adolescence than to class consciousness, she attributes them to her politics rather than to her age. She suffers from shyness, a sense of inferiority, a basic loneliness, and a sense of isolation from the other teenagers around her—those who go to all the dances (she has never been to a dance, has never dated, says she never will) as well as the politically active kids and the trippies.

"I wish I could find an element, or people, or a person with which I could be peaceful, tranquil, myself, open.

"All this stems from being what I am, being where I am politically. Before I got into politics, everything had its place, but so many things, being lonely, being afraid, stem from this. But those are the kinds of things I'd rather endure than being rah-rah.

"I wish I could leave L.A. for someplace without smog—any place but the Midwest.

"I would like to find out, of all the things I'm capable of, one thing, which everything could be conducive to developing, so that not only I could derive pleasure from it, but other people too—one thing in which I could excel for everyone's happiness.

"All these things are really messing me up. I have to look at each thing as a teenager, as a girl, as a high school student, as a Marxist, as a dweller in Los Angeles, as a person who doesn't want the world to end tomorrow, as a person who opposes the war. It's terrible. It's like sifting sand through finer and finer screens. That's the hard part. That's what's confusing me."

Since Carol entered politics and adolescence at approximately the same time, it is difficult to say whether politics really brought an end to that period of her life when, as she says, "everything had its place," or whether that period ended for her in the as yet unresolved confusions of early growing up. In any case, Carol's intelligence, precociousness, personal charm, political certainty, and relative security at home have failed to provide her with a sense of well being. And that is, apparently, how drugs came to take a place in her life.

Their role for her is very different than the role played by drugs within the Kentwood group. It is highly personal, in no way social, and hardly experimental. She tried pot once and didn't care for it, is scared of acid, has gone no further with speed than caffeine pills. Downers are her thing. She doesn't even know the name of the pills she takes.

They are known as "yellows," and they are probably Nembutols.

"I condemn the use of drugs," Carol said. "It is like temporary suicide. When I first take it I have no desire to move; I can feel my arms and legs and all, as if I were molasses. That's the way it is when I don't like it. But you get so—ethereal. I start spouting poetry. I have this urge to recite all the poems I've never told anyone before, or I just make it up. My sister [Anne, age 14, and Carol's closest friend] was with me twice when I took the yellows, and she once told me she liked me better when I was stoned, which bothered me, so much . . . But I knew why. It didn't really make me different, being high. It's just the way I really was. I knew I would be looser, freer with what I said, but I didn't think I'd go to that extreme. I'd look at things and take them apart, or see things . . . I looked at blades of grass with the wind blowing through them, and saw lots of little green soldiers standing there waving their swords. It was disgusting. I hated it. But it was such a good release, so great. But if anyone asked me, 'Should I?' I'd say stay away from it. Stay away from anything like that. Acid especially."

But Carol gets into moods when she wouldn't hesitate to try acid.

"Depression. A feeling like there's no place for me. There's always unconsciousness to escape to when there's no place for me. But when it starts to work on you, and you think about it for a while, and everything's been going wrong and you have fights with your friends, and it's an especially bad week for Vietnam, it just gets to be too much. As long as I don't go out of my way to get the stuff, I'm okay. Because it's there. For anybody."

Carol said she had one friend from whom she could get anything from grass to speed to heroin, and another from whom she could get all the grass or hash she wanted. Sometimes she would have to pay, sometimes not.

"Someone else I know learned how you grow it in your own backyard and came out with perfect grass every time. I wish it weren't like that. But it just passes from friend to friend. You just have to make a little comment or a joke. One day, at the time I already had one source, I was talking to a friend in class and I made a little joke and the next thing I know, everyone's asking me, "Do you want some? I can get it for you this weekend." Then there are all sorts of things you can mix together. People make hallucinogens in science class. I've had acid offered to me in the middle of Hollywood Boulevard. Things like that happen all the time.

"One parent I know is telling his kid to get it over with now. He doesn't mind that she's blowing pot or whatever, because it's her stage. He says we must try to be sympathetic, and that's bad. There are times I wish my father would just come up to me and say, 'Kid, if you ever put your hand on another joint . . .' "

Carol told her father she'd tried pot, but she didn't tell him about the pills, although she had been stoned in his presence. She excused her euphoria as deep tiredness, and he didn't know the difference—and no wonder. Carol, like so many girls her age, is moody as all hell, with or without artificial stimulation. I have to laugh at most of the popular articles listing warning signals to alert parents that their child might be on drugs, for I'm sure I was putting out most of the same signals at one time or another in my early teens, without having ever smoked even a legal cigarette, popped a pill stronger than aspirin, or tasted an alcoholic drink.

Carol, putting great trust in her younger sister, said, "I told her to watch out for me if I ever do it again. I once told her that—or asked her, that if I was ever missing, if she could calm my parents down, and she said she'd try. If she could make them like not call the police and get all upset. That's the other alternative. When I get too turned off to really know what I'm going to do next or what's going to happen next, I may run away some time.

"I'm so against the use of drugs. I'm a thinking being. I would never take them to enhance my feeling of the world around me. I have two eyes, two ears, a pretty good brain, two hands. God made me the way He made everyone else," she said, sarcastically now, because she does not believe in God. "But I found these are the two main reasons people take them: it's either for escape, because you don't care, or an 'I can get more from life' kind of thing. And along with that comes the social thing. "Let's feel everything together.' I think about it a lot. With me, it's just I get so turned off sometimes with everything, it's not myself anymore. I wish I had someone all the time to turn around and say 'no, no, no,' " she laughed, bubbly. "But it's right there. It's like grabbing a piece of candy out of a dish in the living room. And it's not hard, either, to get an excuse."

29

NO MORE TIME FOR TRIPPING

THE high school Left consists of widely read, intensely political wonder children like Roger and Carol, who were practically weaned on Marx; people who are attracted to dynamic leaders, whatever the cause they are leading; frustrated, previously apolitical people who have just awakened to the possibility of doing something about their situation; and confused adolescents seeking a social milieu into which they fit, and trying revolution on for size.

The political kids I met in Los Angeles, who all moved within the same social group, though they were scattered through the tenth and eleventh grades in Hollywood's two largest high schools, fell into all of these categories. Yet they had enough in common to unite them despite their major political differences.

They all came smack out of the middle of the middle class. They not only had nice homes and nice clothes, but they engaged in nice activities, like folk dancing and sailing, healthy forms of family entertainment, which they actually did enjoy with their families. They were all too young to drive, and they took buses, walked, or sometimes hitched to where they had to go by themselves. Most of them had not traveled beyond the west coast of the United States and Canada, which they had explored on outdoorsy-type family vacations. In almost every way, these kids failed to meet the stereotype of rebels or rabble-rousers. They all argued with their parents over one thing and another, but they all respected the intelligence, the background, and even in most cases the present life style of both parents, though they would have liked to see a greater flexibility, in their mothers especially.

Degrees of parental acceptance of their offspring's involvement varied from whole-hearted support to threat of disowning; but all these kids were in communication with their parents and their environment. Many smoked pot now and then, but few had an involvement with drugs even as serious as Carol's. Drugs and politics, as adolescent life styles, plainly have nothing to do with one another. The average American teenager is exposed to pot and pills. Many try pot, find they like it, use it now and then. But, like Roger, who has enjoyed pot for a long time, they put down those kids who make pot a way of life. The smartest, healthiest, most productive adolescents in any field don't have the time or energy or desire to get further into drugs, or even further into pot, than that. And that's all there is to it. Consistent, goal-oriented activity in any field does not mix with heavy drug use; it will neither be found that the kids in a bad drug scene are into politics, nor that politically active kids are into drugs very much. It should be obvious that the children of Marx and Coca-Cola are physically, emotionally, and mentally in a better state of health than the speed-freak offspring of Kentwood, in Pennsylvania's political and intellectual stagnation. And it should be equally obvious that whatever Roger and his friends want to do to our system, and however threatening their ideas may seem, it is they who represent the greater hope for the future of our country than those who are spending the major part of their young lives in another dimension.

Brenda, Roger's girl friend, and a good friend of Carol's younger sister, Anne, feels more or less the same way about drugs as Carol and Roger do. But Brenda has a slightly different viewpoint, in that she licked a heavy drug scene, and a mild drug problem in making the transition from teenybopper to student militant.

I was introduced to Brenda in a large, and (by Eastern standards) plush, coffee shop on Hollywood Boulevard and Highland Avenue, called Coffee Dan's, where high school kids congregated in large numbers after school. She had just bought Roger a single gold earring, and Roger had accepted it willingly enough (there was definitely something of the gypsy in him, despite his clean-cut-ness), but now they both agreed that it did not suit him, and Brenda felt a little silly.

Brenda was a tall, fragile-looking girl whose hairdresser had carved an ash-blond shoulder-length pageboy out of her naturally curly hair. She had large, beautiful blue-gray eyes, and her clothing came right out of the pages of *Seventeen*. She looked in a way very much like the nice Jewish girls I went to school with, except that they got a "y" into the spelling of their names somewhere, and they wore their cashmere sweaters with the labels on the outside. And, of course, their skirts were not as short as the cute minis of this ex-teenybopper, ex-trippie, who had made it through acid and had somehow emerged into a slightly saner world, now, six months later, looking still a little pale, a little confused.

At 15, the oldest of four girls whose father is a top nuclear physicist for the U.S. Government, and whose mother is a working archaeologist, Brenda could hardly boast that her parents share or encourage her political interests. Yet her parents had known Roger's family since before she was born, and it was they who introduced her to Roger.

"Before that, I was completely apolitical. I still have no background. We never talked about it at home. I never talked about it with anyone until I met these people."

Brenda had been one of the many teenyboppers who used to hang out at Fischer's restaurant on Fairfax Avenue, which, at that time, seemed almost like an extension of the Sunset Strip scene.

"We all started meeting there. We all started smoking. I never should have. I have asthma. But it became a thing just to sneak a cigarette and go up on a roof or into an alley and smoke it. Our minds were deteriorating in a sense. The kids I met there didn't read, didn't care about school. The best time you could have was if you were stoned. My grades fell. I got C's and D's in everything. I was unhappy. I guess it showed."

Brenda had gotten into the group under the influence of a girl friend, Lois, who lived across the street, and it was Lois, and other friends Brenda made in the group, who kept her there, as she sees it, almost against her will.

"During the summer we went to this pool every day, to do nothing. It was very boring, but we kept going, every day. Some people didn't mind talking about it, but I tried to impress them by not saying anything. I was ashamed of what I was doing.

"The families of the other kids in the group were different from ours. They had their 2.5 kids, and that's it. The kids aren't stupid. They get their C's. But they have like twenty books in the house. And like at Lois's house, they hired a decorator, and they didn't even change anything. And Lois is like that. Nothing is of interest to her.

"I got very sick of it. I wanted to get out of the crowd, and then I met Roger. He is the opposite. He got me out of it. He wouldn't let me see Lois. And that's what I needed. I needed someone to tell me, 'You're not going to.' I didn't read. I didn't do anything. He gave me books. He said, 'Read this. Do this.'

"I liked the people, but they weren't good for me. They weren't stimulating. There were no conversations. Just gossip. I'd get into things where I'd try to talk to somebody about life, and I'd get, "Oh, that's what so and so got when he took acid." And I'd see friends who were on acid, and they'd tell me all these insights, and I'd say I'd thought about all those things before, and they'd say, 'Well, it took you all this time to think about it, and we did it in a couple of hours.' "

Brenda, who eventually was coerced by her friends into a relatively bad acid trip of her own, said that if she could change something about herself, she'd make herself less impressionable.

"I'll be listening to Roger, and I'll agree with all of his views, and I'll talk to my parents, and I'll still think Roger is right, but when they're talking to me, it sounds like what they are saying is right also. This is partly because I don't know too much about politics. But not entirely. That's the reason people were able to do what they did to me so well. I think I could change that, I really do. I just have so much confidence in myself right now."

In terms of her own political activities, Brenda has been forbidden by her parents to do as much as take part in peace demonstrations, even when accompanied by Roger's parents.

"I asked my mother, if I wanted to join S.D.S., which I don't, would she let me? She said 'No, because you're living in my house. When you're going to college, if you're still interested, which I hope you're not, then you can do it.' And then she's always saying we should be *exposed* to these things. So when I mention this to her, she says, 'You are. You're reading about it. You're exposed.' So I say, what if I become interested in some of these things, and she says, 'You can think what you want, but you may not act on it while you are living here.' "

Brenda felt they were afraid of her becoming involved with the law in some way, and afraid especially because of her father's job.

"But they don't give me direct reasons. We've been having fights a lot, about what I do. They're making me join Jewish youth groups. They want me to stay Jewish and live the good life. But I'm doing a lot of things now, like folk dancing and getting good grades, that they said *before* they wanted me to do, when I wasn't doing anything they liked. But now it doesn't mean anything to them that I've changed. And if I did what they want me to do now, soon that wouldn't mean anything, and they'd want something else."

30

IN AND OUT OF S.D.S.

SO Brenda goes on, growing a little stronger, but still under the influence—if not of drugs, of people whose views may or may not coincide with her own ideas, ideas she has not yet given herself a chance to discover.

How many bright but confused young people like Brenda are in or on the fringes of radical groups? Enough to create some difficulties for the organizers.

"One of our problems is, we're catching these people at a stage, and as quickly as they go into one, they can also pop out of one," said Garth Haskell, a 15-year-old S.D.S. member.

Garth, a tenth grader who had attended junior high school in Chicago and had been in California and S.D.S. for only a few months, was like Carol and Roger, a child of radical parents. But Garth has never really known the comfortable family life, and uncomplicated middle-class existence that Carol and Roger grew up with. Garth is also one of the few kids who will be mentioned in this book who has never taken any kind of drugs. He's probably the only one I interviewed who I believe never will. He grew up with a father and later a stepfather who were both junkies. His stepfather, much to Garth's apparent relief, finally died, off junk and on booze, early in 1968.

Garth didn't look at me once while we talked, sitting side by side on a couch. He spoke quietly as he stared straight ahead at the opposite wall with liquid brown eyes. I found it difficult to tell if he was very uptight, merely a little shy, or if this was just his manner. There was something slightly sad, trapped, or beaten in his demeanor, not in his clothing, physical attitude, or expression, except perhaps in the tone of his eyes. It was somewhere on an emotional, invisible, almost imperceptible level. But I could see how the very same thing that I interpreted as a kind of negative (or at least questionable) vibration could have communicated the kind of dynamic tension that attracts followers to a leader.

"I feel sorry for S.D.S.," Garth said. "It is one of the most unorganized, sporadic organizations that is in existence. You ought to attend an S.D.S. meeting sometime. It's pitiful. Everyone is always agreeing, yeah, yeah, yeah, but nothing happens.

"Why? Maybe it's fear of retaliation of some sort from the administration, but maybe it's also insincerity. I've had a fear lately that revolution is going to become commercial, and people are going to capitalize on revolution, just like other things, like in clothes and stuff like that. That can't *not* happen, really, and it scares me. I can just see it now— 'Three black berets for one dollar! One old .45! One wall poster of Che Guevera! *Quotations of Mao* now on sale!' And if that happens, we're not going to have the sincere people, we're going to have the fad-crazy people, and I don't particularly want them."

I asked Garth what would be his first goal for S.D.S. at his school, from the stage in which the group was currently operating. He said it would be to enlighten the fifteen members of the group and strengthen them so that they could better carry on the message to other students.

"A lot of people seem to have called the regional office,

and wanted to know if there was a movement on our campus, but we never seem to find them.

"What we are trying to change is this channeling for society which is going on in the schools—where you are supposed to be a certain type. For instance, the L.A. schools in general are channeling you for the middle class, capitalistic type of society where you do as you are told. I've had the thought that private schools are channeling you for leadership, and also Beverly Hills High and other schools that have relaxed codes of dress could be directing you toward leadership. And I've also noticed that in many of the poverty areas, they take the little students to the side and say, 'Why don't you get interested in mechanics and woodshop and things like that?' Like Malcolm X's teacher took him aside and told him, 'You don't want to be a lawyer, you want to work in wood,' even though it was obvious that someone half as smart could become a lawyer."

Aside from the problem of students going through stages, and general faddishness, Garth found that fear was the main factor preventing more high school students from rebelling against the school's channeling actions.

"They can't legally do anything to you, but they make you think that they can. Like they make you wash dishes in the cafeteria, which they can't legally do to you, or they say they won't give you a recommendation to college, which sometimes you need, or they say they'll make sure your teachers won't give you good grades, or they'll suspend you, and a lot of people are afraid, including me."

"What can they legally do?" I asked.

"Not much of anything. If a teacher sees fit, they can shake you. But they can't hit you. Legally they can only call your parents and complain."

"What, specifically, are you doing that they want to punish you for?"

"Many of us are disorderly in assemblies; we don't stand up for the flag salute, or sing their songs, or do patriotic things, and we criticize the administration and are very political on campus, and they don't want that. They say that's a terrible thing, to be political on campus. And they are always coming up with little laws, which they say were passed by the Board of Education, which they say overrule the Constitution of the United States, which they do not. The only trouble is, if you want to fight them, you have to go to court. Meanwhile, you are out of school, suspended while the trial is going on, so you miss a year and they get you one way or another.

"I'm quite afraid, and I really haven't been faced with it that much. But I think I would go through with what I am doing now, and disagree with them continuously. But it's quite a serious problem, especially if you have high goals for yourself. They can knock them down, but I just keep trying to remember they really can't legally do anything to you when it comes right down to it."

Garth also blamed fear for the lack of participation in the election-day walkout that Roger and Carol mentioned earlier.

"We were very strong last year. The teachers started getting on us, and the students got very angry and started to come over to our side. So they started something else: student against student. They sicked the football team and the R.O.T.C. on us, and broke up a rally and starting beating up people. And what the principal said to Roger, who was hit, was, 'Gee, if you're taking away their freedom and they don't like you, it's not my fault.' Yet if we attacked the football team and broke their legs and things, there would be a lot of repercussions all over the place."

And Garth's girl friend, Liz, small, blonde, wispy, determined, 15 years old, doing eleventh grade courses in the tenth grade:

"I don't go to rallies, I don't go to demonstrations. In many ways, I think S.D.S. is too radical, in many ways too conservative. They have the basic opinion that all people are bad, and I have the basic opinion that all people are good, so . . . You've got to really think people are bad to want to change them in such a radical way. I think it will happen anyway. I don't think you should try to force people to change—because that will only foul them up, psychologically—and there are too many fouled up people now. It frustrates them.

"I'm talking about S.D.S., Neo-Nazis, and anyone else. I'm not a conservative person, I believe that what S.D.S. is doing and is about is for the better, and it would be very good if we could all live the way they want us to, but I don't believe that's possible.

"I think Communism and socialism would be fantastic— if people were ready for it. If people could *take* sharing. But I don't think they can do it on basic, ordinary levels."

I asked Liz how she would start working toward the goal of a socialistic society. She said, "I'd probably do it underhandedly because I know that's the only way it can be done. S.D.S.ers are very idealistic, and they think they can just go out and rally. But you have to reeducate the people completely, first of all—psychologically, especially. They have to want it. You can't get anywhere unless they want it. You have to use a lot of propaganda, really. It can't be done in a very honest way. That's why I'm not involved in it. I'm too honest about what I do. But if I were going to do it, that's what I'd do.

"Since Garth is in S.D.S., I get very rejected sometimes. People say, 'You mean you're not in it?' But I think that's my right."

31

ACTIVISTS WEST AND EAST

I HAVE heard it said that California, Los Angeles in particular, breeds a species of precocious monsters who start
on cigarettes at 3, dope at 6, sex at 9, driving at 12—who
have private phone numbers at 11, color T.V., water skis,
surfboards, boats, record players, tape recorders, etc., etc.,
practically as soon as they are old enough to differentiate
their own property from someone else's. I have found it true
that California kids do seem to start earlier to do whatever
they do; and whatever kids across the country start to do
later in epidemic numbers, they were doing it in California
first. However precocious Western kids are, though, it seems
that in the East precocity more quickly becomes an emotional, intellectual, or spiritual cynicism that often stunts
genuine growth and stamps weary age on children.

Politically, the activists I spoke to from a large high
school in Westchester County, New York, had many things
in common with the radicals I spoke to in Los Angeles. Most
people in both groups had asserted their radical politics
without affiliation with S.D.S. More than half in each group
had either inherited some background in the life and literature of the Old Left, or had started out in the early Sixties,
under parental guidance, "being for" civil rights and peace.

In most nonpolitical aspects of their lives and personalities, however, the Westchester radicals were quite different from the Hollywood radicals as, I think, all children of the East Coast are different from those of the West. I am not merely generalizing my observations from the New York and Los Angeles areas, but I have found that traits I observed in New York area teenagers were usually present in those from Pennsylvania, New Jersey, and New England, and that many things I noted about Los Angeles teenagers were also true of those from places like Colorado and Washington.

Western teenagers smile more, speak more freely, express less tension in their physical presence, and are more interested in other people, perhaps even less self-centered, than Easterners, who, on the other hand, seem more refined of intellect. That is, I found them more specific in intellectualizing their opinions and ideas, and more respectful, aware of, or interested in the intellectual as an adult figure. In their personal lives, the Eastern kids express more aggressive self-confidence, and convey much more sense of being in battle than West Coast kids discussing comparable conflicts. Easterners seem to have greater difficulty communicating with parents, yet are a little less intimidated by systems and structures, such as The School and The Government, than Westerners are.

Specifically comparing New York area kids with Los Angeles area kids, I found the New Yorkers culturally far more sophisticated. They are more likely to be aware of films as an art form rather than as mindless entertainment; they read more books, listen to more different kinds of music, visit museums more often. They do far less with their bodies; socially, they are quite adept but not always genuinely comfortable, and they seem to enjoy themselves less.

West Coast kids seem to have more time than Easterners

do. The New York teenager's "cultural activities" are busy, busy things. In Los Angeles, a teenager is more likely to entertain himself with some physical activity, spends his spare time more casually, is more likely to make plans on the spur of the moment, and generally has fun at a far more leisurely pace. It also seems that the average middle-class Los Angeles teenager has more space, more room to grow, more freedom of movement, than a far wealthier teenager in the East, whose large house with spacious grounds cost three times as much as an L.A. ranch house. Perhaps it's a difference in the way one uses space that was fought for, and space one takes for granted. The house in the Eastern suburb was not casually acquired; it is something to be careful of. The Pacific Ocean is free, and freely used.

In general, there seems to be less of a need to fight for things in the West—less competition in the schools, less value placed on sophistication, less petty snobbishness, which may be partially due to the fact that Westerners are up against less competition in getting into prestige colleges that use a geographical quota in their admissions policy. However, I don't think an Eastern high school radical would have commented, as early as Roger did, that the disco-thèquers and dopers are radicals, too. In the East, at least at the time of these interviews, radicalism among high school students belonged only to a certain intellectual elite.

I was also impressed with how little the radicals I spoke to in the East seemed to need and like each other as individuals, and at how many different levels they were compulsively competing, as opposed to the California kids, who demonstrated warmth, respect, and genuine concern for one another. I spent more time with individuals in the California group, and they had much more opportunity to gossip to me, but they did not do so; whereas the New York kids quickly took advantage of any chance to cut their friends.

32

"AS LONG AS I CAN REMEMBER,
WE WERE ALWAYS FOR PEACE"

SIX Westchester County high school students (who assured
me that they were not a group nor any part thereof) were
selected for me by a school official as "politically interesting
kids." When I arrived at the school's offices to meet them,
all six were sprawled in a disorderly arrangement of chairs,
engaged in shrill, boisterous conversation that prickled with
antagonism—toward each other, toward me, toward the
school, and toward the world at large. I picked out the three
most disorderly of the six—Joel Tannenbaum, Ross David-
son, and William Ziff—and we went into an office that had
been set aside for our use, while Angie Kline, Allison
Bronstein, and Jim Haig waited noisily outside.

Joel, Ross, and William immediately, as if they'd planned
it, pulled up three chairs behind the big desk, and set themselves up in a shaggy-haired triumvirate. Although I had
interviewed many teenagers in the past eight months, individually and in small groups, until now I had not been
reminded of the defensive, childishly insolent classroom
behavior that I had not seen since the days when I was
passing notes and munching crackers behind my books

while the spit-balls and paper airplanes flew overhead. However, it did not take us long to get down to business (these kids seemed as accustomed to being subdued as they were to rebelling), although it took a while before they forgot about trying to make an impression and got down to talking.

Joel Tannenbaum, 16, was an S.D.S. member who was, in his own opinion, at least an important political force in the school and community, and at most, *the* leader—of what I'm not sure. Joel was short and dark and slight. His black hair curled around his neck, and he was wearing an olive drab sweater and a peacoat. During our discussion he sucked on cigarettes, a pipe, and a cherry tootsie pop, in turn. Both in the group, and later in private, he demonstrated an irritating unwillingness to converse in anything but monologue. He put down middle-class values, and in the same breath espoused them with snobbish remarks about the colleges that had produced the most Rhodes Scholars, and he was adept at maintaining a stream of chatter on similar subjects—an ability I had always associated with the Right rather than the Left. Then he expressed reverse snobbishness, in putting down the "pigs" by detailing his arrests and near-arrests, the most recent of which had been for corrupting the morals of a minor—a younger girl with whom he'd been caught drinking on a local sidewalk one sunny afternoon. ("She'd had an illegal abortion about two months ago, so I would not exactly say her morals were corruptible.")

He also volunteered information such as: "I've been straight for four days, and William has been straight, too, for about that long" (According to his own story, William had been straight for more than six months), "Scag [heroin] hit town about ten months ago . . ." and "these kids," referring to the other five non-members of the non-group, "are all fucked up."

Ross, who seemed to have paired up with Joel, though they appeared to disagree on most issues, was even harder to talk to. He was an espouser of ideas, a quoter of impressive concepts, and he appeared unable to separate himself or what was happening in his own life from Jungian theories and explanations. In discussions, his friends rapidly became impatient with his digressions. Ross, like Joel, was short and scruffy looking. He had lightish hair, darkish skin, needed a shave, and looked surrealistic with a lollipop.

Each of the kids I talked to privately assured me of how rich the other five were, and I was soon quite thoroughly convinced that Joel and Ross were both very, very rich indeed, and had very influential, liberal fathers. Joel was the most gossipy in private, and conversely, he was the one most talked about by the other five. None of the six smiled much.

William seemed the most mature non-member of the non-group in every way. When sitting with his friends (or non-friends), he looked like an adult by comparison. He was tall, broad-shouldered, alert-looking, and oddly clean-cut, despite hair that was just as long, shaggy, and formless as that of the other boys. Yet his behavior did not immediately set him apart from the group, all six of whom could scarcely have created a worse impression had they been littering the waiting room with spit-balls.

When we finally got to real talk, however, I learned to my surprise that all six were involved in creative and practical programs for community reform that made Roger and Garth and their friends in L.A.—all much more likable people than this New York bunch—seem like armchair revolutionaries. Community was something that barely existed for the L.A. kids. They tried to work within the structures of their individual junior high and high schools, but they seemed to find even such limited systems overwelmingly large and ill-defined as targets for action. The idea of moving into an even larger sphere to locate something that could be called a community and try to make a political dent in that, would have been beyond considering.

On the other hand, students within the well-defined limits of a smaller city, large, unwieldy, and unresponsive as that city might be, were more easily able to isolate targets for action, and thus, though they might be rebuffed or defeated, they were not overwhelmed.

When I asked if there was an organization comparable to S.D.S. in their school, I was told that there were about seven. Two of these, it seemed, were genuinely active at the time. One was the Student Union, which William called "an attempt to unify all the existing political groups in the school, as an alternative to the existing student government."

"It will operate," Joel added, "on the doctrine of a participatory democracy. If a student has a demand, he goes directly to the steering committee, and we write up a petition and go directly to the Board of Education."

"It will be an attempt to radicalize the school in a way that could be meaningful to people who aren't white or radical, but just have grievances," William said. He felt that the Union would be used by the majority rather than just a politically sophisticated minority of students, "if we get black kids and Italian kids, and make it clear that you don't have to be radical to belong."

"Nor do you have to agree with any past position of ours," added Joel. "You just have to have a grievance."

Like Garth Haskells in L.A., all six of these comfortable white suburban high school students were very concerned with the way in which the school system manipulated and attempted to channel the lives of individuals. Their community, as they saw it, was divided into black, Italian, and Jewish segments, and the school system channeled a child according to his ethnic group from the elementary grades on, to prepare for a life style substantially the same as that of his parents, so that it was extremely difficult for one generation to do much better than the last. One of the goals of the Student Union, as well as that of United Students, an organization for which Ross was spokesman, was to combat the "track system" of course division.

"At the high school, they place students in groups according to their quote ability," Joel said. "It's not so much a question of ability as a question of their training in junior high and elementary school. Because of this, a lot of equally bright students are separated from the college prep program and are channeled into other programs, and we never meet kids of different backgrounds in this school. In elementary school they decide what group you are going into in junior high and in ninth grade they tell you, you want to go into the business, vocational, general or CP [college preparatory] program."

"They don't even tell you," Ross interrupted. "They just put the white kids in college prep . . ."

"They don't even do that," Joel said. "They put the Jewish kids in college prep, the Italian kids in vocational, and the black kids in business. If you're an Italian girl, you're a hairdresser."

"And then if you complain," Ross added, "they say, 'Well, you chose your program in ninth grade.' You chose your program like your guidance counselor says to you, 'Do you want to do very well and go into vocational, or do you want to go into CP and fail every course? We know what you can do.' "

"Kids just can't decide for themselves at that age," Joel said, "so they do what they're told. Then, if they do want to change, in their junior or senior year, to college prep, well, you just haven't got enough math to go into college. You have to repeat your sophomore year. They've just been tracked into programs which they can no longer change."

Ross said that if a black or Italian ninth grader decided that he wanted to go into college prep, he would have difficulty following through on his decision.

"The counselor will tell them, no matter what kind of grades or I.Q. they've got, 'You'll do much better in vocational,' and most of them go where they're told because, well, a lot of them don't give a damn where they are going. In ninth grade, a lot of them are just realizing where they are. They're just realizing they're living in a slum, they're realizing they just don't care about the system, because the system is just trying to destroy them anyway. They usually don't argue. When they get to high school, the majority of them realize a couple of years too late that they have not taken any Regents courses, they have not taken anything that would get them into a college. They have no place to go. Most of them haven't even learned a vocation. They're just in non-Regents, lower track courses that have no placement value.

"This is where the track system is racist. Because it starts at a very young age. One of the things said is, 'Well, if you had better grades, you could be in a higher track.' But the reason they're not having better grades is the achievement test, which . . . tells the school the general I.Q. and the intelligence of the student. Now this achievement test is biased toward me, a white, middle-class Jew whose family has a private pool, and it is not geared to a student who lives in the projects."

Ross gave me an example that he said had been pointed out to him by a sociologist, about tests in which one was required to associate "common" objects that might be unfamiliar to a ghetto child.

Joel went on to say that United Students was interested

in changing the elementary school program, as an essential first step in bringing about changes in the school system.

"But you have to reeducate the teachers, too," William said. "The very nature of an elementary school is you've got a lot of old ladies and strange men teaching."

"There's no incentive for younger people to be there," Ross added.

"And the good teachers would ask to be transferred out of the slum schools. So only the lower ones would stay there, and they wouldn't care about black kids and they wouldn't teach them as well," Joel said.

What I wanted to know was, why did *they* care—these three middle-class and apparently self-centered Jewish boys whose families had private pools and who had done well on their achievement tests and could be busying themselves making excellent grades and preparing applications that would get them into the excellent colleges to which their fathers would gladly send them for as many years as it took for them to prepare for whatever they wanted to prepare for in view of someday eventually, ten or fifteen years from now, making it, really making it on their so-called own in the so-called outside world.

"You can start with the early civil rights movement, in 1962, 1963," said Joel, who would have been about 10 or 11 years old then, and making a transition from an elementary school that was 40 percent Negro to a junior high school where there were suddenly no black people in his classes, and where he found himself quickly losing all contact with his black friends. "I became involved through my parents in the N.A.A.C.P., Urban League, things like that. Then I became involved in the anti-war movement in 1964, through the high school student mobilization (Mobe) committee. I was 12. In 1965, I joined S.D.S., got out in 1966, got in again in 1967, and I'm still in. I'm getting out again now. Gradually, I've been sort of looking at things around me, both listening to other people and forming my own opinions, I suppose the early Sixties brought me into the two major movements that began to radicalize me, and then as I talked to other people I saw that there were other problems than just these two."

When Joel joined the regional chapter of S.D.S., it was "simply not that radical," and this, he said, was one of the reasons he got out. "I'd heard of some very good things they were doing, but I felt a lot of people were just bull-shitting around, waiting for a demonstration to come, and then there were no follow-ups." When he rejoined S.D.S., he was on the regional council, talked to a lot of people at different high schools, and started a chapter at his own school. According to Joel (Ross contested his story) the chapter, consisting of about fifty members, joined black radical groups to sponsor a student strike, took the brunt of the bad publicity that followed the strike, and consequently fell apart.

Joel was once more about to disassociate himself from the organization, this time because of the divisions therein. He described the situation as follows:

"The Progressive-Labor Maoists are saying you must align with the workers now for revolution. It's a lot of shit. The Trots are saying you must lead the workers in revolution now, which is even more shitty. PL hates the Trots, the Trots hate PL . . ."

"The Trots hate the Commies, too," Ross interjected.

". . . And everybody hates the Labor Committee, which came out in support of the teachers in New York, and they've lost sight of any struggle that's going on in the country. They're considering battles more important than total victory. They don't know who the pigs are. They're fighting the cops in the streets, and they're losing sight of the Daleys and the Nixons."

Joel said he was involving himself with other organizations that would approach political radicalization through the education of youth, "But not just to our point of view, and not just to the point of view they are being taught now, but to both points of view. I think if a revolution is impractical, which it is at this point, another end to work toward is a constitutional convention. Because of this, I am now called a pig by the S.D.S."

I pressed Joel further in regard to his personal motivations, in an attempt to get a better understanding of how his activism functions in relation to the rest of his life, or vice versa, but I had little success. Ross was even less illuminating in this regard. He tried to explain himself by saying:

"You could trace it all the way back to the Depression and my parents—of course, my reaction is from my parents. During the Depression, you had people who were living within very bad conditions, and these are the middle class of today, and because of their preoccupation with their own material needs, they weren't able to do what they wanted to do politically . . ."

He began quoting Jung, in an attempt to tell me that today's youth is acting out what their parents were unable to do, and I was about to indicate that what I was asking concerned him personally, and not today's youth or any subgroup therein, when William interrupted him.

"I think psychological reasons are very interesting," he said to Ross, "but I think the reason why a lot of radical students get involved is a basic sense of injustice, and I think that you're right if you trace this back to your parents, but that's not the issue. Probably everything you are saying is perfectly true. However, if your radicalism is motivated, first of all, by reaction to your parents, and second of all, need, then when you grow out of adolescence and these psychological factors are no longer present, then you are going to be conservative, like all the other radicals when they grow out of their radicalism."

Ross, however, continued to quote, growing more and more flustered as Joel and William, sitting on either side of him, attacked his approach to answering the question, and I tried to get him back on the track. Eventually, he said, "The reason I am involved in politics today is I genuinely feel certain injustices, and that most people are trying to fool themselves from the fact that they are being oppressed."

Despite Ross's impassioned delivery, I couldn't help noticing that this was almost exactly what William had said earlier. I asked Ross how he first came to think that way, and he said the first things he'd said so far about himself that were entirely credible:

"Well, that's like last week, because it's constantly changing. I wouldn't really say last week, but you have to realize that youth is constantly changing their ideas, youth is constantly reading things, and someday when I'm eighty I'll be a reactionary in the sense that I will not have any changing of views . . . I simply started reading and becoming aware of things around me through different people's thoughts, and basing a value system on these people." He said he'd been reading mostly Freud, Jung, Marx, the Bible, and the Constitution.

"What got you interested in this stuff in the first place?" I asked.

"Sex," one of the others said, and again it was a free-for-all, with Joel and William, especially William, running Ross into the rhetorical ground.

Ross tried again.

"I had the reaction to my parents and the N.A.A.C.P.

that at the time they were doing all they could, that they were right and justified in not doing any more. Recently I saw that they weren't doing everything possible, and when they say to me, 'Well, you're going to have a lot of things to take care of,' I react to them, and say, 'Well, you had time to do it, too.' It's like taking some shit and saying you flush it down the toilet, and I'm saying, like it's your shit, you take care of it. This is the way my parents are treating me. So my radicalism is a reaction to my parents not doing anything—but I'd sort of like to give myself a little credit before going any further—that I have a mind and can comprehend things and not just react."

Ross seemed to feel less under attack now, and was no longer taking himself quite so deadly seriously as he had been earlier. He then gave the following political auto-biography:

"I was involved first in SNCC, which I joined when I was very young, prodded by my parents, who gave me literature and said 'Here is a great organization.' At that point I started thinking on my own and involving myself in different things. I was in fourth grade. And the teacher said to me, 'I notice you didn't say the Lord's Prayer.' I was brought up as a non-believer in God by my parents— they explained to me when I was young and said you can make up your own mind that God doesn't exist—anyway, the teacher said you have to, so I started to cry. And at assembly I started saying it. I couldn't memorize it, though. I faked it. In junior high, I refused to say the pledge of allegiance, and this I guess was my first big rebellion, and they pulled me in and yelled at me, and I had Supreme Court cases I'd pulled out of books, proving I had the right not to say it, and for the next two years, I had a running battle with the school.

"Then I came to the high school, and I had a period when

I decided the hell with politics, the hell with everything, and I didn't do anything for about a year. After that I went to private schools for a while, and I had been a pacifist for that year, and then I decided that the only change we were going to have was one of motion, and you're not going to have a peaceful change, and I said to myself, Next year I am going back to public school (I had to leave the private school because we didn't have any more money), and now you are going to do well in school and you are also going to enjoy yourself politically in school.

"I had belonged to S.D.S. at one time, but I burned my S.D.S. card at a rally once because of my disgust for them. They're not looking at the entire movement. Only small aspects. At the high school level the movement has gone into token things, and because they've been willing to settle, they've been co-opted. National S.D.S. is entirely different. But locally, they've just settled for the things that were easy for the administration to give—a Swahili course, for instance. Like they gave us a black literature course when we didn't ask for a black literature course, we asked for a black history course, but it didn't cost them anything, so they gave us the lit course.

"I think its irresponsible to go out on the street like kids do and yell at cops and throw bottles at them, because a cop is just a person, and he's just an equal person to you, but when you start getting to people like the administration, or like Daley, they're the people you are supposed to throw bottles at, or yell at, or shoot at. You go out on the street and get yourself hit on the head by a cop, it proves nothing, it does nothing. When you go out on the street and smile at a cop and shoot at the mayor, well, that does something. You're shooting at the source of your troubles at that point."

"Could you kill somebody?" I asked.

"No, not at this point."

"Would you like to be able to?"

"Not really. But it's not about the feeling of wanting to be violent, it's about the feeling of wanting to protect yourself."

"But you realize," William argued, "that if you shoot Mayor Lindsay or Mayor Daley it wouldn't prove a thing."

"I realize it has to be on a much larger scale than that," Ross defended himself. "You can't just shoot at the Mayor and leave it at that. You have to start organizing and working within groups and attacking certain things. You won't have a revolution in this country until you have groups willing to storm the National Archive."

"You won't get it then, either," William said, "because you are not attacking the economic structure. When you talk about revolution, or when you talk about not revolution, but hitting the right power structure, I think a lot of us miss the boat, because the things that have to be attacked in our society are not the people, because there is always someone left to fill in their place. So I think a lot of this talk about revolution is destructive, because I think it would do a lot more for the black people, or for the white people on relief, to go and attack the welfare system than the personalities in the welfare system that are the symbols of this corruption. Yet a lot of the time radicals talk about, 'Well, we shouldn't yell at the pigs because they're people . . .' Well, ultimately, everybody is people, but the point is that the thing that runs the nation, the thing that makes this such an immense, complex problem, and why I don't think there will be a revolution, is that this country is firmly entrenched as a capitalistic entity and the capitalistic system in our country is based on inequalities. Even if you overthrew the government, you'd still have the military-industrial complex and General Motors."

"That's part of the government," Joel said.

"That's part of what you have to attack," Ross said.

"In what way would you attack that?" William demanded.

"First I'd buy sixteen million shares in the stock market, and let it crash. Then I don't know what I'd do after that," said Ross miserably, and those were nearly his final words of the afternoon.

The second group of three, Angie, Allison, and Jim, nearly as rowdy as the first three while waiting outside, were a far more docile trio on the other side of the desk. They were much more agreeable toward each other, and gave the impression of caring somewhat about each other. They were also much more apathetic than Joel and Ross and William.

Jim was just as scruffy as Joel and Ross. In fact, he was physically almost a taller version of Ross—lightish hair, darkish skin, in need of a shave, dirty brown suède jacket, well-worn army boots. The girls, by contrast, appeared almost nun-like. Both were fair-skinned and very clean looking. Angie, who looked as if she had always been plump and always would be plump, was short, with short, neatly curled light brown hair. She wore a gray wool pleated skirt and a short-sleeved white blouse with a little round collar. Allison, also a small girl, but slender and pretty, wore a long-sleeved white blouse with a little round collar, and gray wool slacks. Her hair, the same color as Angie's, was long; it appeared to have been straightened, and the ends were dry and ragged. Angie wore a navy blue loden coat; Allison carried a short, heavy red wool cape. All three were pleasant to talk to.

Jim and Allison belonged to the Y.C.I.A. (Young Citizens in Action), as Joel and William did. For Jim and Allison, Y.C.I.A. seemed to be the major, if not the only, local political group worthy of their involvement at that point.

The organization, which had published a magazine irregularly, and chartered buses for major out-of-town demonstrations, was described by William as a group for "all around community type political action," and by Joel as "a kind of information group, to try to bring people out of apathy." Currently, the group was organizing symposiums, primarily for the purpose of bringing about a working relationship between white and black students.

White/black relations was the only problem this group discussed with me in detail, which was really their own problem as well as someone else's. A relatively new breakdown in communication between black and white students was a part of their daily lives. Instead of being in the role of over-privileged, able whites extending a helping hand to underprivileged, unable blacks, they were just one party in a two-party misunderstanding, trying to get some considerations and feelings out into the open.

"I think if anyone in the high school is getting into communication with black kids, it's us," Allison said. "We want to set up a panel and work with kids' attitudes, work out our fears and resentments toward each other. The problem we've run across initially is we can't even get black kids to sit down and talk to us about sitting down and talking to us.

"We've been friendly with some black kids for several years—these are kids who don't need a Black is Beautiful movement to know that they are black and to know that they are beautiful. Others are very distrustful of us—and of these black kids. Through several discussions, I've tried to work with a particular black kid, and I say why is it so difficult for you to come to a meeting, and he says we're trying to establish unity now in our black organizations and

I say we're not trying to break your unity . . . gradually, I think we are making some progress."

Although all six students spoke out in one way or another against gradual change, Jim, the newest to politics, and perhaps one of the most impatient, justified the Y.C.I.A's type of gradualness, "because you're working with something so direct as changing attitudes of kids, it can come about quicker, because we haven't had time quite yet to become as disgusting as some of the older people have."

Angie, who had been president of a now defunct peace organization, was not particularly enthusiastic about Y.C.I.A. She told me apathetically that she was not involved in anything now. "This year, more or less, everyone is going their own way," she said. She shrugged her shoulders and retreated to some point behind her eyes. She seemed to go into hiding every time she closed her mouth, and when asked a question, had to make an effort, not an unwilling one, but an effort, nonetheless, to come out.

"The peace group was kind of a strange club," Jim said, "because the school would not allow it to be political in nature. It is very difficult to have an apolitical peace group. That meant if we put up posters announcing anything we were doing, this was a political action. For example, we sponsored demonstrations against the draft board, but we had trouble advertising it, because they ripped down the posters in the school, and we weren't allowed to sponsor it as an organization."

Angie emerged again, this time voluntarily. "I sort of felt personally even then that it was very hard for us to get organized at all, and I'm kind of fed up with politics already, if you can call that politics. There's nothing going on now, but even so, I can't see myself getting involved at this point. But there's nothing else really to do other than work with the black radicals, if we can figure out how to do that . . . except this Student Union coming up might be good, working sort of alongside the Government Council but opposed to the Council. Like before, we didn't work in the school, because we didn't see the possibility of anything getting done in the school. Then we ran two "peace candidates" for Government Council officers and they won. They have since copped out and left us. Now we could start all over again . . ."

The peace candidates had apparently copped out by failing to act in the interests of those who had supported them, once elected. "They just got embroiled in the system, the way things are done," Jim said, as if he were still trying to figure out exactly what had happened. "When you work through an organization, like that, things take time, things take politeness, things take orderly, bureaucratic steps."

"There's a right way to do things, and a right time," Angie murmured.

"We were pretty much together last spring," Allison said, frowning, "on the issues of McCarthy and peace and black people. And I don't know what happened over the summer, but everyone more or less came back to school with their politics very different."

Allison thought perhaps the Democratic National Convention, which shook everyone up, had shaken everyone in different directions. But Jim didn't think it had changed him any, and Angie felt the dissolution had started last year.

"I personally couldn't support McCarthy," Angie said sadly. "I just didn't think he was that great a person. The convention just sort of brought a head to that. A lot of the others supported McCarthy. I just worked for O'Dwyer." She mentioned that the summer breach might have been caused by the fact that a lot of the kids went away. Allison had gone to Europe. Other kids had gone to summer sessions at colleges, or to other places where there were a lot of kids, and a lot of new ideas.

"Those two Government Council officers went to Europe together," Jim remarked a little wistfully. "And that brought them even closer together, where they really operate in the same way now."

Despite Jim's discouragement, Angie's apathy, Joel's obnoxiousness, and Ross's neurotic obtuseness, it was my distinct impression, just from the number of political events that had occurred in the school, that this suburban student body of 3,000 was in general pretty concerned with issues. But Allison and Angie assured me that I was wrong.

"They aren't," Allison said flatly.

"It's very easy to live here and not be concerned with issues. It's a very nice little life. There's nothing to be concerned about."

I wanted to know how they had become involved.

Jim told me he'd been thinking about that a lot lately himself. "Even at the beginning of last year, if I thought I'd be doing anything like what I'm doing now, I'd have thought I was going crazy. I think it kind of came to me one day when a kid was circulating an ad against the war for the school newspaper, to be paid for by students. And I kind of apologetically said, no, I don't support what you are doing, and I'd never even thought about it, it was just that way. It had been established in my home that the war was nice. And then I suddenly found myself apologizing for what I supposedly thought was right. It made me kind of stop and look, and some kids were getting together at the Y, and William asked me if I wanted to come so I came along and I got involved."

Politics was a cause of great conflict between Jim and his right-wing parents, who had more than once threatened to throw him out of the house. For Angie, it was a different matter. Angie's mother and her lawyer father were active in the local N.A.A.C.P., of which Angie said, "There wasn't much done here, but whatever got done, the N.A.A.C.P. did it."

She herself had been involved since 1963. "So the peace movement is just a natural step, and my parents support me in my involvement.

"My father still takes civil rights cases; my mother is going to school. We were involved in peace, but there's sort of not much to do now. They're at the same place I am. We're in harmony—politically anyway."

Allison, who also claimed to have inherited her politics from her parents, said she and her father were fighting a lot about political issues. Her father is a civil liberties lawyer who had himself run for office a long time ago on a ticket she couldn't remember the name of. I asked her if it was the Progressive, and she laughed and said, "Yes, that's what he ran on. He lost twice. It's so unreal to me."

Angie and Allison had done mailings and canvassing from the age of 13 on. "Before the peace issue was popular," Allison said. "It was a pretty bad time. If we said we were against the war, we were just completely ostracized. And you just saw the same people working and giving money over and over again, and they just didn't get anywhere. It seemed hopeless.

"So I disagree with my father's general attitude that politics is necessary for change, and everything has to be done through political campaigns. Angie and I and the whole gang were involved in local politics a couple of years ago, and then we just became so turned off by the whole idea of just sitting and doing mailings and canvassing and the whole thing and not getting anywhere, we just stopped.

"It's funny to be saying here I am seventeen years old

and I've had it, but there's nothing else to say. So I disagree with my father, and he tells me I'm just rationalizing my own inactivity. I'm more concerned now with working alongside the black movement—not in it—but doing what has to be done in white communities, instead of running around and campaigning.

"It's harder for me to go work in a conservative white community and talk to people about these things than it is to go down to Harlem and tutor for two hours. I did tutor in the local community action program. But talking to white people is really hard to do."

"For myself," Angie said, "I'm not really sure what my role as a white person is in terms of supporting the black movement. The kids in the black lit course come up to me and say, 'What is the meeting tonight really about?' They want to know what it's *really* about. And that's just the point. We're whitey, and I don't doubt that we're whitey, but the point is I'm not trying to trap these kids into anything. We just want to say, we feel this toward black kids, tell us what black kids feel toward white kids. Then we can set up questions, focus, have a panel, so more people can get things out in the open. I think it's breaking down now, getting more honest."

Jim laughed and insisted that she's wasn't giving up, but Angie was not quite about to admit that she was still a political person. On the other hand, Jim himself, who had not been out ringing doorbells or stuffing envelopes for the past three years, seemed to "have had it," too.

"I keep seeing this picture of everyone saying work within the system because it provides this nice, slow, gradual change," Jim said. "And they're admitting the fault right there. Gradual change. Doesn't make anyone uncomfortable. It will pass right by me. By time I'm gone, this gradual change may just be starting. I still haven't grown up enough to wait for things like that."

Jim's impatience is more typical of the attitudes expressed by the high school activists I spoke to than is his disillusionment. While Jim's experience is obviously not unique to the student come lately to politics, William's more self-assured attitude better represents the many teenagers who recall a very early political awareness with a phrase like, "ever since way back when, we were always for peace."

"I was always very irate and pro-Soviet when they were anti-Soviet in school," William said. "My total outlook, from I don't remember how early, was always vaguely Marxist, and as I get older, gets more and more Marxist, and really more and more subtle, but the basic feeling is still there—that I don't have very much respect for the way this country is run, and if it can be changed, it has to be affected on a local level."

Yet, William's viewpoint is really more liberal than radical; he has hardly jumped on any revolutionary bandwagon in response to the Yippie concept of "revolution for the hell of it," or to the more complex ideologies espoused by S.D.S. groups.

"I think radicalism has to spring from a desire to help people, and a respect for humanity that conservatives don't have," he said. "Conservatives have this contempt for people, and this very thin line between their kind of hatred and their political action. And I think this is what is kind of upsetting about the Yippies and people like that—there is a lot of hatred there.

"The people have to be involved. They have to be willing to give. I don't go for indoctrination because the minute people get away from you and their old feelings come back, then wham, they change their minds and say, 'I don't believe what *that kid* said.' But if their feeling of involvement comes out of a need to help—and I think all people have the need, and a lot of kids are curious about what is going on, but are scared—and when people become involved in working, in feeling they *can* do something to change their own lives, then this is really what politics is, not pushing people along. That's just the sheep and the shepherd."

33

SOME CONCLUSIONS

THE many kids who are "curious about what is going on, but scared" are becoming more curious and less scared. And gradually, the "discothèquers and dopers," the trippies, the alienated, the spaced out, are joining the children weaned on Marx, and the children who, with their parents, were "always for peace," to try to change all sorts of things they don't like—from rules for the length of their own hair to the economic situation of a working class with whom many of them have had virtually no contact.

They are not humble. They feel, no less than the militants, that they have inherited a mess, and many of them have been trying all along to create, at least for themselves in the privacy of their own lives, a better world. Just as those kids who feel they suffer from a lack of experience with life will boldly run away and get some, those who suddenly feel hindered by political naïveté are confident that the knowledge they need can be acquired. And as they attempt to act within the broad context that could be called political, as they seek their own definitions of politics, set up goals, attempt to involve or inform others with their ideas and ideals, they are, at the very least, preparing themselves better for the world, if not preparing a better world for themselves. If what they are doing can be called rebellion, they are rebelling not merely against some all-encompassing establishment, but against the myth of their own apartness, and against the time-honored cliché of youth's idyllic life "in his own world."

In a statement before the House Special Sub-Committee on Education in March, 1969, Dr. Bruno Bettelheim, the Chicago psychiatrist, said:

> To understand why pressures erupt in adolescence on a growing scale nowadays, and why controls seem to grow weaker, we must recognize that adolescent revolt is not a state of development that follows automatically from our natural make-up. What makes for adolescent revolt is the fact that a society keeps the next generation too long dependent in terms of mature responsibility and a striving for independence. And it is this waiting for things—for the real life to come—which creates a climate in which a sizable segment of students can, at least temporarily, be seduced into following the lead of a small group of militants. . . .
>
> The most rebellious students, here and abroad, are either undergraduates, or those studying the social sciences and the humanities. There are no militants among students of medicine, engineering, the natural sciences. They are busy with doing things that are important to them, they are working in the laboratory and at their studies. It is those students who do not quite know what they are preparing themselves for, and why . . . which form the cadres of student rebellion. . . . Their deep dissatisfaction with themselves and their inner confusion is projected against the institution, of the university first, and against all institutions of society secondarily, which are blamed for their own inner weakness.

Although I take exception to Dr. Bettelheim's implied equation of the rebellious with the weak, and have not found in general that student activists are merely unhappy individuals who have been "seduced" into radicalism, I feel that he has cited two basic sources of many adolescent difficulties: that we err first in regarding revolt as a natural and inevitable characteristic of adolescence, and second, in denying our youth "real life."

What is called "rebellion" at the college level usually involves agitation that is genuinely disruptive to the status quo. Such demonstrations have occurred recently in high schools as well, but what is generally regarded as rebelliousness in the public secondary schools is anything that is more aggressive than apathy or submission—any questioning of values, any *interest* in political involvement. And in taking effective action to change the public schools, students have a very long way to go—not only in fighting a basically intractable system, but in fighting the reflexes that have been developing in them since kindergarten, to submit to that system and stand in awe of its authority.

In a recent documentary film called *High School,* Frederick Wiseman depicts this blind obedience, along with the shocking blandness, apathy, and obsolescence that characterize daily routine at a white, middle-class Philadelphia school. We see students being insulted by their teachers, ordered by guidance counselors to feel guilty for failing to live up to parental expectations regarding college, made to feel morally wrong over the length of a dress worn to a school dance, being fed nineteenth-century aphorisms like brain-wash messages first thing in the morning over the P.A. system, being given misleading and unverifiable "facts" by a dirty-talking gynecologist in a sex-education lecture.

We see, with one or two exceptions, an impassive, colorless, and unsympathetic organization of adults making a condescendingly patient attempt to instill a cowed, apathetic, and equally colorless group of young people with values.

The only time we see a student praised and told he has "finally shown some character," is when a boy abandons an attempt to establish the truth about an incident, and agrees to accept punishment for an offense he insists he did not commit. What it means to be a mature and responsible individual is simply to obey, to concede, to accept whatever authority demands.

According to a *New York Times* article, filmmaker Wiseman (who is also responsible for the controversial *Titticut Follies*) reported praise for the school from groups of parents and teachers who saw the film in Boston and New York. Some stood in awe of the Philadelphia school's ability to keep the kids so orderly and quiet, while others "praised the school's efforts at inculcating values and respect."

What is really being inculcated by such efforts is neither values nor respect, but rather fear, guilt, and suspicion. I found an astonishing example of this in Carl, an articulate, sensitive, underachieving, passionately non-conforming senior at Hollywood's Fairfax High School. Carl was one of a group of teenyboppers and dopers, but unlike his friends, he was a spirited rebel and an S.D.S. supporter on the verge of becoming a militant himself.

I had interviewed Carl after school in a semi-sheltered outdoor lunchroom area of the school building. When we finished, around five o'clock, it turned out we were going in the same direction, and I told him to wait for me while I went to the ladies' room across from the bench where we were sitting.

"But that's the teachers' room," Carl said, suddenly as nervous as if I'd suggested we break into the principal's office. "You might get into trouble."

"Nonsense," I laughed, and went on in, incredulous that this could concern him.

Yet, when I came out, he had a look of great relief on

his face, as if he had thought there were closed circuit TV cameras behind every forbidden door in the school, wired to trap doors that electronically opened under any pair of feet that stepped out of bounds.

The following comment, from an article on right-wing rebellion,* expresses in yet another way the common and dangerous attitude that both reduces the potency and increases the anger of the young. The remark is laden with such condescension that I think the *Times* might have hesitated to print it, if its subject had been a racial, religious, or ethnic minority group.

> It is hard to judge these young men, their unlined, pimpled faces. Any discussion is necessarily on an ideological, abstract plane. How do you ask an 18-year-old who he is? He is no one yet, all his experience having been taken up with physical growth and intellectual abstractions which seem to them [*sic*] terribly serious.

Not only can one ask an 18-year-old who he is, one can ask a 15-year-old, or a 10-year-old, or a 5-year-old who he is with a good chance of receiving a more honest answer than a 35-year-old or a 50-year-old would give.

It is indeed a terrified society that must go to the lengths that we do to keep youth and its ideas and energies so suppressed—declaring youth sick, declaring it weak, declaring it spoiled, teaching youth to think of itself as dependent, irresponsible, immoral, escapist. We are fortunate that more and more of our adolescents are rising above our fears and falsehoods and mistakes and claiming their right to a voice in their own lives and the world we all live in.

* Sophy Burnham, "Twelve Rebels of the Student Right," *New York Times* Magazine, March 9, 1969.

APPENDIX

The Questions and the Answers

Although the interviews for this book were conducted in a highly informal manner, they were all based on fifty specific questions. The following eight subjects were covered:

School
Personal experiences and attitudes
Politics
Religion
Culture
Drugs
Sex
Parents

A statistical breakdown of data is not within the scope of this study. But I have included below a few questions that elicited responses that I found particularly revealing about the culture, attitudes, and experiences of the generation as a whole.

1. SCHOOL

Most of the militants, the dopers, and the runaways were prepared to talk for hours on the subject of school, while the trippies and the street kids usually considered it of little importance.

Are you learning anything in school?

It would seem that the kids who were considered good students should probably answer yes to this question, but they answered no as often as those who were doing poorly. Likewise, the pattern of answers to other questions in this category did not seem to bear any relation to whether the student was bright or dull, doing well, or not doing at all.

What do you think school could do for you?

Few kids could really deal with this question. In general, answers indicated that the purpose of going to school had never really been clear. I got the strong impression that most kids—brilliant, stupid, and in between—felt they were in school in order to get out of it, and that they would not be there if the law or their parents or college admission boards didn't say they had to.

Only a few were enthusiastic about school; though many were enthusiastic about learning, there seemed to be a strong feeling that the structure of the public high school hindered the learning process rather than promoted it. Those who were going along with the game—and they saw it in exactly that way—*tended* to enjoy school more than those who were not. But I could not conclude that the "good" students were proportionately more satisfied with the whole experience than those who were coasting or instigating dissent. All of those who were "playing the game" were playing on the basis of their faith in the value of college. Not one person communicated the feeling that high school had any intrinsic value in itself.

What could you do to get more out of school?

Study harder and do more independent work, was a common answer. But few felt that the rewards for this additional effort would make it worthwhile.

Was there a time when you liked school better than you do now?

Almost all reported liking kindergaten and elementary school, but had found the school experience increasingly boring, nerve-wrackingly competitive, or irrelevant to their lives, since about the beginning of junior high. In most school systems, this is the point at which teachers begin to frantically try to prepare kids for college, prepare them to pass exams, fill them with data. And the kids, not quite understanding the purpose of all this frantic preparation, become resentful or disinterested and remain so.

2. PERSONAL EXPERIENCES AND ATTITUDES

These questions were intended primarily to provide some background on each individual. But some of them produced surprisingly uniform responses.

What was the nicest thing that happened to you in the last year?

Nearly 50 percent were unable to recall something "nice" that had happened to them recently, and many said "nothing nice ever happens to me."

If you could change something about yourself, what would it be?

Many named some personality trait, like bad temper or intolerance, that they wanted to get rid of, or an ability, like playing the guitar, that they wanted to improve. Almost all of the girls, no matter how pretty, wanted to improve their looks. But the answer that I heard most often—from about 40 percent— was "improve my poor memory."

If you could change something about the world, what would it be?

About 95 percent, most of them a little apologetically, said "peace."

What was the biggest lie you ever believed?

A few kids had an elaborate personal story to relate here, but there were basically three answers to this question: belief in Santa Claus, belief in the American Dream, and belief that pot was harmful.

Additional comments indicated that many kids considered themselves gullible, and felt they were believing many lies they didn't know about.

What would you like to have accomplished ten years from now?

Very few mentioned vocational goals; most mentioned having completed their education, all mentioned the achievement of independence—and also a certain measure of security—in having their own living quarters and a source of income. "I don't want a lot of money, but just enough that I don't have to hassle it," was a typical part of the answer. The answers communicated much more materialism than idealism. Most kids answered the question in terms of *having* something rather than *having done* something or *being* something.

3. POLITICS

The questions in this category necessarily changed with the times, since the interviewing began in early summer of 1968, a few days after the assassination of Robert Kennedy, and concluded after Nixon was in the White House. The general intent of the questions, however, did not change.

I asked for degree of interest in the Presidential election, and for amount of participation in demonstrations or other activities that could be called political. Most teenagers expressed either interest in the election or guilty feelings about how little attention they had paid to the whole thing. The "guilty" ones assured me, not always convincingly, that if they had had a vote they would have made it their business to be better informed. But most of those who were following the election closely said that they would not have voted if they had been old enough, since they saw no difference between Humphrey, Nixon, and Wallace.

I came across far fewer avid supporters of Eugene McCarthy

than I expected to, and I can only conclude that McCarthy's numerous teenage supporters came from a generally more conventional group than those I sought to interview. If anyone, my kids tended to favor Dick Gregory in the East and Pat Paulsen in the West.

Regarding peace and civil rights demonstrations and similar activities not directly arising out of the school situations, many had participated, none were enthusiastic. They felt that this aspect of political activity had seen its peaks before their time.

4. RELIGION

A number of adults whose opinions I sought—school officials, police officers, civil servants in charge of youth problems —expressed the firm conviction that this is a Godless generation of thrill-seekers, atheistic, agnostic, or hedonistic in character, spiritually sterile, and lacking any sense of values or ethics on which responsible behavior could be built.

I found that the values these kids hold are primarily spiritual ones, and that, in their rebellion, they are usually seeking not kicks, but rather self-knowledge and an ethical and humane way of life. Some of them are even seeking God. These quests usually do not take place in relation to any church, nor do they necessarily occur strictly outside the context of conventional religious thought or ethical teachings, or as part of a drug trip.

About religion, I asked simply, "What is a religious person? Are you? Do you want to be?"

I had expected to find that a large number of kids were seeking religious experience, because this was true of the people I knew personally who had used L.S.D.—most of them in their 20s. I had observed that a great many older dropouts with a basically atheistic world view had suddenly begun to use words like God and religion and spirit in a new way; it was almost as if a whole generation of blasé people had acquired a new innocence.

But the kids did not respond to this question quite as I had expected them to. For the very young and still, in a sense, really innocent, the words are somehow harder to use. Frequently, I had to repeat the question "What is a religious person?" several times before it was understood that I was asking for a personal definition rather than a stock one. I did not have this trouble with any other question. The problem was that kids simply did not want to use the word "religious" or "religion" at all. For most, these were fraught with connotations of dressing up in stiff clothes and wriggling against their will through boring and irrelevant rituals, connotations of hypocritical living, rote thought and behavor, doing what you were supposed to do without understanding any whys—a kind of paint-by-numbers of the soul. They didn't buy it. But God was another matter. Though these people shuddered at the word "religion," they would hardly call themselves atheists or agnostics. Many volunteered that they believed in God, and "spirit" and "soul" were much easier words to use.

When the kids finally did give me a personal definition of a religious person, most described him as someone with a deep belief in man. Most did not consider themselves devout enough in any way to be called religious, though many said they were working toward this, and that the goal of becoming a religious person was a desirable one, and that a truly religious person was someone to admire.

I asked the same set of questions about freedom. The answers were less interesting, and usually less personal, because most of the kids had had so little opportunity to embrace responsibility. All, of course, wanted to be free. Many said, "There is no such thing as a free person, but if there were. . . ." Most had not defined the word or concept of freedom for themselves in any way. The runaways knew much more about it than the others, having dealt with it directly.

5. CULTURE

Do kids read?
I asked them if they read anything other than what school required, and what they liked. The impression I got was that

kids don't read much on their own, and that they are not deeply impressed by the written word. The politically oriented kids read far more than any other group, but they didn't read novels or much of anything not directly related to politics. They had no literary heroes, no favorite books as a generation—though the works of Herman Hesse and J. R. R. Tolkein were mentioned often as "important" books in the lives of individuals, as were A. S. Neill's *Summerhill* and *The Autobiography of Malcolm X*. Most had trouble recalling a book that had recently made a big impression on them or changed their thinking in some way.

The same was true of movies. I found very few who recognized the film as art form, and no one who considered the idea of *making* films as something to do. Most said they went to the movies seldom because there was nothing good to see. Few seemed aware of foreign films, and many seemed to place films on the cultural level of soap operas. There were two movies, however, that everybody made a point of seeing, and everybody liked: *2001: A Space Odyssey* and *The Graduate*.

All kids, however, listen to music. Ask them what kind they like, and they'll probably say all kinds. Actually, most individual preferences are probably more limited than that easy answer would indicate, but kids today do seem to have more eclectic tastes in music than my generation did. I would hesitate to call them undiscriminating in their tastes, but there does seem to be a general consideration that goes, "If it's music, it's good," paralleling one that goes, "If it's a movie, it's bad," and "If it's a book, I meant to read it, but I didn't."

Most kids today are plugged into their radios, phonographs, and tape recorders like communicators at NASA monitoring a manned spacecraft. It is through music that they are most directly and constantly being reached by the outside world—though this "outside world" is populated primarily by artists not much older than their audience. Music is as much a part of the adolescent's environment as the color of his bedroom walls. But he can't tell you why it is so important.

In 1959, I interviewed an average group of suburban high

school students, aged 14 to 16, on rock and roll, and found them almost completely inarticulate on the subject. The kids I interviewed for this book were almost equally inarticulate. Most of the commentary and criticism turned out by rock magazines is not very illuminating either, whereas the most perceptive and literate commentary on post-Beatle pop appears outside the real milieu of that music, in newspapers and literary quarterlies which are probably hardly ever read by kids.

In my interviews, I even found it hard to pin kids down to naming their favorite groups, since they assured me that these changed from week to week. I thought I might get some specifics by asking them what records they owned, but the kids claimed that this would indicate no more than whom they happened to like at the time they happened to have money to buy records.

Yet popular music seems to have much more permanence today than it did in the Fifties. The songs of 1958 were oldies but goodies in 1959, whereas kids who were in grade school when the Beatles made *Rubber Soul* in 1963 are familiar with that album as something more current in their lives than an oldie, and I doubt that many teenagers in 1959 could, even if pressed, recall a single hit of 1953.

One obvious reason for this is that the stereo album has a more permanent quality than the old 45. Another reason may be content and quality of the songs. All rock has become more of a folk music than a popular music, and the truth or social relevance of the songs, as well as the same old factors of star or group, plays a part in their popularity. In the Fifties, tunes and stars—as opposed to lyrics, message, innovation, overall sound—made the hits. One did not expect truth, relevance, or messages of any kind from that music. But during the past few years, popular songs have become symbolic of life styles, and life styles do not wear thin or change as quickly as mere tunes.

6. DRUGS

Nearly all the kids answered yes when asked if they had taken any drugs. Of the few that answered no, one was lying and quickly admitted the truth, three were half-embarrassed and half-proud to say they hadn't and didn't intend to, and the rest said they just hadn't gotten around to it yet, but probably would in the near future. Obviously, most of the questions that follow do not apply to these few.

Pot is the first drug most kids try, though some actively seek an L.S.D. trip as their first high. All those who turned on first with L.S.D. later tried pot. About half of those who started with pot had gone on to try other drugs. They usually did so within a matter of months. The other half had no interest in other drugs, and some had no further interest in pot.

Those who started with L.S.D. typically had to purchase their first high, sometimes going to considerable trouble to import a dose from another city. Almost all of those who started with pot were invited to turn on by a friend (or stranger) of their own age—an individual with nothing to sell and virtually nothing to gain by introducing a novice to the drug.

Do you think drugs have changed your personality?

Most answered no, and then went on to tell me *how* they thought drugs—pot, speed, acid—had changed them. "I am less uptight, more open, more tolerant, and more aware of others," was a typical answer.

Do you think drugs have changed the personalities of others?

Kids who said yes would often mention a friend whom, they thought, was being, or had been, "ruined" by drugs—someone who had been a "nice person" and was no longer a nice person and no longer did anything much and was interested in nothing but drugs.

Should everyone turn on?

Almost all said no, and a few were horrified at the idea, though they could not clearly say why.

How do you get drugs? Do you ever go to a great deal of trouble? Where do you get the money to pay?

A great number quickly said they never bought anything, that it just wasn't that important to them, that if it was there, fine, if not, that was fine, too. I felt that less than half of them were telling the whole truth. When asked the second part of the question, many indicated that they had bought on occasion, and at times did want to get high badly enough to do a fair amount of telephoning, traveling, waiting, or general hassling to score or find someone who would turn them on.

The third part of the question brought a fair amount of hemming and hawing. In almost all cases, the truth was pretty hard to admit: the money came from allowances, hoarded lunch money, money requested for an evening of bowling, a record album, or a date.

If you could get what you want from drugs in some other way, would you prefer that?

Most answered no. The yeses were enthusiastic yeses, from people who were tired of fearing the law, or uneasy about taking foreign and potentially dangerous substances into their bodies, but who felt that the drug *experience* was too valuable to give up.

About 20 percent of those who answered no were quite open in expressing their enjoyment of the illegal aspect of drug use, and/or the rituals involved in getting high.

Was there a time when you thought drugs were bad?

"Of course," was the immediate answer. Some, who were using drugs nonetheless, said, "I still think drugs are bad."

Do you worry about getting busted?

While many described occasional moments of paranoia in regard to police, most had little fear of the law catching up with them, and were much more concerned about their parents finding them out. I was surprised to hear the phrase "busted," traditionally meaning "arrested," applied to being found out by parents.

It seems that most kids who have been "found out" by their parents agree to stay away from drugs in the future, if that is what is requested of them. Those who break this agreement, whether or not they make it in good faith, naïvely, in my opinion, are convinced that their parents do not know they have done so.

Do you ever take drugs alone?

About 60 percent use drugs only socially: if they want to get high, they will seek out someone else to join them, and if they can't find anyone, probably won't turn on at that time. It was my impression that those who do turn on frequently alone are either the hard-core dopers or are using drugs in active search for psychological or mystical insights.

Do you get high more frequently when you're feeling good or when you're feeling bad?

Most individuals had a preference for the kind of mood in which they preferred to get high. But these preferences fell into no discernible pattern, and I found no evidence to back up the myth that people smoke pot to escape from depression. On the contrary, a large percentage said that drugs increase the intensity of the emotional state they were in before getting high, and rarely change it from good to bad or vice versa.

Have drugs changed your relationships with others?

Half expounded the virtues of drugs, especially pot, for producing closer relationships between people who share a high, or for increasing their ability to communicate with and understand all others in all situations. The other half noted that the secrecy involved in their use of drugs had caused a general breakdown in relationships with non-users, or "straight" people, especially parents.

7. SEX

I did not attempt to make an extensive study of the sex habits of teenagers, but merely to discover their attitudes and the general extent of their experience. I found a little reticence about the subject itself, and in many instances, the tone of the interview changed at this point, and it was as if we were beginning the interview all over again. But I did not meet with real embarrassment or reluctance to talk about sex, except in a few instances with very young boys.

Runaway boys, who identified more than any other group with the hippie movement, had had the most extensive experience, and expressed the attitude that sex with anyone with whom there was some spiritual communion was good. Everyone, without exception—and these boys especially—made a point of saying that sex for its own sake was not good, that having sex with someone with whom there was nothing in common, no beyond-body relating, was, in fact, a bad trip.

Almost everyone said they preferred having a serious relationship with one person to "playing the field." But quite a few volunteered that they did not believe in marriage. I was surprised at the number of girls who said they did not think they would marry. They felt that the legal bond of marriage was somehow destructive to real emotional bonds. "I want to be with someone because I want to, not because a contract says I have to," was a typical attitude. An equal number of those who felt this way came from happy homes as unhappy ones.

Of those who had had sexual intercourse, I asked the following question:

Was your first drug experience more important to you than your first sex experience? In which instance did you feel more differently about yourself for having had the experience?

Only a few said they found the first drug experience more significant. Drugs seemed quite taken for granted, as a natural part of a teenager's life and environment, whereas, in contrast, there seemed to be much mystery and confusion about sex.

I was especially impressed by the plight of an otherwise very sophisticated 16-year-old girl, a political activist, who was having an affair—her first—with a college boy. She was sensibly eager to obtain birth control, but she had no idea of how to go about it, and apparently her boy friend was unable to help her. She planned to go to a doctor in another town and lie about her age and her situation, but she knew she looked young, and did not expect to succeed in her mission. She said she suspected most of her girl friends were not virgins, but that her friends did not discuss sex, and that therefore she felt obliged to keep her affair a secret.

What has had the most influence on your attitudes toward sex?

Almost all answered, "my friends." Many mentioned that they had never been told the facts of life by their parents, and that sex was not discussed at home.

8. PARENTS

There was more reticence and emotional charge on the subject of parents than on anything else covered in the interviews. Rather than expressing hostility, anger, or condescension for the older generation, most kids just didn't seem to want to talk about it. They seemed willing enough to try, but were unsuccessful in remembering much about their pre-adolescent relationships with their parents, and many found it painful to discuss their present relationship.

Was there a time when you liked your parents better than you do now?

Most answered yes, but could not say when that changed, or what had happened.

How much do your parents know about you?

About 65 percent said their parents did not know much about their attitudes and feelings.

Do you want them to know more?

Many answered yes. Those who said no did so not because of secrets or fear of punishment, but because of fear of disillusioning and disappointing their parents, or because they felt that there was simply no possibility for more understanding.

Would you like to know more about them?

Almost all said yes.

Was there a time when you decided it was better not to tell your parents personal things?

"I never talked to my parents," was one fairly common answer. Others said they were sure there was such a time, but they could not recall it. Many seemed to feel that time had been around the age of 6. There was a strong feeling that parents didn't want to know more about their children and were unwilling to receive communication on any subject where there might be disagreement.

Does one of your parents have a better idea of who you are than the other?

About 75 percent felt their mothers knew them better.

Do they have a strong sense of who they are?

Some felt their fathers did. Most felt their mothers did not.

In your opinion, are they happy?

Most felt that their parents were either unhappily married or unhappy as individuals.

If you could change something about your parents, what would it be?

Few mentioned fathers. Most wanted to make their mothers less anxious, more liberal, less rigid, more tolerant—"a little more flexible in the mind," as one boy put it, and most of all, less hypocritical.

What do you do when you are at home?

The activity most often mentioned was listening to records. About half mentioned having some household chores, but in general, I got no sense of any activities that were not solitary ones, including watching T.V. In most cases, I sensed little real participation in family life.

Do you have any thoughts on raising your own children?

Most, even those who said they didn't expect to marry, seemed to anticipate child-rearing with pleasure, and seemed to have given some consideration to what they, as parents, would try to achieve. They wanted their children to feel freer than they did—especially freer to communicate—and they wanted to be careful not to impose their own old values on a new generation.